D1095141

The Cultural Prison

STUDIES IN RHETORIC AND COMMUNICATION
General Editors:
E. Culpepper Clark
Raymie E. McKerrow
David Zarefsky

John M. Sloop

The Cultural Prison

Discourse, Prisoners, and Punishment

The University of Alabama Press Tuscaloosa and London

Manufactured in the United States of America

∞

The paper on which this book is printed meets the minimum requirements of American National Standard for Information Science–Permanence of Paper for Printed Library Materials, ANSI Z39.48-1984.

Library of Congress Cataloging-in-Publication Data

Sloop, John M., 1963–
The cultural prison : discourse, prisoners, and punishment / John M. Sloop.
p. cm.—(Studies in rhetoric and communication)
Includes bibliographical references and index.
ISBN 0-8173-0822-9
1. Prisoners in popular culture—United States. 2. Mass media and criminal justice—United States. 3. Discourse analysis—United States. I. Title. II. Series.
HV9466.S66 1996
365′.973—dc20 95-38732

British Library Cataloguing-in-Publication Data available

Contents

Acknowledgments

Portions of chapter 6 originally appeared as " 'The Parent I Never Had': The Contemporary Construction of Alternatives to Incarceration," *Communication Studies* 43 (1992): 1–13, copyright 1992 by the Central States Communication Association; used by permission.

Thanks to the Drake University Center for the Humanities for funding portions of this project.

While I would like to express particular thanks to the following people, I recognize that the collaborative nature of all writing means that I will leave many other very important people off this list: I am indebted to the members of my dissertation committee—Bruce Gronbeck (adviser), Michael Calvin McGee, Sam Becker, John Lyne, and Rudy Kuenzli—as it was central to the completion of my dissertation, upon which this manuscript overlaps in part. My ongoing relationships with several of my graduate school peers cannot go unnoticed, as I am deeply in debt to the following people: Todd Boyd, Dana Cloud, Fernando Delgado, and Ben Attias. Accolades for her patience and insight go to Jennifer Gunn. For keeping me aware of what's really important, I thank Christopher Sloop. Inspiration and a payback of a different kind to my friends Sara Romweber, Michael Rank, and Andy McMillan—I owe the three of you very much. For support and inspiration when the editing and rewriting processes seemed at their darkest, I must thank the colleagues, friends, and students at Drake University, especially Robert Hariman, Bill Lewis, Allen Scult, Jon Ericson, Jody Swilky, Richard Abel, Barbara Hodgdon,

Andrew Herman, Joseph Schneider, Rachel Buckles, Jennifer Stiff, Jon Shectman, and Shari Stenberg. For keeping me company in my office on my Sony CFD-440, I thank Kristin Hersh (*Throwing Muses*) and Thelonious Monk (especially "Ruby, My Dear"). Finally, my most sincere thanks go to my friend-peer-teacher-collaborator Kent Ono, to whom my debt is deeper than I care to imagine.

The Cultural Prison

1

Introduction

The Historical Force of Rhetoric and The Disciplinary Force of Culture

In late 1987, after having been convicted of drug possession and driving while intoxicated, Maria Arnford was to be sentenced by Texas District Court judge Ted Poe. Because Texas prisons were at the time filled above suggested capacity levels, primarily because of laws that either lengthened sentences or mandated imprisonment for virtually all classifications of crime in Texas, Judge Poe found himself faced with what has become an increasingly common problem: balancing the legal and popular demand for imprisonment and the spatial and economic constraints that create prisons so overcrowded as to constitute grounds for claims of "cruel and unusual" punishment. In this case, Poe chose to utilize one of the few alternatives available that would not increase the population of any of the state's prisons. Arnford's home was transformed into what was in effect a mediated prison: a video screen, camera, and transmitter were installed to assure authorities, who would call at random, that Arnford was "home," constantly ready to transmit her image back to them. Furthermore, Arnford was asked at random times to provide urine samples as evidence that she was following orders to abstain from drugs and alcohol for the duration of her punishment. According to the conditions of her sentence, Arnford was permitted to leave her house only for preapproved therapy appointments, community service activities, and church meetings. The gaze of the state was fixed intently upon Arnford, its probe monitoring not only her movements but the composition of her blood.

While the form of Arnford's punishment is provocative on its own grounds, it is not the most engaging or troubling aspect of this narrative, a story told in the pages of *People.* Rather, Arnford's personal assessment of the monitoring system is simultaneously both more chilling and more intriguing. When asked to comment on the effects of this experimental punishment, Arnford noted, "This program has been like a parent to me, the parent I never had" (quoted in "Outside the Walls" 23).

From the moment I first read this statement, Arnford's words have haunted and engaged me. Her assessment is one positioned for polyvalent reactions; it is sure to bring encouragement to those interested in the rehabilitative possibilities of punishment, tears to the eyes of civil libertarians, and slightly nervous nods of recognition from those familiar with Michel Foucault's thesis of the carceral society and the panopticon. As a person's body and subjectivity are overtly open for testing, therapy, and control by the state, she neither protests nor stands by numbly accepting what is her due. Instead, she expresses a feeling of gratitude, one that encourages a continuance of her correction. While Jean-François Lyotard has recounted the death of the metanarrative and the advent of the postmodern condition, and while Jean Baudrillard has been busy living the life of a postmodern, noting that our condition is one in which "we are gorged with meaning, and it is killing us" (1988, 63), I take pause on the basis of this and similar stories. Maria Arnford is not represented as confused about the stability of metanarratives nor is she represented as being laid to waste by excess meaning; instead, in embracing the state as parent, she appears to have found a strong shoulder, a strong metanarrative to provide a renewal of both life and meaning.

If we approach this story from a rhetorical angle, assuming the influence of discourse on creating social issues and subjectivity, a number of questions arise. First, what are the rhetorical circumstances that create a reality in which a claim such as Arnford's could be published in *People,* a widely distributed popular journal, without attracting much attention? Second, what are the possible cultural effects of a shared reality that encourages such complete penetration of one of its participants, albeit a "criminal" one? Third, what is the cultural significance of the gender, class, race, and sexual orientation of Arnford, each at least implicitly suggested in the article (i.e., Arnford is a woman, middle class, Caucasian, heterosexual), in this representation of discipline? Finally, and perhaps most important, what type of social world is implied by our uncritical acceptance of her words, and what alternative visions might be offered?

In approaching these questions and their accompanying problems, I am interested in understanding how it is that we, as a culture, have constructed a reality that allows this particular configuration of discipline. In order to gain this understanding, to comprehend the present discourse about punishment and about those who are punished, I have also found it necessary to examine the history of public discourses dealing with punishment and prisoners in the United States. With this perspective, I could work forward to see how the layers of discourse from the past continue to act as forces in shaping the contemporary construction of prisoners and punishment. In short, I wanted to know how we had arrived at our current condition, and could only do so by understanding the discursive undergirdings of our current conceptions of prisoners. In the chapters that follow, I present the lines of argument about prisoners that have developed over time and the characterizations and narratives that shape our contemporary cultural understanding of prisoners and punishment in an attempt to answer this initial line of inquiry.

Assuming that the discourse surrounding prisoners and punishment acts as a material social force that creates space for the current discussion of punishment, particularly alternatives to incarceration, I investigate the general cultural positioning of prisoners. Theoretically, this project requires an inquiry into the relationships between culture, mediated images, ideology, hegemony, rhetoric, and discipline.

Because I am less interested in how prison sentences are enforced than in how dominant culture "talks about" their enforcement, my primary focus is on how the institutional punishment of our society's offenders is represented in mass-mediated and popular outlets. That is, I am more interested in how we talk about prisoners and punishment than in a discussion of what prisoners and punishment "really are." I wish to claim (and will clarify this claim below) that the behavior, morality, and subjectivity of all members of a culture are tied to the way misbehavior, particularly via characterizations of prisoners, is represented in mass-media outlets and public arguments. In what follows, I argue that mass-mediated representations of prisoners function as a public display of the transgression of cultural norms; as such, they are a key site at which one may investigate the relationship of the individual to culture in general, as well as the cultural articulation of "proper behavior." Hence, the cultural articulation of the prisoner and the punished teaches everyone, convict and law-abiding citizen alike, his or her position relative to cultural institutions that constitute the culture at large.

Because my particular orientation toward discourse and the study of culture may be unfamiliar to some readers, I will begin below by briefly outlining my understanding of the impact of rhetoric in culture as a disciplinary force. Moreover, I will describe the particular discourses that are the subject of this study, noting the ways these choices shape the claims and observations I make throughout the book.

Rhetoric and Culture, Energy and Mortar

The assumption with which I begin is that rhetoric acts as an extraordinarily powerful and historical basis by and through which cultures and "individuals" are constituted.[1] The relationship between rhetoric and culture is a fairly slippery one, however, and while I'm not one given to definitional moments in an essay or book, it seems here that an attempt to provide some sense of that relationship will be helpful in understanding how I approached this study. In noting that culture "is the very material of our daily lives, the bricks and mortar of our most commonplace understandings" (184–85), Paul Willis provided a double-edged definition of culture: while culture is positive in the sense that life could not be experienced without the bricks and mortar that give it shape and substance, it is also negative, or constraining, in that bricks and mortar have a discursive materiality that privileges existing discourses, existing ideology. As discourses and definitions become generally accepted within culture, they are assumed and hence act as sedimented practices. Particular orders of discourse, shared definitions, must exist if human beings are to have consciousness of themselves and the world around them. Yet, the need for regularity gives such discourses a solidified nature in which change and transition become difficult.[2]

If culture refers to the "bricks and mortar" of everyday understandings, rhetoric is the "energy" of culture. That is, just as energy in the material world represents the "work" of material objects, rhetoric is that which is the energy or movement of the symbolic or cultural world.[3] These conceptualizations have at least two implications that are relevant to this study. First, rhetoric and culture cannot be studied separately. When we study the movement or "work" of bricks and mortar, we necessarily investigate the bricks and mortar themselves. When we investigate culture, we are almost necessarily interested in the ways in which culture hangs together, how strong is its pull on those who are held together by it. Second, if rhetoric is the energy of the symbolic world, the ease with which we perceive it is related to its power. Hence, rhetoric that is the most obvious can also be the most harmless in that we can most easily protect ourselves from it by shying away from it. Just as one knows better than to touch the exposed wiring in an electric cord, one can also learn to shy away from get-rich-quick schemes after being burned once too often. The task of the rhetorical critic, paralleling that of someone whose job is to measure low levels of radiation in residential areas, is to measure and reveal the energy of the bricks and mortar that have become so commonplace that we no longer notice their power. Through awareness, we can seek to change our reactions.

Saying that one is studying the bricks and mortar of everyday life and the ways in which these bricks and mortar constrain and enable is more problematic than it may sound initially. Two sets of questions arise: first, what locations and types of discourse does one study in order to examine the bricks and mortar of a particular group of people? How broad a set of claims can be made on the basis of those discourses? Second, and in some sense most important, what is the status of a work that purports to be a study of the discourses on a specific topic? How does that work itself operate as a part of the energy of culture? Indeed, how does the critic position rhetorical criticism that purports to be doing cultural criticism?

In that this is an investigation of a series of discourses about a particular cultural topic, it is a cultural history of "prisoners" and "punishment" that assumes that such representations work to offer knowledge and subject positions to cultural participants, providing part of the material that allows them to exist while simultaneously constraining their knowledge/understanding. In attempting both to justify the particular set of discourses that I am investigating in this text and to explain the status of this work as a discourse in itself, I want to be clear that my investigation focuses on dominant discourse, dominant ideology. My attempt is to provide a practical edge to what has been called "critical rhetoric."[4] As Robert Hariman recently has pointed out, discourse theorists and critical rhetoricians have been guilty in part of theorization without the performative edge they so often claim to valorize ("Afterward"). This book should be seen as an attempt to draw from the critical rhetoric perspective but to put in play its critical and performative promise.[5]

The promise of critical rhetoric was made by Raymie McKerrow in 1989 when he delineated a critical practice that would pull together "disparate scraps of discourse which, when constructed as an argument, serve to illuminate otherwise hidden or taken for granted social practices" (101). Based on the assumption that the discourse and communications of contemporary culture are fragmented, critical rhetoric gave over to critics the role of pulling together the multiple layers of communication that take place in culture and of drawing them together to show the ways particular "objects of discourse" are created, how relationships of power aid in the determination of these definitions, and the senses in which different people have varying opportunities to speak on different topics.[6] If one wants to understand how a particular term or idea has cultural meaning, this perspective requires that rather than investigating academic or philosophical discussions of the topic, one focuses on the public discourse surrounding it (McGee, "Origins" 25).[7] It is what is in the open, what is accepted as true, what people are willing to claim in public places, that acts as true and provides meaning for those who embody specific terms and positions. Only to the degree that an idea "is convincing to a large number of people will it carry social force and gain materiality" (Condit, *Decoding* 9).[8] Hence, prisoners and punishment only have meaning to the degree that their usage acts upon members of a particular culture. We cannot understand the enacted meaning of the term *prisoners* by looking only at what philosophers or sociologists of crime and punishment mean by it unless such philosophers and sociologists have taken their discourse into the public forum and made claims in the ideological struggle over its meaning.[9] By looking at philosophical debates over the meaning of punishment or the nature of criminals, we perceive how the term operates within philosophical communities. By looking at popular discussions of the same arguments, we understand more fully how the dominant culture uses and shapes the concepts in everyday life.

To respond to the first few questions I asked above in problematizing this perspective, the "pulling together of disparate fragments" from a culture is the study of dominant culture; it is the study of what the most popular voices have had to say about a particular topic. While dominant ideology is certainly important in that it influences, positively or negatively, the ways in which all members of a culture constitute not only given objects of discourse but also, and importantly, their selves, I should also be clear that this study is limited to a reading of the dominant discourses of a culture, rather than of overtly resistant ones or of marginal ones. While resistant themes may run through some of the discourses that are dominant, as a whole such discourses tend toward stability of the overall system.

I have suggested that the way in which a term works in practice in the present is highly dependent on how it has functioned in the past. I have also suggested that understanding the present meanings of a term, the culture's brick-and-mortar understanding of a topic, requires that the fragments of dominant discourse be assembled and an argument or story drawn from them. However, asserting that a particular term gains its meaning in material usage provides a virtually never-ending set of locations from which to investigate its cultural usage, even if one is studying dominant discourses. Where, then, from all of the available discourse, does one look to find the dominant meaning of, say, the term *prisoner* in practice?

When Michel Foucault posed this question during his "archaeology" phase, he claimed that "there must not be any privileged choice. One must be able to read everything, to know all the institutions and all the practices" ("Order" 3). Foucault posited himself as the ultimate discursive positivist, uncovering all discourse surrounding objects and unearthing the rules and relations that allow objects to appear, presumably separating himself from, and exhaustively researching, contemporary discourse, investigating every instance of a term's usage, every treatise, every legal document, every utterance, every grunt (*Archaeology* 185). In practice, this claim is absurd, although certainly admirable. Realizing the impossibility of such a search, Foucault's genealogical perspective tightens limits on what would be analyzed in that the guiding criterion of genealogy can be argued to be persuasiveness rather than comprehensiveness. That is, while genealogical investigations continue the turn away from transcendentalism, they are also more pragmatic. Hence, Foucault provides discourses from a variety of types of sources (daily papers, diaries, journals, discussions, and so forth) in enough detail to persuade his reader that he has indeed come to a thorough genealogical investigation ("Truth" 117). My own choice of discourses borrows perspective from Foucault's claims about both archaeology and genealogy.

Hence, I have attempted to be comprehensive within a particular domain of discourses (popular journals) while at the same time fleshing out my readings of these discourses with spot checks of discourse from other domains (primarily newspaper accounts and films).[10] In order to investigate the popular meaning of *prisoners,* I have comprehensively collected and investigated all articles from popular journals under the heading *prisoners* (or under relevant subheadings)[11] in the *Reader's Guide to Periodical Literature* from 1950 to 1993. In this way, I provide a comprehensive study of one set of discourses while simultaneously checking on other forms of popular discourse. In full, this approach provided my study with 642 popular articles dealing with prisoners.

The second set of questions that this perspective demands be answered concerns the status of the critical work itself (that is, the text you are reading). If discourse has meaning in the interstices of power and knowledge, this text itself cannot be purely descriptive; nor, on the other hand, can it be "scientifically" explanatory, as it is itself one discourse that adds to the overall understanding of the terms *pris-*

oner and *punishment* (as well as terms that are often represented alongside these two, like, say *African American* or *homosexual*).

When Foucault moves on to his genealogical phase, he focuses more on the relations of power that shape the creation of subjects within local conditions and examines the influence of the past on the present. Here, with more of a Nietzschean flavor, he closely investigates the operations of power, particularly as it operates in and through bodies in the production of knowledge and subjectivity. Whereas archaeology depicts the subject as a fictitious construct, genealogy attempts to understand and illustrate the material context of the construction of this fiction, to illustrate the political consequences of subjectification, and to draw out possible lines of resistance ("Clarifications" 189).

In *Discipline and Punish,* Foucault questions his own desire to write a history of the discipline of the body and answers, in a now oft-quoted passage: "Why? Simply because I am interested in the past? No, if one means by that writing a history of the past in terms of the present. Yes, if one means writing the history of the present" (31). Here, and again in "Nietzsche, Genealogy, History," Foucault moves to reappropriate "history," to see the writing of history as a task with roots and effects in the present. In writing a history of the present, one writes a history that highlights the present, that comments on it, and in the process of discussing matters particular to the present, transforms the present and its objects. A history of the way the meaning of homosexuality has developed culturally, for example, might lead the present members of a given culture to acknowledge the groundlessness of our ideas on homosexuality and homosexuals and, in the process, transform the overall cultural representation and positioning of homosexuality. As Foucault notes, "History has a more important task than to be a handmaiden to philosophy, to recount the necessary birth of truth and values; it should become a differential knowledge of energies and failings, heights and degenerations, poisons and antidotes. Its task is to become a curative science" ("Nietzsche" 90). Discourse, then, including genealogical studies, is always already a material force acting upon the knowledges and activities of the present.

Hence, in that all discourses about the past act as forces in creating the present, the genealogical study is itself a force of intervention. This book does not escape such a status. It cannot be seen as purely descriptive, nor can it be seen as an "objective" description of the causes of shifts in the representation of the prisoner. While I have attempted to be thorough in constructing a fully developed narrative, my text is necessarily also an "effective discourse."[12]

The Cultural Prison: Institutional and Cultural Discipline

As the title of this section notes, "discipline" operates on two levels throughout this text: the institutional and the cultural. Discipline not only refers to how institutions (such as governments, schools) literally and physically discipline individuals (for example, by incarceration, whippings) but also refers to how discipline takes place on a cultural level through the reactions of the "looking-glass self." Ignoring Louis Althusser's structuralist leanings, one could claim, in his idiom, that I am interested here in looking at the way in which ISA (ideological state apparatus) discussions of RSAs (repressive state apparatuses) themselves act as a form of discipline; I am interested, then, quite literally, in critiquing public discussions of disciplined subjects. In that I will argue that public discussions are themselves a form of discipline, I am interested in the disciplinary power of discussions of discipline, the discipline of "discipline."

In *Discipline and Punish,* Foucault delineates a line of difference between forms of punishment in late eighteenth-century and early nineteenth-century France. He is taken with the shift from public executions of criminals and the focus on the discipline of bodies to the 1970s' conception of a punishment aimed at the soul, directed toward the rehabilitation of the individual. He notes that "ever since the new penal system . . . has been in operation, a general process has led judges to judge something other than the crimes . . . and the power of judging has been transferred, in part, to other authorities than the judges of the offense" (22). Foucault indicts our current society as "disciplinary" and points to the normalizing procedures that affect every aspect of our lives, procedures masked by the link between power and knowledge. He claims that each of our institutions and the representatives of these institutions—law and lawyers, education and educators, religion and priests, and so on—are on the lookout not so much for the violation of laws and rules as for departures from what is normal (298–99).

The creation of this "carceral society" has encouraged the emergence of a new form of law— "a mixture of legality and nature, prescription and constitution, the norm"—and places each of us in the role of the judge (304). We need only add the title *judge* to our occupational and cultural roles to understand the implications of this claim; we are a society of teacher-judges, doctor-judges, social worker-judges, psychoanalyst-judges, friend-judges, spouse-judges, and so forth. Through the human sciences and our disposition to rehabilitate the individual, our job descriptions necessarily include watching for those who fall outside the boundaries of "proper" human behavior and thought.[13] The growth of the carceral society necessarily leads to the deterioration of even an imaginary private space in which the individual can freely or easily behave outside of "normal" behavior. We live in a carceral society in which a large number of forces work to hold individual subjects within certain grounds of behavior, to discipline them.

I contend that this notion of discipline may be transferred to the general behavior of mass-mediated discourses, which, as a characteristic of operation, work in tandem with the dominant social structure and the dominant ideology by disciplining all opinions counter to it. In other words, I am conducting an investigation of ideology and culture through a discussion of the disciplinary nature of the mass media. I suggest that ideology and the mass media are interconnected because the media and its operators reflect ideological demands not by intent but simply as a matter of operation.

Although I have emphasized that rhetoric (discourse) operates as a force in culture, I am not attempting to construct a "prison house of language" argument. My focus is on the public construction of prisoners and punishment and hence on the starting material with which people operate; what people individually do with this material is a different question. I do not mean to suggest that displaced subjects have no agency within their constructed boundaries. Indeed, recent work in cultural studies has witnessed a reemergence of discussions on how human subjects are able to provide individual interpretations of cultural artifacts that provide resistance to dominant cultural discourses. From the early 1980s onwards, work within cultural studies shifts attention increasingly away from the production of discourse (writers, producers, schools, and so forth) and the product (books, newspaper articles, broadcasts) and to the ways in which the "weak" in society make use of cultural artifacts in order to create a sphere of autonomous action and self-determination within the constraints imposed upon them.[14] Essentially, this shift represents a move to a Gramscian theory of hegemony, one in which it is made clear that in order to have control over subordinate groups, the ruling group must win and shape consent so that the power of the dominant classes appears both legitimate and natural. If consent must be won over, there is room for resistance from nondominant groups within culture.[15]

I place myself in a central position between structural theories of discourse and those that search for signs and room for resistance in all activities engaged. My position is somewhat similar to that articulated by Celeste Condit in her response to cultural critics and theorists who emphasize the power of audiences to control, with relative autonomy, their interpretations of mass-mediated discourses.

Condit suggests that the audience's ability to shape its readings is limited by factors such as the "audience member's access to oppositional codes, the ratio between the work required and pleasure produced in decoding a text, the repertoire of available texts, and the historical occasion" ("Rhetorical" 104). Rather than autonomous audiences or totalizing media, Condit views media and audiences as interactive in the assessment and creation of mediated messages. Furthermore, Condit notes that because television or any mass medium addresses upscale viewers for the purpose of attracting advertisers, these media are constraining simply because their economic interests encourage them to address this dominant audience and promote its interests ("Rhetorical" 112). The audience has power to interpret, then, but that power is limited both by its own characteristics and by the economic interests of the media. Unlike arguments claiming that audience reception has very little effect on the ultimate meaning of a mediated message (for example, its sexism or racism), Condit sees media outlets as placing constraints on how a message might be read even though audiences place the ultimate value on what is essentially a shared meaning of the text.[16]

The most important conclusion to draw from this argument is that mass-media outlets, due both to the position of the producers of mass-mediated texts as members of mass culture and to economic constraints that require marketable output, will necessarily reproduce, albeit with minor changes, the dominant culture's ideology and its perspective on any topic given voice. Hence, while a representation of a woman or an African-American male prisoner, for example, might be different than the "empirical reality," it cannot be outside of what is ideologically acceptable to a great number of people whom advertisers wish to reach. Change can occur, but only change that is already somewhat acceptable to the audience. As Raymond Williams might say, it is necessarily a "long revolution." Otherwise, the images, not appealing to viewers, will not appeal to advertisers and will themselves be "disciplined" out of production.

I have said that this is a study of the discipline of "discipline." To that end, I am assuming that mediated messages generally constrain interpretations not only because they are often constructed in the interest of gaining the attention of their audiences but also because they have the inherent feature of disciplining those subjects who speak against this audience's interests. When individuals find it possible to offer critiques of the dominant ideology through mass media outlets, such outlets, by virtue of those who run them, operate efficiently to critique and discipline these individuals. For example, when Jimmy the Greek offered his interpretation of why African Americans were better athletes than whites or when Professor Griff of Public Enemy suggested that Jews are responsible for the majority of wickedness in the world, their claims were quickly described in mass media outlets as intellectually corrupt. The media exposure and negative description of the claims force actions from other institutions; for example, sponsors threaten to pull out, and boycotts are planned. This functioning of the media ceases only when public, mediated apologies from the offending parties are forthcoming (see, for example, Sloop). Such discipline protects the established culture's ideological security by reproducing the morals, values, and epistemology of that culture.[17]

This is not to say that outlets for resistant voices do not exist. Indeed, this would be a ridiculous claim in an age with hundreds of cable television options, an endless number of special-interest magazines, and a plethora of resources on the Internet. However, even these voices are mediated, filtered, and diluted by the discourse of dominant culture. As Condit notes, public argument has a "universalizing influence." As topics and themes are argued publicly, the options of what may be uttered publicly change. As African Americans were slowly brought under the banner of civil rights on a cultural level, it became more and more difficult for individuals to utter racist comments publicly even if in their "private" circles they continued to do so ("Democracy" 15). Large pockets of various discourses may exist, but there is less room for them in public forums.

This "universalizing effect" of public argument also impacts the structuring of laws and public policy. As Condit notes of post–civil rights legislation, "Laws were made in the new vocabulary rather than in the old; public policies were framed in the new vocabulary rather than in the old, and social practices were experienced by many through the new vocabulary as well" ("Democracy" 15). This "cultural discipline" or universalizing influence limits the effect of private or marginalized voices and makes the public forum the arena for ideological struggle over the meaning of who we, as a people, will be.[18]

Thus, this disciplinary nature of culture or ideology is experienced as an accumulation of all actions and discourses, emerging from and through all institutions and subjects, working to reproduce dominant interests through a reproduction of the ideological relations of domination. One of the primary routes through which this discipline is carried out is the mass-mediated construction of cultural objects. These constructions do not occur as a result of mindless controllers of the media. Rather, those who control media outlets, just like you and me, have an interest in maintaining the current system of power relations; it is constitutive of their senses of "self," their subjectivities.

We live in a "cultural prison" in the sense that our self-understanding grows from depictions and discourses found in mass culture. To the degree that deviant activities and subjectivities are represented publicly as being disciplined, symbolically or otherwise, our options in terms of behavior and being are similarly limited. Our sense of who we are, what we can be, and how we can behave is somewhat limited by how those representations that guide our behavior are treated. At the very least, such images work in a loosely dialectical exchange with our current viewpoints.

What is specifically interesting ideologically about the study of prisoners or punishment that we cannot find in the study of any mass-mediated messages? In brief, as a nation, we establish certain laws, procedures, and institutions (Althusser's RSAs or "repressive state apparatuses") to discipline our "outlaws." Rhetorically and ideologically, however, it is in the media coverage of these outlaws/ "prisoners" (and in popular arguments) that the most "effective" disciplining of the people at large takes place. Articulations of the term *prisoner*, as it emerges in mass media outlets, are reflections of contemporary dominant power relations. As Richard Ericson, Patricia Baranek, and Janet Chan argue in their analysis of Toronto media coverage of crime, "News represents order—morality, procedural form, and hierarchy—through constituting an active and influential discourse about the ordering activities of the people and organizations reported on. . . . News becomes an agency of social control, not merely describing the crime, law, and justice processes but serving as an integral part of them" (i). Hence, not only does law and its enforcement parallel our definitions of community and culture, but our representations of law and its enforcement in mass media outlets also allow the law and its links with morality to become integral parts of our relationships with each other and the culture at large.[19]

While the general definition of the term *prisoner* has remained factually the same since the 1950s, the institutional means for dealing with prisoners has changed and, of more importance and significance, we as a people look at prisoners differently on a cultural level. It is on this cultural level that we learn to enact or avoid a term like *prisoner* and learn the deeper cultural relationship of that term with others. The benefit of focusing on the cultural meanings of a term of this nature lies in drawing out the subtle workings of ideology; it is here that persuasion and discipline work at their most silent and therefore their most effective level. Studying the articulations that surround a term like *prisoner* aids us in understanding the cultural definitions of institutional discipline, the "discipline" of discipline. Furthermore, to the degree that we identify our legality with morality (that is, outlaws behave immorally and moral people follow laws), the study of mass-mediated depictions of outlaws and prisoners provides suggestions not only as to how we need to behave to be moral or simply how we should view or treat "immoral beings." It is much more important that a study of the discipline of "discipline" suggests what our relationship to the state, the disciplinary apparatus as a whole, should be—at least according to contemporary dominant ideology. As I make this observation, I am again taken back to Maria Arnford's inviting adoration of the state, and the silent acceptance of this adoration, and I am once again alarmed.

Headings

As noted, this text represents a close and comprehensive reading of articles focusing on prisoners from periodicals representing dominant discourse from 1950 to 1993. In addition, I have checked the consistency of general cultural representations of prisoners and punishment by investigating films and newspaper articles throughout the same period. The narratives that follow are the result of this reading and of my own interests. Those interested in a discussion of the theoretical representation of prisoners during this same era should refer to Appendix 1. Others should feel free to skip the Appendix all together.

Now that I have raised the specter of appendixes: Appendix 2 provides a numerical description of the recurring themes, narratives, and characterizations of prisoners that appear throughout the period under study and comments on the periods of discourse that emerge as a result of my investigation.[20] Appendix 3 provides a numerical breakdown of the types or categories of people who actually were counted by the U.S. government and its various agencies as being imprisoned during this period as opposed to the people who are represented in popular media outlets.

The characterizations and themes that emerge from the narratives of the prisoner are many and varied. Gender, race, sexual orientation, determinism, autonomy, patriotism, nationalism, drug use, economic status, and childhood behavior all make up the inks from which various portraits of the prisoner are drawn in popular media. The lines I draw between the changes in these topics are chronological and thematic; while admittedly fuzzy at the borders, they are the ones suggested by my reading. The "snapshot" summaries that I provide in this chapter are not meant to touch on all of the themes I cover later but only to touch upon the strongest elements of the emergent characterizations.[21]

Before presenting my reading of the representation of prisoners, I have provided, in chapter 2, a short summary of traditional histories of punishment and prisoners from the colonial period of the United States to the early period of my study (1950). This chapter provides an entry into the readings that follow and an explanation for placing the beginning of my own study in 1950. Chapter 3, covering the period 1950–1959, begins my description of the representation of the prisoner in United States popular culture. Here, the prisoner is fairly homogeneously represented—he, the male prisoner, is humorous, patriotic, Caucasian, and hapless. The female prisoner, while ambiguously "raced," is a naturally virtuous being who has been corrupted by external forces; her task is to become rehabilitated in order to assure the continuation of the species and its morality. Both male and female prisoners are infinitely redeemable and persistently drawn as having altruistic motives, as desiring a reunion with the culture previously shunned. It is almost as if there is something true in 1970s representations of the 1950s, and we are reading about the imprisonment of characters from "Happy Days" and "Laverne and Shirley." The implied culture itself is represented as homogeneous, sharing a common set of values and goals. Prisoners are part of this homogeneous culture; even if they have stepped outside of its bounds for the moment, they will return.

Chapter 4, reading the period from 1960 to 1968, paints a decade of transition. The failure of rehabilitation programs and a renewal of prison riots are cited as evidence for two discrepant and often competing depictions of the male prisoner. This bifurcation of the redeemable prisoner of the 1950s provides on the one hand the continuation of the altruistic Caucasian; on the other hand, it also provides space for the emergence of a different prisoner, one who, as the decade proceeds, is "African-Americanized" while he simultaneously becomes increasingly violent. It is in this second characterization of the male prisoner that we begin to see the growth of the "essential" criminal, a convict whose very nature is one of criminality, a convict tied more and more closely to racist stereotypes in the decades that follow. The representation of the female prisoner, however, is the model of consistency; she continues to be mother and moral guidepost of the culture. The primary concern expressed in representations of female inmates is that such inmates be reunited with their families after finding redemption through incarceration. Although the representation of the prisoner becomes increasingly complex as the decade proceeds, the culture itself continues to be represented in a homogeneous fashion. That is, while the prisoner might be represented alternatively as essentially "moral" or essentially "immoral," this judgment is made according to the criteria of one homogeneous value system.

Chapter 5 covers the period from 1969 to 1975, wherein lies another split in the dominant representations of the prisoner. While the white male prisoner remains forever open for rehabilitation and reunion, the "other" male prisoner divides. The products of this bifurcation, while both violent, take on opposite valences. The violence of one is justified in that it emerges in reaction to an unfair social system that imprisons the African-American male while it protects a racist society. Riots and violent behavior are the reasonable reactions that any human being would experience if forced to live under the same conditions. Indeed, there is a certain sense of nobility articulated with this characterization of the male prisoner and the courage of his struggle to preserve a cultural heritage. Furthermore, this nobility acknowledges a respect for cultural diversity, a cultural acknowledgment of varying value systems. The other product of the division is once again predominantly African-American, but in this representation, he is violent for the sake of violence alone. This prisoner is a rapist, a liar, a spoiler of white youth. Rather than struggling against a racist culture in order to preserve his heritage, he is represented as following his nature, behaving in ways that defy transformation and thus demand restraint.

The representation of female prisoners continues to crystallize the representations seen earlier. It is the nature of females to behave morally; their imprisonment is the result of corruption triggered by external forces early in their lives. When female prisoners are discussed, it is in order to note their separation from their children, their rehabilitation, and their eventual reunion with their families. The behavior of female prisoners in prison is generally positive in force. Hence, when they enter coed prisons, they bring a "calming influence," tempering the violence and homosexuality of males.

Chapter 6 covers the remaining period, 1975 to 1993. It is this period, weighted by the depictions of the past and plagued by economic and political events that increase the number of "convicts" while stabilizing the number of spaces for them to be held, that creates the conditions for a Maria Arnford. Indeed, it is during this period that numerous criminals characterized with similar desires and similar attitudes about discipline emerge.

Simultaneous with (and as a product of) this emergence of willing prisoners, the philosophical position of "just deserts" gains merit as a popular orientation toward imprisonment. "Just deserts" dictate that convicts receive the exact equivalent in punishment that is due for their crime, without consideration of other factors, including race, gender, or evidence supporting rehabilitation. This philosophy provides a surface belief in the heterogeneity of values. That is, to the degree that "just deserts" are enacted only in regard to the crime committed, people may hold various moral systems. However, because they live as citizens of the United States, they are required to follow its laws, keeping their behaviors within those limits. While the philosophy of "just deserts" is persistently articulated in essays that claim that prisoners are punished for crimes, regardless of other factors, the weight of past narratives and characterizations of the prisoner work as social forces in shaping the depiction and motives of the prisoner of the present and hence force the issues of race and gender. Because the public has a memory of the discourses concerning prisoners, however ephemeral, all new constructions of the prisoner begin with past characterizations as a base. Hence, while all prisoners are supposedly treated equally under a system of "just deserts," the arguments of the past serve as a force in the present in such a way that African-American male inmates, depicted as untrustworthy, are represented as receiving their just deserts through prison sentences, while Caucasian inmates and female prisoners in general (the former represented as redeemable and the latter as needing reunion with family) are more frequently represented as serving their sentences through alternative systems of punishment.

Nonetheless, the depictions by race may be the least troubling aspect of the discourse of just deserts. The call for just deserts and stronger antidrug policies, along with government budgets that disallow the building of new prisons, inevitably leads to overcrowded prisons. It is not only the race of those depicted as partaking of alternative forms of punishment that is implicated by past discourses but also the ways in which the participants go on to characterize the experience of their punishment. Hence, because the idea of just deserts disallows rehabilitation unless the participant chooses to rehabilitate himself or herself, those prisoners who undergo alternative forms of punishment (be it home monitoring, public confessionals, or boot camp) do so of their own volition. They "choose" to invite the state to monitor them for their own good and then praise its results. Furthermore, to the degree that just deserts respect the heterogeneity of values, the cultural praise for punishment represents a praise of a morality that is not necessary but chosen. Ironically, those who undergo the less violent, alternative forms of punishment, become the strongest spokespersons for Foucault's panopticon, while the imprisoned are the only ones left with room for critique. Those represented as imprisoned do not choose to invite rehabilitation and hence offer one of the few spaces for a critique of the carceral society.

In chapter 7, I am in some sense trying to deal with the "terror" with which I began this study. What I learn, however, in no small way disappoints me. I began this study with the specter of Maria Arnford pushing me. In the end, I not only have an entire cast of problematic characters to concern me, but I am also far less optimistic about the role of arguments as a social force for quick change in the public forum. Instead, I have become all the more convinced that, once grounded, depictions and arguments do indeed become material in the sense that they solidify and crystallize in public memory. One cannot simply wish away the depiction of the African-American prisoner as a rapist, no matter how much one wants to. One cannot wish away the representation of the female as forlorn mother, no matter how hard one tries. One cannot simply dismiss the problems of "justice" in "just" deserts, no matter how loud one shouts. This is not to imply that there is no hope, or that different stories cannot be told; if anything, it makes it all the more important that we do not "post" ourselves completely into the realm of academic theorizing, but that we take more seriously our roles as the doers of deeds and tellers of tales.

Prelude to the Present

American Histories of Punishment

Histories of the emergence, growth, and transition of the theory and practice of punishment in the United States are relatively plentiful, and the explanations each offers for the changes in systems of punishment in the United States and their tellings of the historical narrative itself are equally plentiful.[1] I hope it is clear that my intent is not to provide yet another overarching explanation of the changing conceptions of the characterization of the prisoner or of punishment; such explanations necessarily take what is a complex and multifarious set of social changes and crystallize them into one or two causal factors (e.g., economics, moral systems). This is not to say, however, that my study has not been informed by these histories and by the differing explanations others have offered concerning the changing nature of punishment. Indeed, by drawing upon some of the metahistories of punishment and their explanatory structures for my own telling of the story of punishment in the United States in recent decades, one gets a fuller sense of the rhetorical, temporal, and cultural backdrops that make up the contemporary positioning of the prisoner.

My goal here is to trace out some of the points in existing histories where one finds consistencies (the information that each story assumes to be "fact"), assuming that such points are part of the cultural narrative that have had, and continue to have, rhetorical force however they are interpreted. That is, because particular events and practices are talked about as "having happened," their status has influence within each historical venue where they appear. As such, these residual practices and events influence the ways in which punishment is carried out historically as well as the ways in which prisoners are represented. In short, such stories allow an understanding of the constraints of the rhetorical field from which cultural discourse about the prisoner arises and also provide a complex and varied picture that suggests some possible factors that influence historical changes in punishment and in the prisoner, be they cultural, material, or both.[2] It is in such a spirit that I attempt to draw together in this chapter the threads of other stories of the history of punishment, moving from early American history to the waning years of the twentieth century.

Histories of punishment are by no means perfectly consistent with each other. Indeed, the reason multiple histories are written is that disagreements exist over precisely when and where the penitentiary was "born" and what and how strong the philosophical roots of the penitentiary system are. Nevertheless, it is surprising that the situation they describe, especially in early U.S. history, is remarkably similar.[3] Regardless of the perspective taken, the reader is persistently reminded that in colonial America the prison did not exist in any significant sense. While it is difficult for the contemporary mind to comprehend a time when there were no prisons or prisoners, they did not come into existence in a contemporary sense until the late eighteenth and early nineteenth centuries. The narratives provided separately by such historians as Adam Jay Hirsch, David Rothman, and Lawrence Friedman (and Foucault in France) point to a culture in which the spectacle of punishment (whippings, stocks, public shaming) was very much the norm. Prisons were typically constructed to be little more than temporary holding houses, containing prisoners until their "real" punishment could be publicly applied.

As Friedman notes, because the colonial republic was one built on a hierarchical system that ultimately modeled spiritual hierarchy, civil laws were tied together with spiritual ones, supporting and codifying moral behavior. Because the "government of men" was to serve as God's instrument on earth, the legal system served rhetorically to translate divine law into criminal statute, transforming the act of "breaking the law" into the commission of sin. Rules banned those types of activities that were considered immoral; hence, courts were provided with the atmosphere of an inquisition: "the judges, who were religious and political leaders, dominated the proceedings. They believed unswervingly in their right to rule in the name of God and according to the divine plan. They ran the show; juries rarely sat"

(L. Friedman 24).[4] One man, reflective of God's plan, sat in judgment of the morals of others, seeking to squeeze out a confession and repentance from the sinners/criminals. It is not so much that criminals were supposed to be rehabilitated as that, in breaking the rules of God, some punishment was warranted. In that the punishment could deter others by illustrating the shame of sin, punishment was open and public, shaming the sinner as a reminder of the moral system to be followed by everyone.

While the specific moment of the transition to the use of buildings for the holding and punishment of criminals is clearly arguable, the openings in the late eighteenth century of Pennsylvania's Walnut Street Prison and New York's Auburn Prison have historically been marked as the beginning of the prison system in America.[5] While the underlying reasons for the transition to the prison are of course multiplicitous and have been given a different focus by each historian who has studied them, certain characteristics of this transition are so common as to seem to be, if not undeniable, then certainly historically influential. In part, this transition to the prison was a move made possible by transitions in ideology. Hence, as leaders of the republic became ideologically removed from the role of the representatives of God's law in the move to democracy, they too became bound by popular law with "the people" and were no longer pictured as God's representatives, as the ultimate arbiters of justice. Because law was supposed to be based on a common system of justice shared by all, a cultural impulse existed toward the professionalization of law, a system based not on favor but on equality.[6] As Friedman notes, the focus of punishment left the body (stocks, whippings, spectacle) and went toward imprisonment of the criminal because whipping, public execution, and other forms of public discipline acted symbolically as attacks on republicanism: "Somehow, whipping was . . . unrepublican. It was an offense to the citizen's dignity" (74). Hence, whipping and physical punishment could only exist in locales where republicanism did not: situations of private tyranny, such as the school, the prison, the navy, the family, southern plantations (L. Friedman 74).

Imprisonment itself was no uniform and stable venture, however. Indeed, the way individual prisons functioned, and the purpose of punishment within these prisons, was in a process of transition. Historians of punishment generally do agree, however, that imprisonment was meant to remove the individual from the temptations of bad company, vice, weaknesses—to remove the individual from one particular environment—in order to reclaim his or her soul.[7] In Rothman's telling, while the original prisons were built as a means of deterring crime based on principles of punishment described by Cesare Beccaria, by the 1820s, it was obvious that Beccaria's solutions could not fulfill their promise. With crime on the rise, the purpose of prisons and punishment went through a process of transformation and rethinking, a transition that led the Jacksonians to attempt the rehabilitation of criminals. Hence, the prisons of the Jacksonian era were structured in order to "treat" criminals and then return them to the community as reformed citizens. Because the social environment was argued to be the root of crime, an artificial environment might rehabilitate some of the prisoners by removing them from the root cause of crime and allowing them to learn proper behavior in a proper environment. Even if rehabilitation was an idea in existence before the Jacksonian era, as Hirsch suggests, the Jacksonians forced attention on "reclamation" of the individual—a more complete takeover of the soul of the prisoner than previous notions of rehabilitation.

The control of individuals within prison walls is also telling of what was expected from imprisonment. The focus of the early penitentiaries was on the maintenance of silence and hard labor: silence in order to allow reflection and redemption, labor in order to make the criminal "productive." In early debates about criminal justice, the argument was not over whether prisoners should be silent or work at hard labor but instead, whether their hard labor and silence should be practiced in isolation or in the company of other inmates. Hence, in the Auburn system, the prisoners worked in silent groups, while in the Philadelphia system (both Walnut Street and Cherry Hill), the prisoners lived and worked in silence and separate from each other (L. Friedman 79). Moreover, the prisons stressed uniformity and detail in every aspect of the prisoner's life: prisoners wore the same clothing, ate the same food, worked and slept according to the same time system, and so on. Each day, each prisoner ate at the same time while sitting in the same seat: "Unlike the corrupt, haphazard, filthy jails of the past, the penitentiary was a place of strict justice, a place of penitence and reformation" (L. Friedman 80). Again, the idea for such rules was based on the theory that otherwise "normal" men (and prisoners were almost always men during this period) turned to crime because of their weak wills and their unfortunate social situations. Prison could cure these problems by providing what was missing from the prisoners' lives. Prison was meant to provide the training, the backbone, and—as Friedman notes in a way that is hauntingly echoed by some of those punished today—prison was "a caricature of the unyielding, disciplined, incorruptible family that the prisoners had never had for themselves" (80).

While I cannot reconstruct a picture of how prisoners were represented publicly during these eras, John DiIulio has provided a useful breakdown of the penological theories that supported imprisonment and provided it with theoretical justification. DiIulio provides a distribution of penological theories that fall rather loosely within chronological periods: the old penology, the new penology, and the new old penology. What he refers to as the old penology was clearly the norm from the founding of the republic through the nineteenth century and well into the mid-twentieth century. Some of the characteristics of the old penology include its stress on prison administrations rather than on prisoners, and its stress on the control of the body and mind of the prisoner rather than on the rights of prisoners.[8] There was little if any discussion, among either penologists or prisoners themselves, about the self-government of prisoners in the old penology; there was no talk of the rights of inmates as individuals. In short, the old penology acted as a child-rearing manual that highlighted the multiple forms of control available for punishment while excluding chapters that dealt with the feelings or subjectivity of the children.

Hence, when Gustave de Beaumont and Alexis de Tocqueville published their classic text *On the Penitentiary System in the United States and France* in 1833, they voiced their admiration for the American prison administration on the basis of its ability to maintain peace efficiently while removing "criminals" from corrupted environs. Their research, based on disparate sources, including interviews with the prison staff, indicated that "given decent leadership and a well-trained staff, prisons could be run in a safe and humane manner and . . . a rigorous regimen of prison discipline, education, and labor could probably help some criminals to contract habits of obedience and industry, which render them useful citizens" (DiIulio, "Understanding" 68). While Beaumont and Tocqueville certainly did not ignore the humanity of the prisoner—they indeed saw him as neither "brute nor saint"—the focus of their work remained on the administration of discipline, not on the prisoners themselves. Order came first and foremost, to be attained at almost any cost. Moreover, as DiIulio notes, the two basic elements of Beaumont and Tocqueville's penology, "the sympathetic focus on prison administrators rather than on prisoners and the idea that those prisons are governed best that are governed most," remained very much at the center of American penological thinking throughout the nineteenth century ("Understanding" 70).

Certainly, not all of the characteristics with which prisons began in the early part of the eighteenth century could, or did, last. Over time, due in large part to the great increase in the number of prisoners who were entering prison walls and with the increasingly obvious failure of prisons to stop crime or to rehabilitate prisoners to any serious degree, many of the practices of the original prisons fell to the side. No longer were prisons the great halls of silence, for instance, but instead became places where men worked and talked together, although still according to a fairly stiff regimen.

Moreover, the racial composition of prisons also led to transitions in punishment. After the Civil War, the black population of prisons rose nationally as crimes by blacks were increasingly prosecuted by "legitimate" systems of justice rather than by vigilantes, in order to provide a semblance of justice. Nevertheless, even when prosecuted in the court system, both because of subtle and overt calls for prison segregation and because of calls of legislators for prisons to become self-supporting, many black inmates ended up in chain gangs and/or were leased to work in fields or mines where conditions were such that the punishment often led to the early death of the inmate.[9] Hence, the racial composition of prisons encouraged the transition of the prisoner from one to be redeemed through hard labor to one who brings profit through hard labor.

In addition, while crimes continued throughout the nineteenth century to be regarded in part as acts against the "moral sense of the community," the overall composition of this moral sense began to loosen, opening space for debates about morality. Hence, as Friedman suggests, the moral climate of the nineteenth century, coupled with decisions by state and federal legislators, slowly brought into existence what he calls the "Victorian Compromise." This compromise consisted of an unspoken climate in which "immoral behaviors" (for example, gambling, drinking, prostitution) were permitted as long as they were either hidden from the community at large or were practiced only within specific, generally geographical, parameters.

Other characteristics of criminal justice in the nineteenth century include an increasing tendency toward a professionalization of criminal justice as a system, from police departments to judges to the prison itself. Again, however, even as the system professionalized, it remained solidly within the old penology camp, with the focus of criminal justice always on the administration of justice rather than on the personal needs or rights of the prisoner. While numerous arguments became apparent between different discourses and professional communities about specific questions of criminal justice (for example, branches of the medical and psychological communities began to argue for insanity as a defense,[10] geneticists argued that criminal behavior could be traced to genetic make-up and thus called for the sterilization of criminals as a long-term solution), prisons remained in general a place where men who had given in to the temptations of a poor environment were to be taken, made productive, reclaimed, revamped, reshaped, and then returned to a community in which they could show their improvement through productivity.

What we see, then, in the transition from the colonial period to the nineteenth century is a move to the secularization of morals and the privatization of punishment. While no longer ostensibly based on the ruling classes' direct relationship with the divine, punishment still remained centered on what was defined as moral behavior, indeed public moral behavior. Moreover, as legislation began to allow individuals to behave differently in public and private settings, punishment itself was carried out more often than not in private; it was no longer motivated by public shame but by private productivity. The prisoner was constituted in some sense as one element of the communal machine, to be taken, repaired, and made to work again, with no question of what the prisoner himself thought was best, with no imagination that a criminal could have rights. In addition, given the higher death rates of blacks in prison due to the more dangerous tasks they were assigned, one could argue that only white prisoners were meant to be productive upon their release, and hence they alone were rehumanized (perhaps because only they were considered human from the start). The old penology shaped criminal justice and carried with it the assumption of the prisoner as malleable object.

While it is of course illusory to provide the year 1900 as a breaking point in changes in the prison system or in the ways in which justice is carried out, it has often been offered as a point of transition and change in criminal justice. However, there are several reasons for marking the twentieth century and the midpoint of the twentieth century as the starting and ending points for eras of punishment. For example, it is in the twentieth century that the federal government began to take a more active role in the business of justice by attempting to provide some form of consistency and order to state judicial systems. As the federal government began dictating court procedures, it also became more active in defining a number of activities as crimes. As Friedman notes, the great growth in federal regulatory apparatus is the most obvious source of new, regulatory crimes (for instance, antitrust laws, securities fraud, civil rights violations, pollution of air and water) (283–89).

As a result, the federal government was establishing procedures for justice, defining legality, and building and maintaining more prisons. On a rhetorical level, during the early twentieth century, crime became a leading motif of the political process in that, as a topic for debate and national interest, crime and responses to it became matters of public interest, matters on which votes were based (L. Friedman 283). Another major transition in criminal justice was the atrophy of the system of trial by jury. As a number of alternatives began to develop in place of the lengthy process of trial by jury (for example, the negotiated guilty plea, the judge as jury), it slowly lost its role as the prominent means of justice.

While each of these changes takes place throughout the twentieth century, it is clear that the midpoint of the twentieth century provides the clearest point for historians to delineate changes in the "process" of justice. In narrative after narrative, and for multiple reasons, historians and criminologists alike point to 1950 as the date marking the clearest transitional point in the administration of justice and hence in the location from which the concept of the prisoner was articulated publicly.

On March 23, 1946, the U.S. Congress passed a set of rules that had been drawn up by a committee put together by the Supreme Court. That legislation provided rules of pleading, practice, and procedure for all federal and state courts. As a result, the years after 1950 saw a growth in uniformity in the many ways that justice was carried out within the courtroom. Because federal law trumped local law, federal courts could make sure that the standards drawn up federally were enforced at the local level (L. Friedman 294–97).

Moreover, it is only after 1950 (primarily in the 1960s) that a number of court orders and court decisions, reflecting a new form of prison activism, enabled prisoners to sue the prison system for "human rights," such as the availability of particular forms of worship or special dietary needs. This change is perhaps the most "effective" one in terms of transforming the prisoner as an "object of discourse." To be specific, while prisoners had been unable to have any "real" legal rights in the earlier portion of the twentieth century, the more activist Supreme Court after 1950 provided the criminal, and hence the prisoner, with a different identity. Rather than an object unto which "discipline" was directed, the courts repositioned the criminal as an independent being who was also the responsibility of the state; while the state could impose discipline as a reaction to the individual's disruption of community morals, it also had to respect the criminal as a human being with the same rights as all other human beings when it imposed its discipline (L. Friedman 313, 418).

Social transformations, separate from the courts and the changing demographics of the prison, also impacted the treatment of prisoners after the 1950s. Specifically, the 1950s witnessed an increase in the number of African-American prisoners held in federal and state prisons, an increase that was coincident with changes wrought by the discourse of the civil rights movement. That is, because African Americans and prisoners (and especially those constituted by both categories) are in relatively powerless positions culturally, the civil rights movement, claiming basic human rights for all people and especially blacks, strongly influenced the positioning of African Americans, prisoners, and African-American prisoners. African-American prisoners were transformed, reconstituted in one set of discourses as humans who could demand the rights, dignities, and privileges of their position as humans.

While politicians had begun to highlight crime (and their accompanying "law and order" mentalities) early in the century, large increases in the national crime rate, which clearly began to climb precipitously in the midpoint of the century, also served to place questions about crime, punishment, and criminals into the foreground of political discourse. Indeed, Friedman notes that it is only after the 1950s that the crime problem became intense enough in people's minds and lives to become one of the central factors upon which voters based their political decisions (449–51). While in some ways crime and criminal activity have always been part of the public consciousness in that they are based on the moral sense of a community, it is only during and after the 1950s that it becomes a pressing political topic and hence highlights the difference between criminal and "moral" behavior, criminality and citizenship.

It is in multiple ways, then, that after 1950 criminal justice and criminals were changing, rhetorically, procedurally, and materially. In addition to an increase in the number of prisoners, there was a simultaneous change in the way in which the criminal justice system dealt with crime. Rather than procedures and operations that differed from state to state and county to county, uniform procedures were prescribed nationally. Rather than prisoners who were legally positioned at the complete mercy of the criminal justice system, legal decisions refigured the prisoner as a human being with legal rights and human dignity. Rather than a peaceful merging of prisoners of different ethnicities, prisons witnessed a growth in the consciousness of African-American prisoners as different rather than the same, as deserving of the same rights that were being demanded by African Americans outside of prison, be they Malcolm X or Martin Luther King, Jr. (although Malcolm X's discourse certainly appeared to have struck a much stronger chord among African-American prisoners than did King's).

In addition to changes in the constitution of prisoners on the basis of demographic statistics and legal decisions, change was also developing in the theory and practice of criminal justice. If the penology labeled by DiIulio as "old penology" provided a sympathetic treatment of prison administrators and others who carried on the workings of the criminal justice system, the "new penology" turned the two main premises of the old penology on their heads and refocused the way in which policymakers discussed criminal behavior and the treatment of prisoners. In short, the new penology focused sympathetically on the plight of prison inmates and argued that prisons work best not when the prisoners are governed strongly from above but instead when prisoners are allowed to set up their own systems of judgment, their own community norms, within the prison ("Understanding" 72). DiIulio traces the theoretical development of the new penology through a number of prominent theoretical works, placing the advent of the new penology in Donald Clemmer's 1940 book *The Prison Community.* Here, Clemmer argues that penologists could not understand the position of the criminal (and hence how punishment works on "him") unless the penologist included a systematic investigation of the prison's unseen environment, its "social community." After Clemmer's work, this movement grew. Hence, 1958 found the publication of Gresham Sykes's *The Society of Captives,* an influential monograph that argued that prisoners often survived because of their subcommunities, and that if penologists attempted to disrupt these crude communities and their relatively autonomous systems of justice, a totalitarian environment that bred corruption and conflict would begin to cultivate itself within prisoners. One element of Sykes's solution to such a scenario was to allow prisoners to write their own rules, to construct internal systems of justice according to their own needs, needs that no one from the outside can begin to understand.

The move to the new penology grew stronger throughout the following decade. In 1960, the Social Science Research Council published its *Theoretical Studies in Social Organization of the Prison* in which the collective authors treated the ideas of the new penology as assumed knowledge. What the new penology assumed was that prisoners must be allowed, to some limited degree, to maintain their own systems of rules and justice, to act as, and be treated as, competent human beings. DiIulio argues that the move toward the new penology reached its peak in 1980 with the publication of sociologist and former prisoner John Irwin's *Prisons in Turmoil,* a work introduced as a "discourse on democracy." Here, Irwin asserts that prison officials are little better than ill-educated racists, while prisoners are "humans just like us . . . [who] will act honorably, given a real choice" (124–26).[11] Irwin retells the stories of the prison riots in the 1950s, 1960s, and 1970s in such a way that they become the result of a lack of inmate empowerment and autonomy rather than (as conservative discussions of prison riots suggested) a surplus of inmate empowerment and autonomy. While others justified the need to limit the autonomy of inmates, Irwin critiqued almost all existing constraints. Instead, Irwin prescribed a system of decision making "in which inmates, through their democratically elected leaders, participate in all phases of prison governance, setting conditions of work and confinement, formulate the results of the situation, and negotiate the special problems and grievances of different parties, reconciling problems between inmates and staff" (241).[12] The position of the prisoner had changed remarkably since the beginning of the century, from a cog in the state disciplinary machine to a "human" who deserved to practice democracy and self-rule, regardless of the crime.

DiIulio, a former student of James Q. Wilson, established the lineage of the old penology and the new in order to position his offering of a "new old penology." DiIulio's "new old penology" contains elements of the old penology in that it provides respect and sympathy toward prison administration and the problems involved in maintaining order in a prison environment, but his move is not simply to recoup the old penology. Instead, while he is certainly less than enthusiastic about prisoner self-management and is supportive of a "law and order" mentality, DiIulio describes the new old penology in such a way that it is *not* the opposite of the new penology, *not* the same as the old penology, and *not* a synthesis of the two. Instead, the new old penology "is an approach to understanding prisons that gladly admits administrators back to the bar of attention, is inclined to treat them at least as sympathetically as it treats their charge, and attempts to translate empirically grounded research on prisoner behavior into ideas about how to move toward more safe and humane conditions behind bars" (85). The new old penology is a move, in other words, to do whatever works to manage the prison. It neither errs toward administrative restrictiveness nor toward administrative permissiveness; its attempt is to run prisons in the best possible way that works without necessarily having to pin its function on "rehabilitation" or "retribution."

Enough backdrop. With this brief historical survey of punishment, both its theory and practice,[13] I hope to have established a suggestion of some of the multiple rhetorical factors that will come into play in the representation of prisoners over the past forty years. The representation of prisoners and the representation of the relationship of the criminal to the state do not take place in isolation but instead in a rhetorical field with a powerful history. The weight of rhetoric on culture in this case comes from a history in which the breaking of laws contains suggestions of sin and immorality, in which prisoners are struggled over as objects of the state and as freethinking, rights-bearing subjects, in which the administration is positioned as tyrannical or as underappreciated, in which race, class, and gender all have their bearing. As I trace out the characterization and narrative of the prisoner, these elements of the rhetorical field in which the prisoner is located all have their pull. Moreover, with the economic and spatial constraints of penology in the last decade, the various and contradictory positionings of prisoners and punishment merge and intertwine in some potentially frightening ways, as the case of Maria Arnford has already illustrated.

3

Rehabilitation and the Altruistic Inmate, 1950–1959

> At one point [prisoner Teddy] Green's eyes filled with tears. "I've done a lot of bad things," he said, "evil things. My only wish is that some time I might do a good thing. Like giving my eyes so that a blind child might see. . . . Isn't there some way I could do something good?" ("Ominous" 24)

While not a universal characterization of the prisoner of the 1950s, this excerpt from a 1955 *Newsweek* report serves well as a characteristic anecdote of representations of this era's prisoner. Teddy Green, along with three other prisoners, took five guards hostage at the Massachusetts State Prison in Boston after the guards had foiled the prisoners' attempt to escape. With the hostages, the prisoners effectively were able to take control of the Cherry Hill section of the compound. Green's escape motive was to recover the reported one million dollars he had buried following the bank robbery that had led to his imprisonment. Significantly, the *Newsweek* article notes that, in a conversation with his daughter, Green claims to have needed the money in order to provide for his wife and children. Hence, even when Green and other prisoners riot and take hostages in this period, their representation in the popular media calls for general sympathy toward their plight. Green knows the difference between good and evil; he aspires to the former and eschews the latter. He and his cohorts obviously have the best interests of others at heart and share a common morality with those "on the outside." While one might not condone their actions, their motives are, for the most part, impeccable. Green's attempted escape comes as a result of his familial obligation rather than of an inherently evil disposition.[1] Indeed, given the same set of circumstances, anyone might have behaved in a similar fashion.

While the prisoner of this era, as any other, has multiple and complex representations, this in no small way is the quintessential portrait of the prisoner of the 1950s. Not only does this prisoner share a morality with the culture at large, but his general failure to behave properly is understandable, the result of uncomfortable and unfortunate living conditions forced on prisoners and outside of their control. Even rioters and escapees such as Teddy Green are represented as redeemable if given proper attention and care.

In their separate treatises on punishment, John Irwin (40–49) and Larry Sullivan (61–93) both point to the 1950s as the decade in which the rehabilitation model for the treatment of prisoners flourished. Both claim that arguments for rehabilitation grew after a number of prisons throughout the nation experienced rioting and as blame was placed on the conditions of imprisonment rather than on the prisoners. They further argue that rehabilitation as a model began to decline near the end of the 1950s as the initial promises of rehabilitative practices (practices such as indeterminate sentencing, counseling, educational programs, and parole) met with criticism from convicts, prison administration, and politicians alike. The rise of the rehabilitation model proves to be a strong element of the discourse of this period; however, it does not begin to fall off in popular discourse quite as rapidly or as smoothly as it does in theoretical and historical discussions. In the popular press of the 1950s, the convict maintains a sense of decorum and patriotism; in general, imprisonment is the result of a single life episode when, after falling on hard times, he or she makes a mistake in judgment. The prisoner shares the dominant cultural morality; he or she is simply faced with circumstances that encourage misbehavior. These prisoners will "do their time" and return once again to contribute meaningfully to the social order. A survey of some of the titles of the magazine articles of this era evinces this stance toward the convict. Hence, we find "Michigan's Happy Convicts" (Titus), "My Convict" (Small), "Convicts Can Be Heroes" (O'Brien), "Big Hearted Guy," "Good Samaritan," "Prisoners Who Volunteer, Blood, Flesh—And Their Lives" (Wharton), and "A Criminal Saved My Life" (Reed).

As appendix 3 illustrates, despite the fact that the racial makeup of state and federal prisoners empirically remained near its 1950 average of 69 percent white throughout the decade, the prisoner of the 1950s is clearly represented as Caucasian when race is mentioned at all (Langan 5). As a result, when race goes unmentioned, the reader is encouraged to imagine the prisoner as Caucasian if only because the most common representation of the prisoner in the collective past has been Caucasian.

In terms of gender, the prisoner of this era, with rare exception, is male. Indeed, while I will deal with the female prisoner more intensively later in this chapter, I will use masculine pronouns throughout much of the chapter in order to make it clear that this prisoner is generally represented as male. The statistical ratio of male to female prisoners may account for part of this. In 1955 and in 1985, the 96 percent to 4 percent ratios of male to female prisoners is indicative of the entire period of this study (Flanagan and Maguire 582).

The prisoner of the 1950s emerged during a cultural moment in which riots and escape attempts were reportedly on the rise in prisons throughout the country. While several reactions to such behavior were obviously available to prison officials and media observers (prisoner segregation or harsher punishments for instance), the chosen reaction was an assertion that prisoners simply needed more attention; the riots became a symptom of malignant prison conditions rather than of unruly prisoners. Because prisoners shared the larger culture's sense of morality, their actions were configured as mistakes in judgment rather than proof of an evil nature. Riots acted as a signifier that the social body must work to improve the prisoner's ability to make judgments. It is not that these public representations of the prisoner are a clear reflection of the theoretical move toward the "new penology," for the argument is not that prisoners are individuals whose rights are being trampled upon (although this is sometimes the case); nor is it the reflection of the old penology, for the focus is not only the prison administration alone (although this, too, is sometimes the case). Instead, the representation of the prisoner of this era focuses on the way in which the prison administration must begin to do more for the prisoner, albeit a prisoner without a great deal of legal rights. The prison remains in control although it must perform its task more effectively.

I begin this chapter, then, with an investigation of the major characterization of the male prisoner of the 1950s, the altruistic and redeemable inmate. I then move on to discuss some of the minor characterizations of prisoners and of prison life, including homosexuality, irrationality, and immorality; finally, I provide a short sketch of the female prisoner. An understanding of these minor and latent characterizations proves important in understanding the shape of future characterizations and the major rhetorical forces of later decades. For instance, while consideration of the constitution of the prisoner as a naturally immoral being is minor in the 1950s, it becomes a more dominant representation later, as criminal justice officials attempt to explain behavior that would be considered inexplicable if coming from an altruistic inmate.

The Altruistic Inmate

Medical Experimentation

Throughout the 1950s and 1960s, it was common practice for pharmaceutical corporations and research institutions to utilize inmate populations as the subjects of experiments focusing on the safety and effectiveness of new medications, vaccinations, and treatments. This type of experimentation was justified on the grounds that prisoners constituted the quintessential controlled population. Because prison rules controlled diet, exercise, activities, and overall lifestyles, prisoners were considered less likely to engage in individual activities that would offset differences in experimental treatment. Moreover, insofar as prisoners were incarcerated for having committed wrongful acts, there is little reported concern about the potential exploitation such experimentation might represent. Instead, rather than emphasizing that prisoners partake in such experiments with secret hopes that participation might lead to early parole or easier work loads within the prison, prisoners are represented as exercising free choice and of working with altruistic motives when "volunteering" for the various experiments.

While a variety of these assumptions (for instance, that prisoners strictly follow the rules of prisons, do not have black market means of securing contraband, or that "free choice" is possible when one is incarcerated), are clearly unsound from a contemporary perspective, the framing of these experiments as the result of choice from both the corporations' and the prisoners' points of view is clearly the most fascinating element of the experiments. Just as Teddy Green hoped to give sight to the blind during the midst of a riot that could have led to the deaths of numerous prisoners and guards, inmates are represented as giving of themselves without any hope for reward other than the satisfaction one derives from helping others and making amends for one's mistakes. Such prisoners do not condemn the social body that has sentenced them; indeed, they are helping maintain it in a disease-free fashion. While some prison officials and criminologists will later publicly indict the prison system for failing to serve the inmates properly, prisoners themselves are praised for their willingness to serve the culture at large. As one title suggests, prisoners are "heroes," paying their debt by benefiting the culture at large at some risk to their own health (P. Jackson, "Prison Heroes Conquer Malaria" 40).

The representations of these experiments can be divided into two broad groups. In the first, recounted here, testimonials are provided from prisoners who have engaged in such experiments. In the second, observers such as reporters and pharmaceutical representatives describe the heroics of the prisoners who choose to become experimental subjects. Inmates at the Ohio State Penitentiary, for example, were asked to volunteer to receive live injections of a cancer strain in order to see if the human body could naturally fight specific cancers. *Reader's Digest* reports that the experimenters asked for twenty-five volunteers who would receive only a nominal reward for their research; over 130 volunteered for the experiment (Brecher and Brecher 63). One of the prisoners who had undergone the experimental injections, when asked why he had decided to participate, reflected the sentiments of Teddy Green in noting that "this is a decision I reached after much thought and a good many prayers. I hope I can be of some good after being no good so long" (64). Several other prisoners noted that they were willing to take part in the experiments because they had either friends or family members with cancer, and the experiments were the only type of aid they could offer from within prison. Similarly, after participating in experiments to find new ways of treating malaria, inmates at New York's Sing Sing were given certificates that commended their participation. When offered the certificate, one inmate placed his hands behind his back and said, "I don't want to touch it—this was the only decent thing I ever did" (Wharton, "Prisoners" 54). Given the opportunity to help others, then, prisoners are represented as doing so in a manner heavily flavored by altruism.

Observers of the experiments also vouched for the altruistic makeup of the common prisoner. For example, when psychologist Austin MacCormick was asked to characterize the motives behind an inmate's decision to take part in such experiments with little promise of either a monetary or social payoff, he noted in *American Mercury* that "prisoners volunteer chiefly because of a social conscience that *many of them do not realize they have.* Selfish motives play a secondary role. They welcome the chance to balance some of the harm they have done" (Wharton, "Prisoners" 55; emphasis added). MacCormick recounted a number of these experiments, including research on malaria at Sing Sing, influenza and syphilis at Stateville, and hepatitis at McNeil Island. He noted that, when asked, prisoners are often embarrassed by their altruistic motives and cover these motives with more selfish ones. Notice that MacCormick, as a psychologist, claims that prisoners have altruistic motives despite their own protestations to the opposite. This characterization of the prisoner who has a need and desire to help society crystallizes throughout the era: thus,

Nathan Leopold is commended for "volunteering as a guinea pig for malaria experiments during the war" ("Nathan" 61); in "Convicts Can Be Heroes," an article in *Today's Health,* a majority of prisoners are said to be willing to donate time and discomfort to provide skin grafts for children and to serve as guinea pigs in experiments (O'Brien 29); and the motive of the prisoner who takes part in these experiments is always to find a way to "help the society they offended" (Cozart 17).

Aid to Youth, Inmates, and Former Offenders

The altruism of the prisoner's personality goes beyond his service as a guinea pig. Narratives provide 1950s culture with prisoners whose sole concern is finding a way to aid others, often by their own sacrifice. For example, *Coronet* reported that Bob McCoy, formerly of Utah State Prison, made parole by inventing a set of metal-cutting shears in a workshop at prison and then gaining the backing of his warden and other prison administrators in creating a corporation to sell the tool. When the corporation became successful, McCoy began to make plans for the excess cash that it provided him. Rather than spending the money on himself or saving it, he planned to build a tool shed for underprivileged children, both to help them learn a useful skill and to keep them out of trouble until they were employable (Snarr 129). In effect, McCoy noted that he wanted to build the type of place that would have kept him out of trouble as a child.

Depictions of altruism are not limited to aiding others against the future; they also operate in situations in the here and now, situations that threaten the safety of the prisoners. At the Oklahoma State Penitentiary, two prisoners attempted an escape by taking a chaplain hostage. The *American Mercury* narrative of the event focused on the risk that any prisoner would take who chose to break the "prisoner code" (which requires prisoners to be loyal to other prisoners regardless of circumstance) and help the chaplain. Such a prisoner would be open to physical and verbal attacks by all other inmates, regardless of how long he remained incarcerated. An enemy of one prisoner, the *American Mercury* reports, would be regarded as an enemy of all. Hence, "snitching" could be seen as the ultimate act of altruism. Despite such risks, the chaplain's inmate assistant, with no promise of reward for doing so, broke away and alerted authorities, thus saving the chaplain's life. The chaplain noted that the prisoner "broke criminal codes but not human ones" (Reed 92).

Two other narratives reinforce this point. One popular news story of this era focused on the generosity of inmate Jimmy C. Henderson of Huntsville State Prison in Texas. Henderson, who owned 23,000 acres of land and had $500,000 in different bank accounts in Texas, despite having been convicted of the murder of his common-law wife, was dubbed the "Good Samaritan" in *Time* and the "Big Hearted Guy" in *Newsweek.* Henderson picked up these nicknames when, on two separate occasions, he gave $10,000 or more to prisoners who were being released to help each lead a more productive life. While both squandered the money and returned to various criminal activities, Henderson asserted that he would continue to provide others with financial aid and stood by the prisoners he had given money to. A picture of Henderson in *Time,* rather than being labeled "Convicted Murderer Henderson," represented him as "Philanthropist Henderson: As Good As Gold" ("Good Samaritan" 24; "Big-Hearted" 27).

In another tale of altruism, we find the romantic tale of a crime partnership broken by imprisonment. The narrative centers on John Carroll, who was being held at the Federal Penitentiary in Leavenworth, Kansas, and his wife and crime partner Mabel, held at the Leeds Prison for Women. When Carroll learned that Mabel had tuberculosis, he slowly plotted his escape. Receiving a note from Mabel in which she said that her death was imminent, he broke out of Leavenworth and into Leeds. Carroll then took his wife from Leeds, rented an apartment and committed a series of robberies so that she could live the last years of her life in comfort. When she died, Carroll willingly returned to serve the rest of his life in prison (Ross 102–6). The crimes Carroll commits, rather than being represented as motivated by a callous disregard for law and social order, become yet one more sign of the ultimate good of all human beings, despite their mistakes in judgment. Crime is not motivated by selfishness but by altruism. Again, Carroll's acts are ones that anyone, put into the same circumstances, would do.

What is common to each of these characterizations and narratives is the inclusion of the prisoner as an individual to be related to on a human level. While some of their activities would always be considered praiseworthy (such as volunteering for experiments) and others would generally be considered criminal (like robbery), their motives make most all of their activities altruistic. At base, we understand the prisoner's actions; prisoners are cut of the same cloth as the rest of us but have been placed into different circumstances.

Rehabilitation and Humanity

Supporting and paralleling the characterization of the inmate as altruistic is his portrait as explicitly redeemable, compelled to return to the social whole, to become "human" again. This depiction arises in reports on rehabilitation programs, the attitudes of those running prisons, and the attitudes and behaviors of the prisoners themselves.

I was tempted to subtitle this section "Duffy's Inmates" because of the sizable body of discourse outlining the career and philosophy of Clinton Duffy, warden of San Quentin during the 1950s and known for radicalizing the treatment of prisoners. Not only is Duffy often cited as a positive force in those articles focusing on and supportive of rehabilitation programs, but he also wrote a series of eight articles for the *Saturday Evening Post* in which he rearticulates the meaning of prisoner, aligning "prisoner" with "human being," a person in need of aid and understanding, rather than the opposite.

Duffy became the warden of San Quentin after an uprising had brought about the kidnapping and stabbing of then-warden James B. Holohan by several San Quentin inmates. Rather than taking an anticipated "hard stance" toward the entire inmate population, Duffy immediately began instituting a series of changes, some seemingly superficial, each of which moved closer toward a "rehabilitation" model of punishment that framed the prisoners as human. For instance, Duffy ended the ritual of shaving prisoners' heads when they arrived at San Quentin, claiming that imprisonment itself was embarrassing for the inmate and that no human being deserved more punishment than imprisonment ("Part Three" 43). Because these changes garnered widespread publicity and were slowly instituted in other prisons nationwide, his testimony is particularly important to the 1950s construction of the prisoner. On taking over San Quentin, Duffy claims to have decided to base punishment on his personal view of prisoners: "I've thought of men behind bars as my father saw them—human beings in trouble and needing a helping hand" ("Part One" 148); and, "Even the most savage of men need and appreciate a friend" ("Part One" 149). Consistent with these representations from the first of his essays, Duffy persists in drawing the inmates as human beings in trouble, needing the help of a friend. Throughout the series, Duffy recounts stories of prisoners whom he and members of his family had visited and notes with pleasure the many times that these prisoners later wrote long letters of thanks ("Part Three" 99).

One of Duffy's central messages throughout the series is that both the public and the penal system have misunderstood the nature of prisoners and of the problems associated with prisons. Of prisoners, he notes that while many people have traditionally viewed prisoners as violent individuals prone to recidivism, in reality they are often rehabilitated, with 98 percent returning to a "normal" life upon release ("Part Eight" 179). Indeed, Duffy blames what many consider to be faults of the inmate on the prison itself. For example, in recounting the story of an inmate who attempted to escape, Duffy puts the blame on his own actions rather than those of the inmate. His brief apologia is stunning: "I failed to reach a man's hand to make him understand how we are trying to help" ("Part Seven" 162). In this statement, we find the highly visible warden of one of the nation's largest prisons refuting what was the dominant depiction of the prisoner of the past and arguing a representation of the prisoner as prone to redemption, a human being who needs to know that others care. Duffy's prisoner is a troubled human being failed by the prison system rather than an inherent criminal who fails his fellow citizens. While Duffy's philosophy was labeled "radical" at its inception, it is a prominent one, demanding a great deal of public space and gathering a great deal of attention. With less focus on control and more on the human rights of inmates, Duffy represents a public move toward the institutionalization of the new penology.

In another example of the recognition of the redeemable nature of prisoners by administrators, we find the surprising case of the riot at the Michigan State Penitentiary at Jackson. Reports about the case were widespread, including a four-part series in *The Saturday Evening Post* that attempted to understand the basis for the riot (J. Martin, "Why," Parts I–IV) and a *Collier's* essay written by the prison psychologist, Vernon Fox, who was responsible for the controversial ending to the riot (Fox and Fay). As reported, two inmates, Earl Ward and "Crazy" Jack Hyatt, virtually took over one block of the prison after first kidnapping one guard. What is important about the episode is not the riot itself but the representation of the way that Fox negotiated its conclusion with Ward and Hyatt. After a number of days of rioting in which several prisoners were injured and several others murdered, the riot was brought to a close with Ward and Hyatt being returned to their cells. Immediately after the riot was brought to a close, Fox gave a speech to the population of the prison in which he claimed "Earl Ward is the head leader, he and the other boys are to be congratulated on the ability with which they have bargained; their word has been good. My word has been good. This may project a new era of good sound interrelationships between inmates and administration. They have done a service: Congratulations to you, men in fifteen block" (quoted in "Convicts Bully" 30; cf. J. Martin "Why, Part Four" 146). Even though Fox later resigned from his position and the prison administration condemned his praise of a man who had killed one of their guards, the speech itself and Fox's opportunity to comment on it in *Collier's* reveal the degree to which prisoners were being represented as human beings with needs and abilities. Rather than murderers and rioters, in this representation, Hyatt and Ward became "leaders" who had "done a service" to the men of fifteen block.

Even toward the end of this era, with the general representation of prisoners in transition, those prisoners who never become "rehabilitated" are for the most part represented as growing and caring individuals. Taking the classic film *The Defiant Ones* as a case study, it becomes evident that even two escaped convicts, one imprisoned for armed robbery and one for attempted murder, can learn the lessons of humanity. The film at first appears as an anomaly in the decade, not only because of the race issues it raises but also because the prisoners are never rehabilitated, never return to the social order. Indeed, in the end, viewers are assured that their escape ends in failure and that the sheriff will return them to their rightful place in prison. However, the film is replete with demonstrations of the two characters' ability to learn about their nature as human beings—to care and to give. Not only, then, do the two convicts, chained to each other for the greater part of their escape, learn to help one another and thereby learn to respect the other's position in life (that is, one as a poor white, the other as a black), but the film also signifies their basic humanity in numerous ways. For example, the pursuing sheriff reminds his newly deputized and overanxious aides that the chase must not be treated as a hunt; prisoners are human beings with full human rights. In the film's climax, the black convict cradles the injured white one in his arms, singing to him, while the sheriff, who has finally caught up with them, returns his gun to his holster, knowing that they will return obediently. While the convicts' pasts may have been violent and while their racial differences may have led to fights, they have a clear aptitude to learn the higher lessons of caring and brotherhood.

Indeed, as a result of discourses that reify the representations drawn by the cases of Duffy, Fox, or *The Defiant Ones,* little struggle is left between rehabilitation and punishment as attitudes toward criminals. By the end of the fifties, Richard McGee, director of a program that trained California prisoners to work in skilled jobs upon their release, could assert nonchalantly in *Reader's Digest* that "primitive people take revenge. A civilized society should try to rehabilitate" (Harmer 128). The same essay provided two narratives about prisoners who participated in the program; one, "a three-time loser—with 100 burglaries on and off his record," now "has a prospering public-relations business; he is married and has earned the respect of his community;" the second, "a convicted forger. . . . with the encouragement and financial aid of his employer, started his own factory" (Harmer 128).

In an equally blatant manner, psychiatrist Fredric Wertham, in a review of Nathan Leopold's *Life Plus 99 Years,* noted that "crime and punishment is now old stuff; what's discussed today is neuroses and rehabilitation" (18). Rather than a need for the criminal to be punished, there is a greater need for the citizenry of the United States to view the prisoner as a human being needing and requiring aid from the populace at large. If we treat prisoners' "neuroses" and rehabilitate them in the process, the rewards are great for all: rehabilitated citizens who create business and families.

Simultaneous with the 1950s stress on rehabilitation is the stress on understanding that circumstances, rather than essences, are the bases for criminal behavior. The stress is on how circumstances create the criminal rather than on how criminals create crime. Hence, Gladys Duffy, wife of San Quentin's Clinton Duffy and also the author of several essays on prison life, provided a narrative about a jazz band made up of San Quentin prisoners who sought air time on a local public radio station. She noted that the band "wanted people outside to realize that most prisoners were not conscienceless brutes, but men striving to regain places among their fellow men" (212).

In a series of articles in *The Saturday Evening Post* with the express purpose of providing the public with an understanding of who and what convicts are, Frederick Baldi, head of the Philadelphia County Prison, noted that "criminals are not something apart, like zebras. The men and women in prison are somewhat more representative of the general population than you might care to admit" ("Part I" 18). A sampling of various characterizations of the period only serves to solidify the point: New Jersey State Prison warden William Carty noted in *Collier's* that "only 15% of the inmates are troublemakers; the rest are decent men who deserve kindness and consideration" (70); in discussing prisoners who had broken their own legs in order to protest treatment by guards in Georgia's Rock Quarry, Louis LaMarr, an Atlanta attorney, noted in *The Nation,* "I don't care what the criminal has done. He's still a man. He has a right to be a human being" (Byron 568). Ruth Slack, a former secretary at the Michigan Prison Camp Program at Waterloo, asserted, "I have learned that even when men are serving terms for murder, larceny, burglary, kidnapping, arson, mayhem, and the rest of the punishable crimes, they are first of all human beings" (14). Slack made note of particular prisoners, including "the shoeshine boy who is an enthusiastic student of yoga and Rosicrucianism, and can discuss Freud. . . . There is the truck driver who hums arias from all the great operas" (14). Finally, in attempting to explain how prisons can properly serve the nation, Reed Cozart, former director of Louisiana prisons, asserted that "we need to remember that prisoners are people created in the image of God, even as you and I" (18).[2] In each case, we are reminded that we must refigure the image of prisoner as human, as human as each of us.

The redeemable nature of the inmate is detailed as well in narratives concerning younger prisoners. For example, a prison camp for first-time offenders in Butner, North Carolina, run by Jim Waite garnered a significant amount of publicity for its apparent ability to transform youthful offenders. In *Reader's Digest,* Don Wharton noted that although most of Butner's inmates came filled with resentment toward the prison system and society in general, their attitudes changed with the discovery that Butner had an ethos of rehabilitation: "In city after city, men holding down good jobs have told me how Butner opened a new world to them" (Wharton, "Jim" 63).

More remarkable, however, is the way in which "failures" of the Butner program are characterized. During the 1950s, inmates at Butner were warned that those found guilty of transgressing any of Butner's rules would immediately be taken away from the camp and moved back into a "regular" prison for the remainder of their sentence. Don Wharton reported that when two youths at Butner were caught attempting to escape, Waite immediately proceeded to have them transferred to a prison chain gang. As Waite drove the two youths to their new prison, the car they were riding in was involved in a collision that resulted in Waite breaking both of his knees, making it impossible for him to move from the car. Rather than attempting to escape, which obviously would have been easy, the two inmates flagged another car over and helped Waite receive medical attention, fully aware that they would immediately be taken to the chain gang to begin the remainder of their sentence (Wharton, "Jim" 64). Even Butner's "failures," then, learn to behave in a civil manner.

Prisoners themselves testify to the virtues of rehabilitation programs and indeed represent themselves using terms supplied by these programs. As John Irwin noted of his time in prison, "Many of us accepted the altered self conception contained in the new criminology. We began to believe that we were sick, and we started searching for cures" (60). Prisoners were publicly presented as infinitely curable, and some portion of them began to believe that cures were necessary—that they were, in fact, ill. Hence, in the aptly titled "Michigan's Happy Convicts," an essay narrating the lives of prisoners who were chosen to work in groups in camps and park sites rebuilding public wilderness areas, participants in the program acknowledged the benefits of the program in changing their attitude and behavior. For example, one participant noted, "Out here work changes every few days . . . every so often you'll see a new way to do it. You talk it over with the boss and chances are he'll let you try. I tell you, when you see your own ideas tried out, it makes you feel like folks" (Titus 60). Here and elsewhere, prisoners are represented as more than capable of rehabilitation, as just "folks," normal human beings in abnormal circumstances.

Furthermore, prisoners testify that they desire rehabilitation to such a degree that they behave especially carefully to assure that they are not jeopardizing their participation in any of the available rehabilitation programs. For example, several prisoners in an Iowa State Penitentiary program were allowed to fish unguarded in order to bring food to the prison. Several years into the program, no one had attempted to escape or return late (Eddy and Runyon 17), both of which were feasible in that the prisoners were alone throughout the day. Similarly, when "Michigan's Happy Convicts" realized that the program that allowed them to work outdoors building campsites would end if any of them acted improperly and that "an idea that might be priceless to them was on trial, [they] went all out to make it acceptable" (Titus 58).

In short, the dominant ideology of the 1950s reveals the assumption that, if respected as humans, criminals will respond in kind. Hence, one inmate of Stateville Penitentiary in Illinois noted that "I have a good record here. I think they'll take that into consideration . . . and the progress I've made in rehabilitating myself. It's done me a lot of good here. . . . How rich everyday life is" (J. Martin, "America's, Part I" 67). Another inmate at the same institution, after having become an expert on diseases and having studied hematology and parasitology by working in the prison's blood laboratory on an army study of malaria, noted, "When I do get [out], if I ever do, I'm going to make them glad I came" (J. Martin, "America's, Part III" 161). In the Texas prison system, moreover, an observer of the annual prison rodeo noted that "no convict has escaped in this mass movement—probably at least in part because the prisoners don't want to mess up their own grand show" (Nordyke 25); another inmate observed, "The prison [has] been trying to do things for us and, by our code, we cooperate" (Nordyke 36).[3]

Two brief narratives solidify the overall description of this era as one in which inmates are represented as redeemable and as desirous of redemption. While both would probably bring censure or alarm today, they are intriguing in that in the rhetorical field of the fifties, each brought praise to the inmates and prisons involved. One is the case of Conrad Maas, an inmate of the Oklahoma State Penitentiary who first came to prison convicted of murdering his wife after accusing her of adultery. While in prison, Maas not only became a Christian but also learned to paint, beginning a series of religious paintings that he gave freely to both inmates and guards in prison. Because of his obvious change, Maas was offered parole three times. On each occasion, Maas turned it down, desiring instead to repay his crime through painting (Bistro). While a narrative of this type would later signify a problematic situation in which a prison system offers convicts so much security that they dare not leave, it is here seen as a celebration of Maas's changed mindset. After Maas's death, Sheriff Tom Horton of the Oklahoma State Penitentiary asserted that Maas "died a convict because he wanted to paint religious pictures for churches and for the prisoners. This was the way Conrad Maas apologized to God" (Bistro 58). His willingness to stay in prison is a willingness to seek forgiveness, to become more human, not a sign of a pitiful soul who has become dependent on the state for his care.

In a second narrative, one that portends the alternative sentencing policies of the eighties, prisoners in Tulane County, California, were praised for volunteering to be rehabilitated by an "in-house" alternative. Those who volunteered for the program would listen over earphones to a barely audible taped message that played each night while they slept. The message was meant to work on their subconscious minds, similar in theory to the way subliminal advertisements are said to operate. The message, as reported in *The Nation, Newsweek*, and *Commonweal*, was spoken by a local minister and read in part, "You are filled with love and compassion for all. You do this with the help of God. . . . I am filled with love and compassion for all, so help me God" ("Hypnopaedia" 62; cf. "Sweet" 21; "Talking" 326). While such a program would now be certain to raise the ire of the American Civil Liberties Union and others as an infringement of individual liberties, the inmate of the fifties is one who may partake of such forms of rehabilitation with little alarm because to be rehabilitated means to return one to an "ideal" state. Because the nature of this "ideal" is not problematic on a mass cultural level, an invasion of rights is not a legitimate concern.

More than thirty years before Maria Arnford, then, we find prisoners praising the system that tends to their rehabilitation, refusing to leave its arms, hoping to make the prison system proud; they accept the dominant and clearly recognizable ideology of the period with little or no resistance. The problem with the 1950s representation of the male prisoner, then, is that he is unquestioning of the worldview to which he is rehabilitated. The state assumes his redeemable nature and moves him unquestionably toward that end. The prisoner's sole option is to choose between good and evil. To be disciplined, then, is to become a player in the one common morality, to choose good. This public representation of the prisoner parallels what Friedman has argued that criminal justice theory claimed for prisons prior to the twentieth century; the penitentiary provides a space for individuals to remove themselves from unhealthy surroundings and then, through work, to redeem themselves. There is no discussion of specific "prisoner rights" and little recognition that alternate moralities may be legitimate. One morality is shared, and the prison provides space for the criminal to discover or rediscover this morality, to return to it, and to help others make a similar move.

Riots: The Problem Is with the Prisons

The early fifties witnessed a rash of prison riots across the nation. The public responses to these riots by prison administrators, agents of the media, and prisoners themselves are telling of the overall representation of prisoners. In articles with titles such as "Prisoners 'On Strike'—The Meaning," "A Riot Is an Unnecessary Evil" (Wilson and Barnes), "Why Convicts Riot," and "Behind Those Prison Riots" (MacCormick), there is an evident cultural concern with why prisoners, who are positioned as being able to change their behavior freely, have continued to wreak havoc within prison walls. While the riots could have been represented in multiple ways, the dominant response was to view rioting as a signifier of the deplorable prison conditions forcing prisoners to riot, rather than as a sign that the prisoners were in fact irredeemable. While riots, a factual event, later indicate that prisoners are inhumane subjects who take advantage of a system that tries to treat them humanely, the discourse at this time invites a different symbolic interpretation.[4] Riots are illustrative of the plight of human beings held under inhumane conditions; it is said to be "a year of shame" for the wardens because "it takes a long period of abuses to set the stage for a full fledged riot" (Wilson and Barnes 138). Riots are not abuses by prisoners, then, but signs that prisoners have been abused. Any human being held under such conditions would riot, given enough time; there is nothing "inhuman" or special about prisoners that moves them to riot when others would not.

Just before the riot at the Michigan State Penitentiary at Jackson, two inmates were asked to write an article for *American Mercury* describing the conditions they experienced on a daily basis. In their essay, the two expressed their gratitude to Vernon Fox, the aforementioned prison psychologist who had been pushing for an increase in the number of rehabilitation programs available at the prison. However, they simultaneously warned readers that a riot at the prison was imminent because of the abusive conditions in which prisoners were forced to live, including overcrowding and inactivity (Shelly and Mazroff 118–25). In 1952, a year that saw many prison riots, this representation of the root causes of the riots is reified. Riots are positioned as a result of overcrowding, poor food, and lack of psychiatric care ("Life in Prison" 543). Riots result from guard brutality, the intermingling of sexual perverts with the "normal" prison population, and unfair parole practices ("Prisoners 'On Strike' " 20–21; "Break" 467). New Jersey State Prison warden F. Lovell Bixby freely admitted that prisoners rioted as a result of overcrowding, mental disturbances, and parole discrepancies, and Kentucky State Penitentiary warden W. Jess Buchanan noted that a lack of conjugal visits was the basis for a great deal of the problem ("Why Convicts Riot" 18–20). In each instance, riots are articulated as the result of prison conditions that could easily be changed; prisoners would not riot if they were treated humanely.

The most often cited cause of riots throughout the 1950s is the nationwide scarcity of rehabilitation programs. Utilizing similar metaphors, psychologist Austin MacCormick noted that "caged, idle men are the dynamite of which prison explosions are made" (98), and Ralph Banay, former head of psychiatry at Sing Sing, observed that "prisons make and install time bombs in the personalities of the men and women confined there. That these bombs will explode in time is almost certain" (13). The prison becomes a "graduate school of crime," a place in which prisoners are likely to become completely incapable of operating as normal people. While they may have been competent humans before entering prison, the prison experience on its own is enough to transform each prisoner from human being to walking explosive.

Similar narratives and characterizations emerge throughout the period. In a four-part series of articles in *The Saturday Evening Post* investigating the prison riot at the Michigan State Penitentiary at Jackson, one essayist explored cases in which healthy prisoners lost control of their mental faculties during their prison tenure. In one part of the series, subtitled "How the American Prison System Completes the Ruination of a Young Man," readers are provided the narrative of the prison life of inmate William Manus (J. Martin, "Why, Part I" 48–51). Manus is described as an inmate with behavioral problems who was constantly moved in and out of Jackson and other prisons. Early in his prison term, Manus was diagnosed as requiring neuropsychiatric treatment and observation, which he never received because of his constant displacements. As his behavioral problems manifested themselves in one prison, he was quickly moved to another, where the problems would once again manifest, and Manus would again be moved. The riot at Jackson, according to Martin, was the event that finally pushed Manus into a state of insanity. The prison psychiatrist, Dr. David Philips, notes that when Manus was first convicted, he was "a hopeful case. . . . If he had gone to a psychiatric ward for treatment, he might be alright now. But instead he went to Jackson, and its pressures broke him" (81). As the subtitle of the article seems to indicate, this is not just a problem with the Michigan prison system but with "the American prison system"; the system completes the ruination of the criminal rather than assisting in his rehabilitation.

More than the treatment received or denied by the prison system, the physical makeup of the prison is itself represented as a contributing factor in the deterioration of prisoners. One of the pinpointed causes of the riot at Jackson is the unfit condition of the cells: "They have solid steel doors. Some cells have tiny windows set high in the outside wall; others are totally dark. None has a light bulb. There is no bed; a man sleeps on a wooden bench. There is a tiny drinking fountain and a toilet but often neither works; there is no washbowl. A man in the hole never sees anybody, except that every hour a guard opens the peephole to make sure he hasn't killed himself. Twice a day a half a ration of food is slid into him through a slot in the door. . . . Living in the hole becomes for some men a stark question of survival. Some have gone mad there" (J. Martin, "Why, Part II" 42).

Prison is represented as distorting the minds of the very prisoners who are most amenable to following social laws by assimilating them to the moral and social order followed by "criminals." Former congressman J. Parnell Thomas, imprisoned at the Federal Correctional Institution in Danbury, Connecticut, for receiving bribes, commented on the everyday occurrences at the prison in which young inmates "receive instruction in crime from the old and hardened criminals" (143). Similarly, upon visiting The Tombs in New York, Gertrude Samuels noted in *The New York Times Magazine* that "the guards and the boys freely called the place a school for crime. Robert [a young inmate] said he'd learned an awful lot about how to commit crimes better while he'd been jailed" ("Forgotten" 12).[5] As a whole, then, the prison system is represented as promoting crime rather than redeeming criminals. Rehabilitation is possible only if the conditions under which prisoners are held are changed drastically.

In short, then, prison riots are represented as exposing the most problematic characteristic of prisons. While prisons are meant to provide a space for criminals to place themselves back on the right track, there are hints here that there is an unsavory nature to them, a drive in the prison that leads prisoners to riot, to learn other criminal behaviors. While all human beings continue to be redeemable within one common morality, this representation problematizes the general characterization of the prisoner of this era in that it suggests that imprisonment may in fact not work, that it in fact reproduces itself. The public discussion of the roots of riots acts in such a way that it preserves the assumption of one common morality while simultaneously providing a critique of what must be done to move the outlaw to this morality more efficiently.

The Homosexual

While the dominant theme of the 1950s is the redeemable inmate who must fight off destructive prison conditions, other prisoners do appear. One such prisoner is the homosexual, a prisoner almost solely identified and constituted by his sexuality. Homosexuality demands attention, not only because it is a fairly common representation, but also because it will later virtually disappear from representations of the prisoner, giving way to discussions of rape based on power relations rather than sexuality. Moreover, it will slowly give way to an articulation based on race, depicting white prisoners as generally the victims, African Americans as the predators. Here, however, homosexuality signifies an aberration from which prisoners rarely recover. Furthermore, it is cited as one other root of violence and rioting within prisons. In effect, homosexuality becomes a condition to be controlled so that "normal" prisoners might be rehabilitated without interference.

Homosexuality clearly is represented as aberrant behavior. Clinton Duffy, generally the most liberal of the wardens to speak in this era, argued that homosexuality must be given attention not only because it is one of the causes of riots but also because "you may also believe, as I do, that they [homosexuals] are suffering from some sort of personality disorder, and that something should be done for them" (Duffy, "San Quentin, Part Five" 146). The two inmates of the Michigan State Penitentiary at Jackson who were invited to write about prison experiences observed that homosexuality "is wicked in its essence. It is a little foul. It is, above all, brutal . . . it is pathetic" (Shelly and Mazroff 120). Lawrence Elliott, in a *Coronet* article that claimed to "describe what happens behind the walls of prisons everywhere," noted the revulsion he felt toward homosexuals in prison (81). Furthermore, because homosexuals are said to have far less shame about their acts than do most other prisoners, rehabilitation is seen as being far less likely (Baldi, "Part II" 96).

As troubling and repugnant as homosexuality is positioned in public discourse, the segregation of homosexuals from the remainder of the prison population would probably be considered unjustifiable without the simultaneous depiction of homosexuality as one cause of violence and rioting. In essays that describe the general architecture of prisons, cells of homosexual prisoners are described as color coded in order to allow heterosexual inmates and guards to escape contact with them (J. Martin, "America's, Part II" 58; Fox and Fay 13). The fact that homosexuality is a cause of violence is agreed upon by those few voices against rehabilitation programs as well as those most ardently in favor of those programs. For example, in describing the riot at the Michigan State Prison at Jackson, John Martin claimed that "wolf packs of homosexuals prowled the cell blocks," raping and beating other inmates ("Why, Part IV" 64). Similarly, Warden William Carty of the New Jersey State Prison noted that prison riots result in waves of homosexual stabbings, deaths, and suicides and are often caused by homosexuals as well (74). Indeed, he noted that "90% of the murders and stabbings inside prison walls can be traced to homosexuals. While I was warden, we had on the average about 80 known homosexuals among our 1,300 to 1,400 prisoners, and they caused trouble out of all proportion to their numbers" (72).

Homosexuality, then, is problematic in the depiction of the criminal for both the left and the right. The prevailing criminal justice model of rehabilitation positions the homosexual as mentally ill and in need of rehabilitation, although rarely amenable to rehabilitation programs. The few voices opposing rehabilitation simply depict the homosexual as not only morally corrupt but also as one of the root causes of violence. That this attitude is pervasive on both sides of the issue seems to suggest something of the negative rhetorical positioning of homosexuality in the culture as a whole. Later, as African-American prisoners are rearticulated as purveyors of prison violence, the sexuality of their acts will be differentiated from that practiced by whites. Indeed, homosexuality will give way as an object of discourse to discussions of the violent nature of African-American prisoners and the rape that results from this nature.

Minority Voices: Irrationality, Immorality, and Responsibility

Outside of the discussion of homosexuality, I have focused my discussion on the dominant representation of the male prisoner of this era. A less frequent and less common representation does appear here, however, as an emergent discourse that will grow to dominance later. In the discourse of those opposing the notion of rehabilitation, a representation of the prisoner drawn with the thematic hues of irrationality and immorality appears and grows stronger as the decade proceeds, to the degree that even those most ardently in favor of rehabilitation admit the existence of a number of prisoners who can only be imprisoned, never rehabilitated.

In his series of essays on the "toughest prison in America," for example, John Martin described the tightly secured conditions of the Stateville Penitentiary and observed that such conditions were warranted as the prison population was constituted by "complete failures." In addition, Martin supplied Warden Joseph Regan's defense of the strict regimen to which the prisoners are kept: "If there was no check on 'em, they'd be running all over the place, conniving, contacting their friends, selling, fighting, trading knives for cigarettes, sending out kites to get guns and junk brought in; . . . they'd take your life and mine and four or five others, and think nothing of it" (J. Martin, "America's, Part I" 52). The terms used here to describe the Stateville inmates stand in stark contrast to the dominant depiction of the prisoner. Here, the prisoners are incapable of rejoining society and are waiting patiently for the opportunity to take the life of anyone careless enough to leave him- or herself unprotected.

While this is a marginal representation of the male prisoner, evidence of the existence of such a prisoner does arise in a number of arguments about the proper treatment of prisoners. Hence, State Representative Norman K. Parsells of Connecticut called for capital punishment for those prisoners who are like "mad dogs and scorpions" (Hopkins and Hopkins 477). The Reverend J. Dinnage Hobden, a Canadian interested in reforming prisons, compared the prisoners he faced in the 1950s with those of the past and, counter to the depiction simultaneously emerging in most popular discourse, noted that the prisoners of the past "were colorful interesting types. They had the old idea of robbing the rich to feed the poor. They weren't like today's criminals who brutally beat up their victims and wantonly destroy property" (Reekie 32). Such statements become all the more common as the 1950s draw to a close; while they never completely unseat the dominance of the image of the "redeemable prisoner," they do create an emergent discursive space of their own and are later drawn upon as the prison riots of the late 1950s lead many observers to assert that the orientation toward rehabilitation has failed.

Paralleling the dominant representation of riots as caused by prison conditions, this marginal representation increasingly places the blame for riotous behavior directly on prisoners and asks them to take responsibility. Indeed, Austin MacCormick, a psychiatrist who generally espoused the "prisoner as redeemable human being" argument, noted that he believed the riot at Michigan State Penitentiary at Jackson could be blamed to some degree on a number of psychopaths who were allowed to roam freely in the prison. Earl Ward, who was described in the dominant representation as a hero for the prisoners, was depicted by MacCormick as a "homicidal psychopath"; his partner, "Crazy" Jack Hyatt, was an "overt homosexual"; their comrades were "wild-eyed psychopaths" (99–100). In the *Saturday Evening Post* accounts of the riots, Warden Julian Frisbee noted: "When you try to find out what is going on from a man like Ward, you don't get an answer. . . . You get an illogical, insane laughing and chuckling" (J. Martin, "Why, Part III" 36). Former prisoner Hal W. Hollister noted in the *Atlantic Monthly* in an essay titled "Why Prisoners Riot" that, when analysts and other observers of prisons attempt to place the blame for riots on prison conditions and on the abusive treatment of prisoners, they disregard "the larger and obvious part played, first, by what can loosely be called convict nature and, second, by deep-rooted convict traditions. Who said convicts were rational people?" (Hollister, "Why" 65).

In another comparison between the prisoners of the past and those of the present, John Martin observed that prison guards had often told him that "in the old days prisons were full of safe crackers and bank robbers, mature and dependable men, but today prisons are full of sex criminals and youngsters convicted of petty thievery—unstable men prone to riot" ("Why, Part IV" 150). Similarly, Ralph Banay, former head of psychiatry at Sing Sing, claimed, "The delinquent we encounter in penal institutions today is usually an emotionally disturbed person, with marked destructive tendencies, who acts out this disturbance at the expense of society. He is full of resentment and hatred. His view of reality . . . may be far from accurate" (56). In short, this vision of the prisoner, one that grows as the decade proceeds, represents him, not as warped by prison conditions, but as bringing a warped attitude to prison.

Finally, not only does this emergent discourse represent the prisoner as unstable and irrational, it also articulates his violence as the product of nature rather than of the external pressures of prison life. While most observers blame violence and riotous behavior on prison conditions, the factual event of a riot is here tied to the nature of criminals. When psychologist Donald Wilson went into Leavenworth to study the mental condition of prisoners, for example, he observed that many prisoners were similar to "law-abiding citizens." On the other hand, he also observed a different breed of criminal, one with little concern for the value of life. As evidence, he recounted his observance of a group of prisoners nonchalantly gathering together and then walking away, leaving one of the group bleeding from a stab wound (90). Similarly, *Time* reported that when Jim Hudson, an inmate who had been involved in the Michigan State Penitentiary riot, was burned to death by fellow prisoner Maurice Hummel in a territorial dispute, Hummel became a hero to many fellow inmates who disliked Hudson ("Iron Bars" 23–24). In brief, violence is a common part of the life of the criminal, articulated hand in hand with prison life.

Similar themes arise in pictorial representations of prisoners. For instance, when prisoner Robert Neese became a photographer while imprisoned at the Iowa State Penitentiary, he produced a series of photographs for *Life* that were intended to provide a well-rounded depiction of prison life. The pictures he chose and the accompanying descriptions speak to the violent condition of the prison and its inmates. Neese described the recreation yard as a place where people die (111), provided two pictures of fights, one for prestige and the other for cigarettes (113), and described the prison itself as a place of "masked emotions, erupting in drunken screams and sudden fights" (109).

While these representations of the prisoner lie only on the margins of this era's discourse, they do exist. Moreover, while the arguments described here exist in a particular historical juncture, their force continues to act on the present, to which they are linked terministically. This is not to neglect the synchronic force of these arguments, but to note that their force lies both in their own time and in the present. As McGee notes, "No present ideology can be divorced from past commitments if only because the very words used to express present dislocations have a history that establishes the category of their meaning" (" 'Ideograph' " 14; see also Railsback 419–20). Tracing out these emergent representations enables us to understand their reemergence and use in later arguments. When representations no longer fit the social conditions of an era, other representations emerge and are shaped to fit more readily as explanations. In addition to their power at the time of their emergence, the existence of these arguments is important in understanding future developments in the representation of the prisoner. Hence, when poor prison conditions cease to be accepted as the sole or primary reason for riots, another explanation will be sought by some members of the dominant culture. The most obvious and acceptable explanations are those that already have some cultural currency; thus, the emergent representations described here are further developed and ready to be taken to a broader level of explanation.

Female Inmates

Throughout the 1950s, women constituted only 3 to 4 percent of the total prison population, and their lack of representation in the mass media reflected this small percentage. Two points are clear about the representations of female prisoners that do exist, however. First, the characterization of women remains remarkably consistent across periods, while the characterizations of male prisoners change more rapidly. That is, while the way in which women are punished changes over time as different penological ideas concerning rehabilitation and methods of punishment gain and lose currency, the overall representation of female prisoners remains fairly stable. Second, gender transcends ethnicity in the representations of female prisoners. That is, female prisoners are not only represented as distinct from male prisoners, but they are represented similarly as women despite their racial and ethnic differences.

While films of the 1950s show female prisons to be hotbeds of rampant lesbian activity and brutality, the representations of female prisoners in print media frame the prisoners primarily as heterosexuals. While male prisoners are rarely described in terms that discuss the "essential" characteristics of men, this is not the case with women. In specific, the essence of female prisoners in these representations is their role as reproducers of the species and protectors of cultural morality. In general, female prisoners are represented as parents, separated from their children by imprisonment and, for the most part, as naturally moral beings, easily reformed if given the opportunity. Indeed, female prisoners are often said to be imprisoned originally because of abuse suffered at the hands of others. The primary concern about female criminals is that they be "redeemed" in order that they may provide their children, and the community's children, with an understanding of proper moral behavior.

While many male prisoners could logically be assumed to be parents, representations of children are negligible, if not altogether absent, in discussions of male prisoners. In representations of female prisoners, however, motherhood is of the essence. In a *Saturday Evening Post* essay on the Westfield State Farm and its 500 female inmates, there is the tale of "Maria," an "undersized Italian girl," arrested for shoplifting who is unmarried but five months pregnant. After describing Maria, the authors noted the regularity of pregnancy among prisoners by observing that "the staff at Westfield take such cases as a matter of course" (Pringle and Pringle 68). Maria's mother was reported to have agreed to take care of the baby while Maria, imprisoned, would take courses dealing with child rearing. Her role in prison, then, is to not only to seek redemption for her crimes but also to learn skills that will prepare her for her role outside of prison, the reproduction of species and cultural ideology. The *Post* article described the role of prison staff to be one of attempting to "teach the inmate mothers to give their children the security they did not have themselves" (Pringle and Pringle 68). To be rehabilitated here, as always, means to be taken back to a proper role, in this case that of the parent.

Similarly, in a series of pictures in *Cosmopolitan* of the California Institute for Women at Corona, there is a picture of an operating table with the caption, "Babies are delivered here (birth certificate does not carry institution name)," and a picture of women sitting under hair dryers with the caption, "A girl may take any subject she is capable of completing; only required subject is 'Homemaking' " (LaBarre, 54–55). In these two tag lines, we find it assumed not only that the female prisoner is mother and housekeeper but that rehabilitation requires a knowledge of "Homemaking."[6]

Indeed, even Ethel Rosenberg was constituted primarily as a mother. In a *Collier's* human interest story describing the life of Deputy Marshal Lil McLaughlin, a federal marshal whose job was the transfer of women from prison to prison or from prison to court, McLaughlin noted that Rosenberg rarely discussed anything outside of "clothes, the weather, and her two boys" (Cameron 11).

In addition to serving as regenerators of the species, female prisoners are represented as naturally "good" but corrupted in their youth, generally at the hands of their guardians. Hence, once given the relative security and distance afforded by prison, the female inmate is expected to remember how to behave in a "normal," moral fashion. A prime example of this characteristic of the female comes by way of an essay John Martin wrote for the *Saturday Evening Post* in which he narrated the life of a prisoner to whom he gave the pseudonym "Anne Milton." Before beginning the narrative, Martin mentioned that Anne's story, as well as the reasons for her failures and successes, are "not unlike that of thousands of other women who are put in prison" (Martin, "Case" 30). Indeed, the story Martin tells parallels closely other narratives of the female prisoner, narratives that at times appear to transcend temporal culture. Of Milton's background, Martin noted, "Her father liked to say he was a railroadman, but actually he was a drunk, and he beat her and her mother. Once, in a drunken rage, when Anne was eight, he tried to kill them. Not long after that he went away. Her mother scrubbed floors in the Railtown grocery store and the Railtown tavern until she died. Anne was ten. The Centre Circuit Court appointed a lawyer named Boles her guardian. He got rid of her by putting her in her grandmother's house" ("Case" 30). Martin goes on to explain that Anne lived with her grandmother, who used her as a maid and later as a prostitute. Committing several robberies, Milton was in and out of reformatories several times, becoming pregnant during one of her releases. Martin observed that Milton was only able to make parole when she found work with a family as a housekeeper. It was there that she learned to understand "human decency." Martin further noted that Milton was only able to rest easy about her child after visiting his foster family during her parole and finding him happy. Martin's narrative provides a familiar representation: the female loses touch with her humanity via abuse, regains it through imprisonment and housekeeping, and utilizes it to assure the welfare of her children.

While the story of Anne Milton focuses only on one inmate, the general representation is clearly a pattern in numerous essays concerning imprisoned women. For example, while imprisoned for her refusal to practice air raid exercises in protest of the proliferation of hydrogen bombs, Eileen Fantino observed of the prisoners, "All their stories were similar; poverty, alcoholic parents, or both, no money and little food, sometimes a relative who was an addict; almost always they had little desire for life and little reason to live" (McCorkle and Korn 94). Similarly, in an examination of the Westfield State Farm in New York, it is noted that the principal crime of the imprisoned women is "that their parents neither understood nor loved them": "Few have known anything approaching family affection or security" (Pringle and Pringle 34, 68). Further, the primary principle of the prison is said to be human decency, a principle that allows the women to develop as they would have under natural conditions. In the same essay, women are said to be "essentially more law abiding" if given a chance (Pringle and Pringle 34, 71).

Female prisoners are not represented as solely redeemable or shaped by childhood problems, of course; as with male prisoners, there are also discussions of drug abuse and homosexuality. But even in these cases, the representation of such behaviors constructs the behavior either as being caused by problem childhoods or as being easily changed or both. Indeed, the representations of female prisoners with problem behavior depict the women as not yet "mature." Misbehavior is more of a passing phase than a career. Hence, although the presence of physical sexual behavior is denied by officials of Westfield State Prison, guards admit that often "a few of the girls write mash notes to each other" (Pringle and Pringle 71). When arguments break out because a "triangle develops," however, all parties "are thereupon confined to their rooms to cool off" (Pringle and Pringle 71). One cannot miss the close connection between such discipline and sending a child to his or her room for misbehavior.

In short, prisons for females are represented as having the function of aiding women to a return to their "essential" state as the reproducers of species and morality. While their problems have grown out of their mistreatment at the hands of others, they are easily transformed, easily reformed, and thereby enabled to raise their children with a sense of cultural morality.

Conspicuous Absences

In a long-term discursive study, it is possible to discuss "objects of discourses" that are absent from a particular cultural configuration even though the "absences" can only be known due to the fortunes of hindsight. Highlighted below, then, are those representations of the prisoner that will prove important later but are here absent, an absence noticeable only from a future stance. I point to these characterizations here in order to pinpoint and understand their emergence as objects of discourse later.

As I have noted, the prisoner of the 1950s, at least as represented in popular print, is primarily Caucasian and primarily male. The paucity of depictions of female and minority inmates is evident in both language use and photographs of inmates. When African-American or Hispanic inmates are depicted, however they are represented as violent, immoral, and uneducated.[7] For example, the murderer of Jim Hudson, the aforementioned prisoner who was burned to death after the riot at the Michigan State Penitentiary at Jackson, was reported to have become a hero because other prisoners despised Hudson and his persistent attacks on others. One of the few African-American inmates discussed at length, Hudson was described as a violent criminal who played the role of the Earl Ward's "violent henchman" ("Iron Bars" 23–24).

A different negative representation of black inmates in general appears in a *Harper's* essay entitled "The Social Structure of the Underworld." Here, Lewis Dent described the universal prisoner "moral code" in which prisoners hold to a line of never squealing on one another, regardless of the nature of a case. Dent organized the social structure of prisoners based on how they respond to this code, and noted that those prisoners who do not tell prison authorities about their disputes but instead settle them on their own are referred to as "right guys"; those who simply stay out of prison circles entirely are referred to as "legit guys"; and those who are untrustworthy are referred to as "wrong." In an elaboration of the social structure of the prison, Dent observed that, "for reasons which I am not prepared to isolate, most Negro prisoners, whose cultural background is in many respects unique in our society, fall into either the legit or wrong categories" (25).

Outside of these brief mentions of African-American inmates, there are only a few references to scuffles breaking out between black and white prisoners. For example, Kenneth Lamott, who briefly taught a high school class in San Quentin, noted that "there are many Negroes in San Quentin, and although there is no official segregation in California prisons, the prison administration finds it politic to separate the races in the cell blocks and mess halls" due to the potential for violent outbreaks ("Socrates" 141).

While empirically there is some degree of racial heterogeneity in U.S. prisons, the mix is not represented well in public discourses.

Although I am not prepared to venture far into a discussion of the reasons behind this, I would suggest that the articulation of "prisoner" with "redeemable" was simply not compatible with the articulation of the African American of the 1950s. The construction of a soft-hearted, nonviolent, altruistic prisoner, judged under a single system of morality, precludes incorporation of African Americans, who were predetermined by the discourse of the time to be violent and uneducated (or uneducatable). That those arguments that do refer to prisoners as redeemable generally ignore the presence of African Americans is evidence for this point. African Americans are evidently so strongly coded as violent that they are necessarily excluded from discussions of rehabilitation.

The 1958 film *The Defiant Ones*, appearing at the crossroads of this era and the next, reveals aspects of the black prisoner as both redeemable and as violent. While the film deals specifically with racism and race relations, it is ambiguous at times about just what and who the black prisoner is. When a young boy happens upon the black and white prisoners chained together, he assumes that the white convict is a law enforcement officer returning the black convict to prison. However, the film's opening scene is the back of the paddy wagon occupied by at least ten prisoners. Of the ten, only one is black; each of the others is white. Further, while the black character is imprisoned for the more violent of the two crimes (attempted murder as opposed to armed robbery), he is also more apt to be physically caring; he sleeps with his head on the white convict's chest, causing some shock to the white character upon awakening; he tends to a cut on his partner's arm; in the final scene, he cradles his injured partner in his arms and sings to him, comforting him. A black prisoner is highlighted in the film, then, but he justifies his crimes as a response to cultural racism and behaves in a caring, seemingly redeemable manner. Hence, while the film in some ways parallels print representations (the rarity of blacks, their more violent crimes, their poor upbringings), other elements are anomalous (he learns and has a caring, thoughtful side) but foretell the representation of African Americans to be highlighted later.

A second characteristic of prisoners that is absent in this era is that of drug abuse. In the entire decade, there are only four brief mentions of drug use, and, in these cases, the purposes of the discussion are murky at best. Three of the essays point to drug use as a reason rehabilitation programs are unlikely to meet with success; prisoners who are "addicted" are less likely to take rehabilitation seriously while imprisoned and are more likely to return to drug usage when they leave (Samuels, "Forgotten" 12; Thomas 148). On the other hand, in a narrative mentioned above in which two "doped up" prisoners attempted to take a prison chaplain hostage, they were stopped from doing so by a "straight" inmate (Reed 88–92). In this narrative, however, the theme appears to center on illustrating that the majority of prisoners can be rehabilitated, since drug usage is only marginal. Again, the strength of the arguments in favor of rehabilitation apparently silences those representations of prisoners as drug users. In short, representations of drug usage would work against the dominant theme of rehabilitation and hence do not gain prominence.

Another construction of the prisoner that becomes prominent later but is for the most part nonexistent in the 1950s is that of the prisoner as a legal being with legal rights. Only three examples of this representation are evident, and two of these actually criticize support of legal rights for inmates ("Prisoners' Plaint" 89; "Captive Congregation" 105; Baldi, "Part I" 19). The general lack of perception of this era that prisoners have legal rights will quickly give way to a growing sense of the importance of legal rights later. However, in a culture whose homogeneous values dictate a moral dichotomy in which the state alone decides the rights of those convicted of crimes, the idea of legal rights for prisoners is apparently a contradiction that cannot be easily overcome. While Lawrence Friedman's history of criminal justice in America suggests that the move toward the recognition of human rights within prison systems gained strength in the early 1950s, this was evidently a transition in the legal status of prisoners and not in their public representation. Public discourse is anchored in the minds and thoughts of those who use it. As such, while the 1950s saw a growth in prisoner riots and the growth in arguments for human rights, the riots were publicly represented as problematic in that they kept criminals from returning to a common morality; prisoners were not represented as yet having human rights as the prison continued to be represented as a place to recoup this basic morality. One does not need separate rights when one is being helped back to a shared position. Only when morality itself becomes fragmented is it necessary to extend the practice of difference to prisoners.

Concluding Observations

As I noted, I am interested in the force of these representations both on the present and within the cultural context from which they emerge. In the culture of the United States represented by mass marketed publications, the prisoner of the 1950s is bound within fairly distinct discursive parameters. In general, the prisoner is male, altruistic, and Caucasian; he is led to riot or misbehave only when the conditions of prisons force him to do so. Again, it is not that all prisoners are represented as wholly alike throughout the period; representations of riotous and violent prisoners such as Teddy Green, "Crazy" Jack Hyatt, and Earl Ward are intermingled with the great number of more sympathetic characters whose crimes go unmentioned while their selflessness is praised. Moreover, the general contours of the female prisoner of the period are constraining, albeit in a different fashion: racially diverse, she is infinitely redeemable as a maternal and moral guidepost. However, while marginal representations do exist, a cultural belief in a deep-seated quality of all human beings as redeemable is evident in the representations of the Caucasian inmate. That is, the fairly clear articulation of what it means to be rehabilitated (for example, helping the blind, steering children away from crime, avoiding homosexual behavior, displaying honesty and a respect for authority) reveals a cultural belief in a homogenized morality and value system to be striven for by prisoner and law-abiding citizen alike. When psychologist Austin MacCormick notes that prisoners volunteer for medical experiments "chiefly because of a social conscience that many of them do not realize they have," he is suggesting that we all share, consciously or not, a unifying value system, perhaps characteristic of all human beings (Wharton, "Prisoners" 55). While I do not mean to imply that other value systems are not available, these other systems go relatively unspoken within popular discourse. In the specific case of the prisoner, cultural discourses encourage a vision of the prisoner, whether he riots or serves his community, as a product of comparatively settled and homogeneous cultural values, a product that the social body must now take responsibility for rehabilitating.

This prisoner is further represented as guiltless. That is, while rehabilitation and the assumption of a shared value system remain dominant themes throughout each of the eras to be covered, here they are so prominent that responsibility for criminal behavior both outside and inside of prisons is pinned on social conditions rather than on individual agents. Hence, rehabilitation cannot be a matter of choice as it will later; since one who was not originally "habilitated" correctly has been failed by the body social, society is collectively responsible for "re-habilitation." Incarceration does not serve the purpose of retribution so much as it attempts to draw individuals back into the homogenized value system of the culture at large. Inmates are not morally autonomous; they have been excluded from shared cultural values and, by cultural imperative, must be encouraged to (re)align themselves with these definitions. The testimony of rehabilitated prisoners illustrates their own belief in a shared value system. Hence, rehabilitation is assumed and not a choice; prisoners are not praising a chosen morality but the only morality readily and obviously available.

The lack of male prisoners of color speaks to the value of rehabilitation and the vision of shared cultural values. That is, the pervasiveness of the cultural belief in the nature of human subjects as redeemable requires the omission of non-Caucasians in discourse about the prisoner because people of color are apparently viewed culturally as morally different from Caucasians. While African Americans and others are certainly imprisoned throughout the period, their virtual symbolic annihilation suggests that their representational presence would have been incompatible with the depiction of the prisoner as a redeemable agent. In short, the presence of a different value system would challenge the belief in a homogenized culture, a culture with one recognizable and valid value system. Even to discuss the African-American male (as will become prominent later) is to challenge homogeneity. It is only when African Americans are discussed prominently in other realms of popular discourse that they begin to be discussed as prisoners.

Although not a dominant characterization of prisoners, homosexuality, almost always associated with male rather than female prisoners, is here a mental aberration that leads to violence. It is interesting to note that, unlike prisoners of color, the homosexual prisoner is not ignored but is dealt with fairly prominently in discussions of the prisoner. The spectacle of a large number of men without access to female companions makes questions of sexuality and sexual behavior inescapable. However, the cultural belief in the redeemable nature of the human being dominates even the specter of the apparent vile nature of the homosexual. When Clinton Duffy noted that homosexuals "are suffering from some sort of personality disorder, and that something should be done for them" (Duffy, "San Quentin, Part Five" 146), he provided a crystallized articulation of a popular theme. Hence, even the sordid nature of the homosexual prisoner is redeemable, if enough is done to cure him. A person does not choose to be homosexual any more than he or she willingly chooses to commit criminal behavior. But like crime, its occurrence is one of nature's accidents, something to be cured rather than celebrated; the homosexual must be transformed and renewed. Homosexuality is not ignored but is articulated in such a way that it does not challenge a homogeneous culture morality.

As McGee notes, cultural ideologies exist in a persistent state of transition with numerous voices arguing a war of positions over key cultural terms or ideographs (" 'Ideograph' "). As economic, material, and cultural factors intermingle, beliefs and ideological claims arise and fade. The representations coded into the discourse of the 1950s do not simply evaporate; they maintain strength as cultural forces. Not only do these constructions leave impressions in bound volumes in libraries, but they also become embedded in the consciousness of the culture and its individual participants, and hence, they impress upon future cultural understandings of the prisoner. While change will occur as the material conditions promised by the rehabilitationists of the 1950s fail to appear (that is, neither the rate of prison violence nor the recidivism rate falls discernibly) and rehabilitation as a goal loses some of its adherents in the ensuing decades, new discussions of the prisoner and punishment must grow within—and hence are shaped by—the logical and rhetorical boundaries of existing representations. When the popular belief in a unified homogeneous morality breaks down, criminals and crime must be judged and understood on different terms. However, past representations act as rhetorical and material forces by which all future discussions of criminality and criminal justice are constrained. While cultural homogeneity and rehabilitation as a philosophy can and will be challenged, they do not die; instead, they impress upon future cultural constructs. Indeed, the following chapter will show evidence of the impact fading representations do have.

4

The Inmate Divide

Rehabilitation and Immorality, 1960–1968

Throughout the 1950s and early 1960s, Kenneth Lamott taught English in San Quentin Prison. Working under the auspices of a program that was designed to provide inmates with a practical education, Lamott attempted to teach survival skills for life after incarceration. In the early 1960s, he wrote a number of essays, primarily for the *New Yorker,* describing his experiences at San Quentin as well as those of the prisoners there. What the narratives display especially well is that the dominant representation of the male prisoner in the 1960s had become muddled, for no longer was the prisoner clearly articulated as altruistic and redeemable. While the male prisoner solidified into two different and contradictory representations by the end of this era, in the early part of the 1960s, his position was not so clear.

In one essay, Lamott provides the tale of an obviously intelligent and self-educated student/prisoner who took an interest in areas as diverse as hypnotism, mysticism, history, and literature. The prisoner was referred to as the "Lung-gom Runner" because of his unusual post-prison goal of traveling to Tibet in order to learn meditative techniques from Tibetan monks, particularly a breathing technique called "Lung-gom Running." According to the inmate, "Lung-gom Runners" are able to run for five days and nights without stopping for rest or refreshment due to their highly developed breathing and meditative practices. Upon his release from San Quentin, the "Lung-gom Runner" promised to mail Lamott a postcard from Tibet, a postcard that Lamott admits to having looked for with great anticipation. Within six months of his release, however, the "Lung-gom Runner" committed a series of crimes that ultimately led to his return to San Quentin. He once again spent his time in prison devising elaborate mental and spiritual schemes as interesting to Lamott as Lung-gom Running. When he was released again, however, his plans were interrupted by yet another trip to prison ("Lung-gom" 151–63). Lamott reports that this cycle of events repeated itself many times and with many inmates.

In Lamott's second narrative, another obviously well-educated prisoner serves as the protagonist. Lamott begins by discussing the types of prisoners that he most enjoyed talking to and notes, "A first rate faculty for a prep school or a small college could have been rounded up in five minutes from the fallen school masters and disgraced graduate students who worked in the prison office" ("We Have" 142). Lamott found himself drawn in particular to conversations with an inmate who was able to engage in philosophical discourses on the purpose of punishment while simultaneously making satirical and biting comments about the low level of education attained by most guards at San Quentin. Lamott admits that his description of the prisoner is influenced by the friendly yet detached relationship he was able to develop with a convict he considered to be of mental acumen equal to his own. What is more interesting and telling about Lamott's narrative, however, is that when he asked his prisoner "friend" to recount the events that led him to prison, the inmate noted coldly that he had planted a bomb in his wife's car after suspecting her of adultery.

Between the blurry lines distinguishing this era from the 1950s and the era that follows, the prisoner is in a period of transition, as Lamott's narratives indicate. While no longer the infinitely redeemable prisoners of the past, Lamott's prisoners are also not the violent, political, homicidal prisoners who emerge more fully later. While the male prisoner will be represented in this era as either fully redeemable (and simultaneously Caucasian) or irrational and violent (and primarily black), the beginning of the 1960–68 period provides a muddled representation of an inmate both highly intelligent and irrational, and also potentially violent.

The representations of this period are evidence of the ways in which public discourses become solidified, sedimented practices. That is, the representation of the prisoner, like all characterizations and arguments, does not smoothly begin and end and is not easily forgotten once adopted by cultural participants. Rather, once created, discursive characterizations and objects exist as material; once an idea is articulated and accepted as "real" or "true" by significant numbers of people, the idea resists sudden change, becoming somewhat residual and persistent (McGee, "Materialist's" 39). Hence, two primary characterizations of the male prisoner can be described here as sedimented ideas. The first characterization is an extension of the redeemable inmate of the 1950s, albeit one in a state of some transition. The second is a prisoner so essentially immoral and irrational that incarceration and physical punishment are demanded. It is in the tensions between these two characterizations that the prisoner is fought over as a site of ideological struggle on such grounds as race and morality. Briefly, because he is now opposed by an "immoral" and "irrational" prisoner, the redeemable prisoner is represented as more highly educated, from a higher social stratum, and more culturally and intellectually diverse than he had been previously. However, the promises of rehabilitation appear lost on him as he persistently returns to crime despite the best efforts of prison programs. The counterportrait reveals a violent and brutal prisoner, uncaring and irrational, deserving only punishment; he is naturally immoral in that his criminal behavior cannot be altered through rehabilitation programs.

A number of other themes that will prove important in later arguments over the prisoner develop during this period. First, homosexuality, which earlier signified mentally aberrant behavior, for the most part disappears as an object of discourse, giving way to a discourse of rape. Acts that formerly constituted homosexuality now constitute rape as an act of violence and power; regardless of its practitioners, the behavior now signifies less a sexual orientation than a form of violent behavior. This move from "sex" to "violence" is accompanied by a not insignificant racial character of prison rape that plays itself out throughout the decade: while all prisoners are viewed early as potential victims of rape, as the period draws to a close, the image of the rapist coheres around the African American and that of the victim around the Caucasian. Second, the notion of "legal rights" for the prisoner, a belief that prisoners do share legal rights with the general populace, gains public acceptance and consequent rhetorical force. Third, female prisoners, still marginalized, continue to be represented in a manner fairly consistent with the representation of the preceding era. Maternity is again a primary characterization of the female, and she continues to be depicted as a naturally moral agent who, corrupted by others, can rediscover her morality and practice it domestically upon release through child rearing and home keeping practices. While the nature of her crimes may have changed, she remains in the end identified by her position as a "sexed" body rather than by any other factor.

Again, the development of these themes is worthy of scrutiny as they serve as forces in the argument and representation of the construction of punishment and the prisoner today. In moving to understand the narratives and characterizations of the many Maria Arnfords that are encountered later, it is imperative that we analyze closely those discursive materials out of which such narratives and relationships develop. However, the different representations and the developing themes do reflect certain transitions and cultural arguments of their own context, for in the midst of these various public representations, one finds implied the theoretical arguments between the old and new penologies, the cultural upheavals with regard to race and youth culture, and the dominant cultural demand for human rights and dignity.

Rehabilitation: A Theme with Variations

Again, then, one of the two dominant representations of the male prisoner that takes hold during this period is that of the inmate who, with aid from rehabilitation programs, can be reincorporated into the body social. While having its roots in the image of the altruistic inmate represented in the 1950s, this image is now a theme with variation. That is, what we witness is not a repetition of past representations, but neither is it a radical shift. Instead, the representation of the redeemable inmate maintains some of its core characteristics while it develops and drops others.

Not only will rehabilitation emerge as an option for the prisoner who already possesses the "normal" trait of altruism and displays it in his attempts to help others, but rehabilitation is also advanced as a form of "treatment" for that prisoner who commits crime as a result of mental aberration or faulty assimilation. Whether in need of treatment or rehabilitation, however, the redeemable prisoner remains a human being whose crimes can be partially justified and understood as the result of a person facing difficult and trying circumstances. In brief, the redeemable prisoner is drawn with two strokes; he is either primarily a "misguided altruist" who can be rehabilitated through prison programs or a mental aberrant who can be cured by disciplinary measures. In both cases, however, the focus is on the prisoner him- or herself rather than on the administration of justice.

Altruism and the Trustworthy Inmate

In a *Saturday Evening Post* essay on prison rehabilitation programs from the early sixties with the revealing title, "Don't Label Them

Incorrigible," we find the story of "Chester," a rapist imprisoned at the rehabilitation-oriented Federal Youth Center in Ashland, Kentucky. Although entering prison "hostile toward authority, blaming the police for his troubles . . . withdrawn, inadequate, insecure, and emotionally immature," Chester slowly and patiently learned to trust and learn from prison officials, eventually becoming reformed to the extent that he earned a college degree through programs offered at the prison (J. Morris, "Don't" 100). Author Joe Alex Morris noted that Chester's attitude change was so complete that it was accompanied by a transformation in his physical appearance: "His hair had been trimmed to a reasonable length. His clothes were neat" ("Don't" 101). Chester himself testified to his change in noting that "if I had been put in a program like this when I first got into trouble, instead of being put on probation, I might have avoided a lot of grief" ("Don't" 101).

The "trust" Chester learns to place in prison officials is a common theme in discourse centering on redeemable prisoners. For example, in a narrative concentrating on a New York prison camp for youthful offenders, Gertrude Samuels noted that teaching trust to inmates had been found to be an effective way to increase their level of maturity (Samuels, "Open Doors" 43–46). Paralleling "Chester," prisoners testified to the benefits of trust in their own lives; one youth at the camp noted that hard work and trust have enabled him to hold a job and remain "unimprisoned" (43).

A case that received a great deal of press coverage, and hence serves as a general guide to the contours of this era's representation of the redeemable prisoner, concerned Paul Crump, an inmate in the Cook County (Illinois) Jail. Crump was imprisoned for the robbery of a Chicago plant in which a plant guard was fatally wounded. While admitting to taking part in the robbery, Crump claimed his innocence of the murder. He was eventually convicted of the murder, however, after one of his accomplices directly accused him, and Crump himself provided a confession. In prison, Crump began to reassert his innocence, noting that he made the confession after being severely beaten by police officers. Moreover, he noted that the accomplice, who had in fact shot the guard, blamed Crump only after being promised legal immunity for doing so. After some initial local press coverage, Crump's case became a nationally celebrated cause when he gained the support of his warden, editorialists at several local newspapers, local ministers, and Billy Graham. The case reached a climax when one local television station aired a three-hour panel discussion of Crump's claims, and three hundred Chicago ministers asked their congregations to pray for his salvation ("Last Mile").[1]

As a result of the support and Crump's record, his attorney recommended gubernatorial clemency on the virtually unprecedented grounds that Crump was completely rehabilitated ("Last Mile" 22). Evidence used to indicate Crump's rehabilitation included his having saved a guard's life by taking a gun away from a would-be assassin, his conversion to Catholicism, and his voracious reading habit, which included works by such authors as Nietzsche and Blake ("Last Mile" 22). His warden, Jack Johnson, called Crump "a classic case of rehabilitation, with whom I would trust my life" ("Case of" 929). Additionally, *Ebony* asserted that Crump's case exemplified the reason that rehabilitation should be highlighted over revenge ("How a Prisoner" 89). In brief, the representation of Crump's case is evidence of the strong continuation of the belief in a redeemable prisoner, an inmate who can be "completely rehabilitated," a prisoner with whom one could trust one's life. Moreover, it also indicates that rehabilitation is signified when the criminal returns to a common morality, a common way of life.

The redeemable prisoner was often called forth to testify to his own condition throughout this era. In the early 1960s, for example, *Harper's* held a contest in which male prisoners were encouraged to submit articles describing their lives in prison. The top ten authors were not only given a small monetary reward but also had their works published in *Harper's*. The resulting feature, "Voice of the Convict," is provocative on a number of grounds. Not only does its title promise to give voice to the previously silenced prisoner, but its very existence suggests that the prisoner indeed has something relevant to say to *Harper's* readers. Hence, each of the published essays humanized the individual prisoner in the very act of letting him speak. Furthermore, each essay offered testimony from the prisoners themselves that each could and would reform his behavior upon release from prison. For example, in his "I Care, You Care, He Cares," prisoner Tim Little observes: "The first few times I have taken a calculated risk by deliberately discarding my shell of indifference, I have felt rich inside. . . . Who knows? This caring bit might be the first step toward a more purposeful life on the streets" (170). A cursory reading through each of the essays cannot help but reveal a pattern in which each prisoner contemplates the use of human "care" as a way to make his life more meaningful.

Moreover, work release programs are represented throughout this era as successful means of transformation. While articles centering on work release programs often were accompanied by disclaimers noting that prisoners enrolled in rehabilitation programs do not represent the prison population as a whole, each article suggested that work release programs hold the promise that all prisoners can be rehabilitated, if only the appropriate means are developed. Evidence of this attitude is pervasive throughout the period. For example, *Business Week* reported that General Electric had opened classes at the federal penitentiary in Atlanta, teaching computer programming to selected inmates. Although the criteria did limit the number and type of prisoners enrolled (to those with either an IQ of 120 or a high school education and with an aptitude for mathematics), a representative of the program observed that the "students' progress has been substantial—greater than that of most college classes," noting that the average grade in the class was 98.8 out of 100 ("GE Opens" 98). In another article on the same program, *Newsweek* noted that prisoners are ideal for computer work because they have learned to function under conditions of idleness and drudgery while incarcerated ("Captive Class" 78).

Other work release programs and college credit programs are repeatedly praised as treating prisoners as human and providing them with a way to develop and utilize their skills in future situations.[2] Further, L. J. Gengler, director of federal work release programs, asserted in *Nation's Business* that "the most important thing is it offers real hope these men will learn work habits and attitudes that will help them make it in society and stay out of trouble—and out of prison" ("Employees" 93). In a general sense, employers who hired convicts through work release programs repeatedly praised the trustworthiness of these workers, vowing to hire more in the future ("Outside on the Job" 33).

Another characteristic of the representation of the redeemable prisoner of the 1950s that continues in this era is that the male prisoner engages in altruistic deeds with altruistic motives. Repeating themes from the previous decade, several essays highlighted the medical research performed in prison and the large percentage of prisoners who volunteer for such experiments. In a general sense, because medical experimentation is represented as painful for the volunteers, it is argued that the prisoners who volunteer necessarily do so with motives that go beyond the minute temporal or monetary rewards they receive. Indeed, Ralph Smith asserted in the *New York Times Magazine* that the strongest motivation for the prisoner partaking in medical experimentation is "the feeling of doing something worthwhile, the chance for self respect" ("Research" 41). Similarly, in a *Coronet* article with the revealing title "Convicts Also Have Hearts," a reflective inmate noted that "twenty-six years ago I took a human life. By giving my blood at every opportunity, I feel that perhaps I am making up, in a very small way, for the life I took" (Kellett 175).

Similar repentant and humane assertions were reported from prisoners participating in a risky series of experiments in the Holmesburg Prison in Philadelphia in 1962. In these studies, prisoners were injected with live cancer cells in an attempt to understand the human body's ability to fight various forms of cancer. While many of the prisoners were said to have voiced some concern for their personal safety when volunteering for the experiment, the *Saturday Evening Post* prominently recalled that one said, "Maybe I was a little scared when we went to get our shots. But the doc showed us some pictures of kids with cancer, and that got to me. Wherever kids are concerned, cons are suckers" (Congdon 64).

Indeed, prison research/experimentation is credited with being the major reason for advancement in several areas of medical practice ("Volunteers" 72). Representatives from Upjohn and Parke, Davis, and Company claimed in *Business Week* that prison research was so profitable for both the interest of the manufacturers and the self-esteem of the prisoners that the companies decided to build research facilities in the Michigan State Penitentiary at Jackson ("Drug" 60). While profits might drive the interests of manufacturers, the prisoners reap the "higher" rewards of altruism and self-respect.

Numerous other narratives and characterizations in this era support the representation of prisoners as redeemable citizens with altruistic motives and a desire for transformation. For example, *Time* reported that Colorado's Canon City convicts created a lecture tour and traveled to schools throughout Colorado with the purpose of dissuading students from lives of crime: "Their message usually goes like this: 'I'm on the road to nowhere. Don't follow me' " ("Crusading" 60). Moreover, a *Coronet* article included the story of a group of one thousand inmates of the Minnesota State Reformatory for Men who adopted a foster child in Greece through an international relief program. After four years of writing their daughter, named Anastassia, and being asked by the relief agency not to discuss their status as prisoners, the group requested that they be allowed to be honest with their daughter, admitting their imprisonment and their repentance for past transgressions. After receiving permission and telling Anastassia of their crimes, she responded by proclaiming that her love for each of them had only increased as a result of their honesty (Sachs 114–15).

At the risk of overkill, one final narrative is offered as a representation of the "base" humanity of all prisoners. In *Coronet*'s "The Fish of Death Row," Lawrence Einstein recounted a day on San Quentin's death row during which a fish mysteriously swam from the local reservoir into the toilet of one of the cells. After receiving permission and a small jar, a death row inmate captured the fish, which was then shared by the men as a "family" pet. The author observed the caring nature of the prisoners as given shape in the plan they drew up for rotation of the fish among the cells. Knowing that any form of life would have special meaning to death row inmates, the prisoners chose to give the fish to whichever prisoner was closest to his date of execution (Einstein 147).[3]

Treatment and Mental Aberrations

The theme of "rehabilitation" is also given shape in a slightly different form as this era proceeds. While still a marginal thesis at this point, a "treatment" model of rehabilitation emerges obviously. The thesis of this model, based on medicalization of criminal science, argues that criminal activity is akin to a physical illness. Hence, it is not simply training that will prepare convicts for reentry in the social whole, but the treatment of the "illness" that will put an end to their misbehavior. For example, Calvin Tomkins noted in *Newsweek* that "convicts are not vicious men who cause crime, but disturbed individuals who cannot help themselves. 'Criminality is a disease and criminals can be cured,' says Dr. Benjamin Karaman, 73, Chief Psychotherapist at St. Elizabeth's Hospital in Washington, D.C., who claims to have cured 'several dozen' of the 100-odd criminals he has treated" (110–11). Similarly, in an issue published on the same day, *Time* reported that a new age in incarceration had arrived with its major tenet the belief that "underlying most criminal conduct is emotional disturbance or outright mental illness. Carried to its logical extreme, this would mean abolishing prisons and putting all convicted criminals under psychiatric treatment" ("Psychiatry" 78). In this same essay, an inmate who was diagnosed as requiring psychiatric treatment rather than punishment testified, "I'm grown up now and I've got to recognize it. Next time out, I'm going to try to get a job" (78).

These two essays, found in widely distributed weekly news magazines, represent the embryonic strands of an argument that will remain as a dominant force in representations of prisoners and punishment throughout the 1960s. Indeed, "recovery from mental aberration" will become a dominant argument in the 1980s and '90s as a way to justify alternative forms of punishment in the face of arguments for "just deserts." During the 1960s, however, it develops primarily in response to the failure of the methods of the 1950s to rehabilitate prisoners. In effect, the prisoner remains redeemable in this strand of argument, but only in the sense that an external force can scientifically "cure" a "mental or social disease" (Playfair 171; see also "Hope for" 371). The inmate is not assumed to have the tools to rehabilitate himself any more than he could perform heart surgery.

Rehabilitation is a matter neither of personal choice nor of self-motivation; it is a matter of behavioral and psychiatric surgery.

While this model is given different degrees of strength in different discussions, it is the stronger forms that are most provocative. Not only will the stronger images of the prisoner as aberrant persist throughout the period of this study, albeit in a decidedly different configuration, but they are also the most startling to readers in the present. That is, the style of the strongest forms of the treatment model from the 1960s have an Orwellian air to them when encountered today, even though, with changes in style, such arguments persist. For example, Steve Allen, in his boldly titled essay, "Let's Brainwash Our Criminals," argued in *Science Digest* that "if Chinese Communists could brainwash our GIs to an alien philosophy, why not use similar techniques, plus the best modern educational methods to imprint reason, honesty and decency on the minds of criminals?" (34). Allen suggested that states commence experiments on the ways in which sensory deprivation, sleep deprivation, closed circuit monitoring, and series of informational lectures would affect prisoners: "What an opportunity to educate and indoctrinate a captive audience," he observed (38). In this strongest form, the prisoner is a human being, but one to be transformed to normalcy, whether he chooses to be or not, with whatever tools are available to the institution. As will become evident, statements such as Allen's, statements that would chill many observers today, will pass unnoticed when criminals are represented as having a choice in whether or not to accept such a method of transformation.

Between the "altruistic inmate" and the medical treatment model of rehabilitation, one finds the struggle between old and new penological theories, between self-motivated prison programs and programs through which inmates are controlled. While both types of program maintain an underlying belief in the transformative nature of the prisoner and the need to move him or her back to a universal norm of behavior, one emphasizes the inmate, the other the programs that motivate such change. Again, such characterizations have roots deep in penological theory. Their continued existence attests to the strength of discourse, once it takes root, never to relinquish its power fully.[4]

Violence, Rioting, and Prisons

While the second primary representation of the prisoner of this period will be seen to construct violence and rioting differently, representations of the prisoner as redeemable continue to attribute violence and rioting to prison conditions rather than to the nature of the prisoner. Hence, John Conrad, chief of research at the California Department of Corrections, argued during this period that those who become prisoners are "produced" and are therefore not to be blamed for their riotous behavior: "We now see him as one who has been caused by unfavorable circumstances to offend against society. The circumstances which led him to crime might be found within him by the psychologist or around him by the sociologist" ("Prisons" 90). In the 1968 film *Riot,* a riot is orchestrated by a cadre of prisoners in order to serve as a front for their escape effort. It becomes clear from the prisoners' dialogue, however, that their need to riot and to escape comes from the mistreatment they receive at the hands of the prison warden. In a similar vein, activist and prisoner Eldridge Cleaver argued that all prisoners should be released from state institutions as such institutions do more harm than good, causing poor behavior rather than stopping it: "I look upon those cats in the penitentiary—I don't care what they're in for—robbery, burglary, rape, murder, kidnap, anything. A response to a situation. A response to an environment" (8). While blaming social and environmental conditions for riotous behavior is an argument with discursive roots that run deep into the previous era, it broadens here to include crime in general as well as prison riots. That is, while arguments of the 1950s blamed riots on prison conditions, some of the arguments of this era take the extra step of arguing that crime itself is a "cause and effect" response to social conditions. Not only is the prisoner redeemable, then, but his entire behavior up to the point of incarceration is constructed as having been beyond his control.

Speaking on a separate occasion, John Conrad noted that while prisoners are relatively nonviolent, their rare violent outbursts occur primarily because the prison is an institution that teaches by example that coercion is required if compliance is to be gained. That is, modeling their behavior on that of the guards, prisoners learn to view mass violence as the only available means of gaining their objectives ("Violence" 115–16). *Newsweek*'s coverage of a widely reported critique of Arkansas's Tucker Prison, a critique upon which the film *Brubaker* was based, buttresses this claim. The report revealed a large number of abuses in the prison, ranging from the illegal buying and selling of goods to sadistic beatings of the prisoners by guards. These abuses would perhaps be uninteresting if not for the response of Arkansas governor Winthrop Rockefeller when the review became widely reported. In *Newsweek,* Rockefeller noted that the abuses, if continued, were certain to cause the most dramatic prison riot in the history of the nation ("Down" 40). Abuse, then, is admitted—by one ultimately responsible for a state's disciplinary branch—to be a direct cause of riotous behavior.

From a different perspective, albeit one that continues the general theme of blaming unruly behavior on prison conditions rather than on the actions of prisoners, arguments become dominant that characterize the prisoner as someone who develops a psychological need to commit crimes because, ironically, the prison provides him with attention he had not received prior to his imprisonment. That is, after being provided with attention and security in prison, two elements lacking from his life before incarceration, the ex-convict will commit crimes in order to return to the security of the prison environment. Hence, Kenneth Lamott observed that "the single great luxury of being taken seriously, of feeling that at last one counts for something, of having a secure, and officially recognized place in a stable and enduring world" is enough to return some individuals to prison repeatedly ("Cells" 21). One would surmise that the prisoner who was praised in the 1950s for turning down parole three times in order to remain in prison would be seen in this configuration as providing a symbolic indictment of the prison system as a whole.

Thus, while this era does provide an alternative representation of the male prisoner, as I will show below, one major strand of characterizations in the 1960s constructs a male prisoner who is not only redeemable but also somewhat guiltless for his behavior. Indeed, the characterizations of this era expand to include the behavior of the prisoner both in and out of prison as being contingent on social and physical environments.

Concluding Observations on the Redeemable Male Inmate

In effect, then, one characterization of prisoners in this era is a continuation, albeit a changed and changing one, of the dominant image of the prisoner of the 1950s, a prisoner both redeemable and human at base. Also paralleling the 1950s, this configuration represents a conservation of a belief in a shared set of values or norms defining how individuals should think, appear, and act. Thus, when "Chester" trims his hair and begins to take on more conservative apparel, the *Saturday Evening Post* notes his reentry into this set of norms. When Paul Crump reads traditional academic scholarly works, converts to Catholicism, and saves the life of one of those who imprisons him, *Ebony, Time,* and the *Christian Century* each claim to observe his rehabilitation. When rehabilitation is posed in the terms of the medical model or riots are posed as being causally linked to the conditions of prisoners, the problem can be solved by a cause-and-effect solution that returns the individual to an ideal state. In each case discussed, actions and appearances signify a move back to what is accepted, a move back to a culturally shared worldview.

Prison histories commonly note that the original purpose of prisons was the removal of human beings from a state of sin to one reflecting a transcendental state of humanity. It is evident that this belief persists to a degree; represented in this period is a culturally sanctioned belief, a hyperconcern, with the use of discipline in the form of medication, "brainwashing," and other programs to move the offending subject from a state of opposition to the social whole to a position of conformity with it. When Steve Allen suggests that we use the techniques of brainwashing to "imprint reason, honesty and decency on the minds of criminals" (34), he pointedly illustrates this belief.

The Counter-Portrait: The Irrational and Immoral Male

Topically, and in terms of policy, one strain of "prisoner discourse" is an extension and transformation of the dominant representation of the prisoner of the 1950s: the male prisoner remains open for rehabilitation and altruism, although he has been shaped by either mental aberrations or social conditions that have prevented his leading an acceptable life. There is, however, a second dominant (albeit somewhat contradictory) construction of the male prisoner. The import of the argumentative competition between the two depictions of the prisoner is considerable; it influences not only the representation of his treatment while imprisoned but also his treatment upon release. Indeed, it evidently has consequences on the ways in which prisoners represent their own behavior to others. That is, the ex-prisoner constituted as irrational and the one constituted as redeemable face two quite different stigmata in the minds of the public they encounter, and, consequently, they are invited to understand their own behavior in radically different ways. The second major representation of the prisoner that arises during this period, then, is that of an organically irrational and immoral human being, one for whom rehabilitation does not, indeed cannot, work.

When repeat criminal Hal Hollister was invited in 1961 by *Reader's Digest* to write an essay that would outline his thoughts on the ineffectiveness of rehabilitation programs, his presence in such a widely read publication initially appeared to indicate that the voice of the prisoner was being taken seriously as a purveyor of critical and analytic knowledge of disciplinary institutions. However, a reading of the essay makes it evident that Hollister distanced himself from "average" prisoners; according to Hollister, he is the anomaly; the irrational inmate is the norm. Hollister indeed saw the average prisoner as not only different from himself but also different from most human beings: "To a degree far greater than normal, most prisoners are impatient, impulsive, heedless of consequences. They are resentful of authority and impatient with the restrictions that personal responsibilities would place upon them. They seem to be unable to learn from experience. And in conjunction with all these traits is a wide streak of irrationality" ("What" 103). Hollister provided a number of narratives of such irrationality, including one concerning Pete, a prisoner who had been released, found employment, and began raising a family. When Pete ran into financial problems, rather than taking the "rational" routes of behavior that Hollister suggested he should have taken (that is, filing bankruptcy papers, attempting to get a loan), Pete purchased a gun and robbed a local grocery store, landing in prison a week later ("What" 104). In a second essay on prison life, this time in *Harper's*, Hollister further suggested that prisons should be restructured so that those few prisoners who are redeemable can be provided aid while those who are "failures simply because they are incomplete human beings" might be kept away from others. As Hollister noted, with shades of social Darwinism, "Nature creates just as many irreclaimable failures among the human species as among any other" ("An Ex-Convict's" 20). Similarly, Steve Allen noted that he was baffled by the typical American prisoner who "has had ample evidence of the misery, the degradation, the monotony and general horror of prison existence. Nevertheless, he is irrational enough to go back to a life of crime as soon as he is released" (35).

The prisoner is constructed in this alternative depiction, then, as naturally and frustratingly immoral. It is not (and this should be underlined) that a rational human subject makes moral choices that are simply an expression of cultural diversity; instead, the prisoner is a "human failure" who continues to make choices that "normal" society considers irrational and immoral. In yet another narrative of prisoner behavior that crystallizes the characteristics of this prisoner, Hal Hollister recounted the story of "Blinky" Taylor, a prisoner who was able to steal from his friends and family with no sense of guilt or shame—indeed, with no understanding that his actions could be interpreted as wrong. Hollister noted that Taylor and other prisoners like him are so impervious to "such normal emotions as compassion, pity, and guilt" that they are "fundamentally non-reformable" ("An Ex-Convict's" 19). He further noted, "They are immune to appeals to conscience and moral sense, and to the painful logic of cause and effect punishment" ("An Ex-Convict's" 19). Finally, in a discussion of the morality of prisoners in the *Saturday Evening Post,* the highly visible Hollister described what he called the odd and yet typical morality of the prisoner in the following terms: "He is unfeeling and ruthless in his disregard for the rights and property of others. . . . He is immoral in that he breaks the conventional standards of behavior" ("How to" 74). The criminal in this construction, then, is both irrational and immoral and is unable to be rehabilitated.

A number of narratives and characterizations lead the reader to conclude that the immorality of these prisoners is also causally connected to violent behavior. In *The Nation,* historian Howard Zinn, surprisingly perhaps, added to this characterization in his attempt to provide support for the civil rights movement. Zinn provided a narrative situated in Hattiesburg, Mississippi, in which attorney Oscar Chase was arrested during a civil rights protest. While he was imprisoned, another inmate, apparently with the permission and encouragement of the prison authorities, beat Chase while guards, police officers, and other prisoners looked on. Afterwards, Chase was taken to another cell where he lay on a cot, bleeding throughout the night. The prisoner who had attacked Chase was given cigarettes and matches and released later that night with no apparent qualms about having beaten Chase for the reward of a pack of cigarettes (502). In somewhat similar fashion, Bruce Jackson made the following characterization in his attempt to describe the problems with imprisonment in the *New York Times Magazine.* Upon visiting several prisons, Jackson noted in his report that violence is a moral norm and recounted seeing thirty inmates stabbed in a single night in a midwestern prison ("Our Prisons" 131). In sum, in this construction of the prisoner, violence is a norm primarily because prisoners are equipped with what would normally be considered immoral mindsets and irrational attitudes.[5]

While I will argue below that these representations of the prisoner will begin to cohere along the lines of race, they also allow for the justification of different policies to be taken toward criminal justice. As John DiIulio notes, "At the core of every penology is some understanding of what the 'typical' prisoner is like" ("Understanding" 69). Just as the altruistic and redeemable inmate allows for the justification of rehabilitation and treatment programs, the representation of the prisoner as irrational and irredeemable is much more likely to justify a more control-centered incarceration, a philosophy of the old penology. While individuals may look at all of the available representations of the prisoner, they are not bound to accept all of them.[6] Indeed, they may assume that the vast majority of prisoners are altruistic and redeemable and that other representations are either wrong or of anomalous prisoners; they may assume that all prisoners are irrational and irredeemable and that altruistic inmates are the anomaly; or they may find some other means of dividing the two characterizations of the prisoner (for instance, by race, class, or gender). In this case, as the decade proceeds, race becomes a characterizing factor, one of the ways in which individuals can interpret the representations of the prisoner. Hence, one will be able to have "mediated" evidence that while Caucasians are redeemable, other prisoners are not. In some sense this provides the seeds of subtle arguments for different forms of treatment for different criminals based on their likelihood for redemption, and underneath that, their race.

Characteristics and Observations on the Irrational Prisoner and Race

To a degree that increases chronologically, discussions of irrationality and violence become intermingled with the inmate's ethnicity. Specifically, African-American and other "minority" male prisoners increasingly become constituted as violent, and irrationally so, as this era progresses. While I will discuss this issue more fully later, a few observations can be made here with regard both to the image of the irrational prisoner and to its linkage with African Americans.

One could surmise that the representation of an "irrational" prisoner reflects the existence of an oppositional worldview within the culture at large, a recognition of the discursive growth of a distinct morality. That is, while the belief in the basic redeemable nature of all people reflects faith in a commonly held value system for behavior, the positing of African-American and other prisoners as irrational suggests that, within the discourse of this era, another set of values has begun to threaten the homogeneity of traditional values and morality. Indeed, that the African-American male prisoner is depicted as violent and irrational suggests that the challenge to those values was at least a marginally popular one, one requiring discipline and marginalization in order to quell its growth. Indeed, the rise and growth of the civil rights and Afrocentric movements throughout this period are sure to have had some influence in forcing the culture to acknowledge African Americans as having an identity with which to be reckoned.

Hence, while the reflection of different moral universes is present, the treatment of the different moral systems within popular discourse indicates that, at least within the dominant media, there remained only one way to judge moral actions. That is, one set of behaviors and actions is praised as fitting within a commonly held set of morals and another set of behaviors or beliefs is condemned. Hence, these discourses do not celebrate difference but condemn it. While the previous era's discourse reflected a celebration of the homogeneity of cultural morality, in this era's discourse, we find an acknowledgment of difference, but a continuation of the praise of one brand of morality. With one set of behaviors linked ethnically to primarily African-American inmates, we find a powerful and subtle form of racism, a racism that is reified as the culture is confronted consistently about questions of race and ethnicity.

As noted earlier, the construction of the prisoner as redeemable represents a belief that criminals could and should be moved back to an accepted state of normality. In the discourse of the irrational prisoner, however, we find that such prisoners are "irreclaimable humans created by nature," that, as Hollister suggested, they are unable to learn from experience. Just as all species have examples who cannot enter the normal social organization, so do human beings. When criminal behavior is constructed in this way, the culture shows a willingness to throw up its hands with regard to a certain class of individuals, to acknowledge that some of its members are natural failures who can only be dealt with through removal from the social body. Once we as a culture accept the possibility of the irredeemable criminal, methods for identifying and dealing with him take on a crucial importance.

Indeed, as this era passes, the common and most likely identifying characteristic of morality is based on race, and once morality is distinguished on the grounds of race, race and (im)morality coexist. As a result, these constructions are problematic to the degree that they encourage the construction of difference on lines of race and thereby silence oppositional value systems on the same grounds. When a majority of redeemable males are depicted as Caucasian and a majority of immoral and irrational inmates are represented as "other," we have a subtle cultural morality in which particular prisoners are deemed to act "rationally" and thus are potentially redeemable, while others, who take similar actions, are considered naturally, and perhaps permanently, inhuman. Indeed, one can perhaps safely assume that such identifying characteristics were widespread throughout the culture during this period, pertaining not only to prisoners but to "law-abiding" citizens as well. The fact that the representations of both a redeemable and an irredeemable prisoner exist simultaneously via race allows members of that culture to choose both constructions at different times in order to justify their beliefs about and behavior toward individual members of the culture.

Emergent Themes: Rape and Race

As in the last chapter, I wish to turn my attention to minor but emergent themes that will loom heavily as rhetorical forces in future discourses even though they remain somewhat embryonic in this period. As mentioned above, the development of particular characteristics on the grounds of race is one such theme. The other, often accompanying characterizations of race, is prison rape.

Rape

In the previous era, male homosexuality was characterized as resulting from mental aberration, and homosexuals not only were characterized as instigators of prison violence but also were depicted as having little hope for rehabilitation. While the violent strand of this characterization persists in representations of this era, homosexuality is now discussed less in terms that constitute a "vile" and "disgusting" nature than in terms of the pragmatics of rape control. Indeed, male homosexuality itself is rarely discussed save a few occurrences, such as in the film *Riot* when a "queens' row" arises whose transvestite members dance for the entertainment of other prisoners. While homosexual rape is discussed, the discussions are far more likely to focus on the violent behavior implied by rape than on the sexual orientation of the participants. Indeed, it is quite often pointedly clear that the participants consider themselves heterosexuals in a situation that leaves little choice of how sexual gratification will be achieved. In short, rape is generally coded in terms of violence rather than sexuality.

During the 1960–68 period, then, descriptions of sex in men's prisons generally highlight the notion of terrorism alone, rarely discussing sexuality at all unless it is to make clear that the participants are heterosexual. For example, in a *Time* report on the Philadelphia prison system, it was observed that no one is safe from homosexual rape while imprisoned there: "Virtually no young man of slight build who enters prison is safe from attack. . . . Most are overwhelmed and raped by gangs of tougher convicts within a day or two of their arrival" ("Catalogue" 54). Again, in a separate analysis of the Philadelphia prison system, in almost identical terms, author Alan Davis noted that "sexual assaults in the Philadelphia prison system are epidemic. . . . Virtually every slightly built young man committed by the courts is sexually assaulted within a day or two after his admission to prison" (Davis 9). Numerous narratives provide accounts of rape and coercive homosexuality in prisons throughout the country. While not the only reports, the ones on the Philadelphia prison system are certainly the most dramatic. The following account from a prisoner in the Philadelphia Detention Center is particularly striking:

> On Tuesday morning, the first week of June at about 9:30 A. M., I was in my cell 412 on D block and I had started to clean up. A tall, heavy-set fella came into the cell and asked for a mirror and shaving brush and a comb, and that my cell partner said he could borrow [*sic*]. He then said that he heard something about me concerning homosexual acts. I told him what he had heard was not true. He then started to threaten me if I didn't submit to him. Then I hit him with my fist in his face before he could hit me. Then about three more men came into the cell, and they started to beat me up, too. I fought back the best I could and then I fell on the floor and I got kicked in the ribs. Three guys were holding me while the other one tore my pants off; I continued to fight until one of the guys knocked me out. One of the guys was holding me on the floor and had my arm pinned to the floor. And about seven or eight guys came into the cell and they took turns sticking their penis up my ass. When they finished they left my cell, and I was still laying on the floor. (Davis 10)

Homosexuality, then, is moved to the discursive underground in making room for the construction of rape. In men's prisons, sex is no longer participated in by mutual consent; it is now an "attack," an "assault." As Alan Davis noted of the prisoners, "The typical aggressor does not consider himself to be a homosexual, or even to have engaged in homosexual acts. This seems to be based upon his startlingly primitive view of sexual relationships, one that defines as male whichever partner is aggressive and as homosexual whichever partner is passive" (15). The focus turns from homosexuality as an act of mental imbalance and toward rape and violence.

In *Newsweek*, author Calvin Tomkins estimated in 1960 that 85 percent of male prisoners in U.S. prisons engaged in homosexual activities either willingly or unwillingly. He further suggested that homosexual behavior "is the main cause of tension and trouble" in most prisons (110). It is evident that while homosexuality as a consensual act is not a dominant theme in this era of discourse, rape and coercive sex are prominent, violence-producing activities that involve a high percentage of prisoners. This line of argument will become a powerful rhetorical force in the following era when portraits of the prisoner as irrational and immoral are articulated with those that essentialize the prisoner by race. As the image of the African-American male becomes solidified as the violent, irrational rapist, the constraints placed on his physical discipline, his treatment, will become solidified as well.

Race and the Prisoner

The racial characterization of the male prisoner during the 1960–68 period is engaging in that it works via a binarism between African Americans and Caucasians, with those of other ethnic backgrounds rarely being mentioned. Furthermore, in these characterizations, there is less concern with the number of African Americans than with the ways in which they integrate with and affect the behavior of white inmates. Indeed, from the first, little is made of the differences between prisoners based on ethnic diversity; instead, emphasis is placed on the self-imposed segregation of prisoners by race. While race certainly becomes more of a distinguishing factor as the era proceeds, distinctions based primarily on racial characteristics are fairly embryonic. Certainly, there are those voices that paint racist characterizations of African-American prisoners, but these characterizations are emergent rather than dominant.

The representation of race takes place on two levels. In the first, the racism of particular prisoners is highlighted; in the second, the essays themselves act implicitly to essentialize prisoner behavior by race. The narrative of Oscar Chase, the white civil rights lawyer mentioned earlier who was arrested and jailed in Hattiesburg, Mississippi, and then beaten by a prisoner whom police had put into his cell for that explicit purpose, is an example of this first level of discourse. The attacker, who was later rewarded with a pack of cigarettes and his release, told Chase that he had been a paratrooper in World War II and that he "would rather kill a nigger-lover than a Nazi or a Jap" (Zinn 502). Here, the prisoner is critiqued for manifesting the same racist attitudes under attack outside of prison; he is explicitly aligned with social ideas that are becoming outmoded.

Similarly, many narratives critique the policies of prisons as racist. It should be noted, however, that the way the arguments are constructed in such narratives works implicitly to substantiate racist representations by universalizing the race of the prisoner. In that such representations maintain an ethnic focus, they indeed contribute to representations by race. While explicitly critiquing racism, their focus on African-American prisoners provides the impression that a majority of prisoners are "other than" Caucasian. For example, African-American prisoner Edgar Labat, described as having possibly been unjustly convicted of the rape of a white woman, provided a narrative in *Look* of the racism of prison life. Labat claimed not only that his arresting police officer called him a "nigger" and that the jury unjustly convicted him but also that the prison system is institutionally racist: "They'd do you all kinds of ways. Take medicine. Say you taking medicine, and they tell you they run out and then, I hear, turn right around and give it to . . . some of the white boys. Or, when you go out to get your clothes, they give you old clothes, with holes in them and give the white boys you know, good clothes" (88). Labat went on to note that when he first entered prison, a white guard openly told the entire cell block that Labat should have been lynched for raping a white woman (88).

Moreover, while investigating a midwestern prison, author Bruce Jackson observed that one result of the segregation of black and white prisoners was that six to eight black prisoners were often placed in a cell together while only one to two whites were. When Jackson inquired of prison administrators the cause of black prisoners being crowded into cells, he was told, "Aw, they're all queer in here anyway" ("Our Prisons" 132).

The racist attitudes of the prison administration are highlighted in a 1967 *Newsweek* report of the escape of four black inmates from the Wilkinson County (Georgia) Prison work camp. After escaping, the four men attended a reception at then-Governor Lester Maddox's house, waiting in a reception line in order to have a chance to meet with the governor and air their grievances about racism and the violent practices of the prison administration. When approached with the prisoners' charges against the prison system, R. T. Bridges, warden of the Wilkinson camp, was noted to respond simply, "A nigger will lie" ("Lester's" 24).

What is interesting about each of these cases is that, while one of the assumed purposes of each is to highlight racism in prisons, one of the possible effects of the articles is to add to and reify the growing conception of the prisoner as black. That is, regardless of the fact that 65 percent of state and federal prisoners were Caucasian in 1965, discursive depictions of the prisoner, including those that attempt to counter racism, aid in the creation of the publicly "black" prisoner, especially because each notes that the majority of prisoners they encountered in prison were African Americans (Langan 5).[7]

Not only does the represented prisoner begin to gain ethnic diversity, but to at least a slight degree, this diversity brings with it the affixation of specific characteristics to ethnic categories. While this depiction is emergent at this point, the move to essentialize characteristics by race will become a dominant and important rhetorical force later. For instance, it is during this period that the number of

Black Muslims in American prisons begins to grow, and they are persistently branded in public discourses as purveyors of a new breed of racism.[8] Simultaneously, and perhaps consequently, African-American prisoners as a whole are represented in popular discourse as holding some of the same racist impulses as Black Muslims.

For example, in a *Saturday Evening Post* discussion of the number of economically lower-class people who are imprisoned, Stewart Alsop noted that the Washington, D.C., Jail has become "a fine breeding ground for hate—it is the best recruiting center in Washington for the Black Muslims" (18). He further claimed that those African-American inmates who do attend Black Muslim meetings "are subjected to an indoctrination which may well wind within them a time-bomb of racial hate" (110). In a separate case, *Time* reported that when prisoner William Howard of Virginia State Prison refused to provide the names of fellow prisoners who, along with him, requested meeting time in order to practice as Black Muslims, he was held in solitary confinement for over four years. In court cases between Howard and the state of Virginia, his lawyers and those representing the state of Virginia debated the reason he was being held in maximum security—either for security reasons, as the state held, or in order to squelch his religious beliefs, as his lawyers maintained. Regardless of the ultimate motives for confining him, it is important to note that African Americans who even requested time for Black Muslim activities were represented as dangerous in popular discourse ("Judges vs. Jailers" 69).

Finally, another racial association made during this period that later proves influential combines both of the developing themes discussed here: race and rape. Although only dominant later, links between the African-American prisoner and rape and between the white inmate and victimization appear as early as the late 1960s. Indeed, two clear references to this configuration of rape appear in 1968, in the blurry transitional period between two of the eras I have distinguished. Both of these references again concern the heavily critiqued Philadelphia prison system. In *Time*'s report, it was observed that "the aggression also has racial overtones. Though Negroes constitute 80% of the prison population, more than half of the attacks by them were against whites" ("Catalogue" 54). In a separate account of the same prison system, Alan Davis noted that he found that "a disproportionate number [of rape cases] involved Negro aggressors and white victims. . . . These statistics in part reflect the fact that 80 percent of the inmates are Negro—it is safer for a member of a majority group to single out for attack a member of a minority group" (Davis 15).

When homosexuals are represented as fairly harmless (for example, as "queens" who are out for pleasure and not violence, as in the 1968 film *Riot*), they are primarily Caucasian. Rape as an act of violence is the domain of the African-American prisoner; as an act of pleasure, albeit a perverted pleasure, it is the domain of the Caucasian.[9]

The discussions of rape and race witnessed in this era reflect a belief that both the rapist and the African American (as well as other nonwhite inmates) operate within the realms of irrationality and immorality. Homosexuality as seen in public discourse has disappeared, or at least is rapidly disappearing, as a curable mental problem; rape is its closest representation in public discussions of the prisoner. While the 1950s belief in rehabilitation encourages an ignorance of African-American prisoners (that is, a lack of representation) and hence prefigures them as irredeemable, the public prominence of African Americans via the civil rights movement forces a public presentation of the African-American prisoner, and this image clearly borrows from cultural stereotypes of African-American men in general. Hence, African Americans move from nonexistence to immorality: they are "queer," they "will lie," they plot violence, they practice the racist policies of the Black Muslims.

I should repeat that while the appearance of African Americans in public discourse does reveal to a certain extent the existence of other worldviews, it is not a celebration of difference. Instead, the alliance of African Americans with irrationality, rather than nonrationality or difference, reflects the existence of the same shared value system of the 1950s. While challenges to it are obvious, these challenges are relegated to a realm of discourse that nullifies their power. There is not, then, a representation of two valid belief systems; rather, there is the representation of one homogeneous moral system under which two types of behavior are judged, one favorably and one decidedly not so.

Furthermore, portraits of the prisoner are important on one level because they reflect and encourage understanding of individuals who are imprisoned as well as those who are not. This being the case, the portrait and discussion of African-American prisoners simultaneously create and reflect a cultural discourse that views African Americans in general in terms of an immorality to be censured, as an illegitimate form of "difference" not to be celebrated. As suggested above, accompanying such a construction of African-American male prisoners must be a similar, although perhaps not as exaggerated, understanding of African-American men in general. Furthermore, it is perhaps more important that this construction indicates that change is not forthcoming; blacks are indeed represented as the key examples of the social failures thought to be inherent to any species.

The Jailhouse Lawyer and the Alcoholic Inmate

Two other characterizations of the male prisoner emergent in this period prove influential in the discursive makeup of prisoners and punishment later. In the first, prisoners are provided with their first voice as legal beings, as citizens with the legal rights of citizenship. Moreover, their status as knowledgeable purveyors of legal counsel provides them with the characteristic of intellectual respectability. This characterization represents the rise of the new penology in public discourse, a focus on the rights and abilities of the prisoner rather than on his or her control by the prison administration. In *Time*, for example, Orange County (Florida) public defender W. O. Frederick, Jr., called "jailhouse lawyer" Theodore N. Turner "a brilliant man. His grasp of law is phenomenal" ("Bar" 88). The article observes not only that Turner had an IQ of 140 but also that his legal maneuvering had forced public defenders to handle a number of prisoner appeal cases they wanted to refuse and forced the courts to abolish a twenty-five-dollar court fee charged to all inmates for appeals ("Bar" 83, 88). Furthermore, convicted murderer Edgar Smith wrote his own narrative, prominently published in the *Saturday Evening Post*, and recounted his having written a legal brief that claimed the death penalty was unfair ("I Don't" 10). Similarly, Lawrence Wright of Clinton State Prison received attention after suing the state of New York for maintaining a prison system that constituted cruel and unusual punishment ("Rights" 46).

While the public image of the prisoner as a person with legal rights is relatively faint at this point, it is a growing conception and one that attributes intelligence and dignity to the male prisoner, enabling him to be situated as responsible for his behavior and actions. It should also be noted that a majority of those described as jailhouse lawyers are also identified decidedly as "white," either discursively or pictorially. The move to see the prisoner as a citizen with legal rights is extremely significant to future configurations of the prison. As the movement develops, it becomes one of the major rhetorical influences in the development and use of alternative forms of punishment. Also, because this inmate is portrayed primarily as Caucasian while the irrational prisoner is constructed as African-American, there is a consistent and increasingly strong association being made between white male prisoners with intelligence, moral autonomy, and rehabilitation, and African-American male prisoners with the binary opposites.

Another characterization that later proves significant is that of drug and alcohol abuse by the prisoner. While public discussions of drug and alcohol abuse do occur in this period, they are rare. As an example of the occurrence of such representations, there is a series of vivid characterizations of alcoholic and homeless prisoners in an exposé of alcoholism among the inmates at the Washington, D.C. Jail. One alcoholic arrested for public intoxication and vagrancy was described in *New Republic* as using newspapers in order to keep his body warm. When guards at the prison began to take the newspapers off his body, layers of skin began to peel off with the paper, inducing one guard "almost [to] lose his breakfast" (Goldfarb, "No Room" 13). In the same essay, a second alcoholic was described who "wore eight pairs of rubbers to keep warm when he slept on the streets. As we took them off and got down to the last pair, part of his foot came off. We sent him to the hospital and they laid him down with his feet out the window in blankets—the smell was so bad" ("No Room" 13). Furthermore, in the movie *Riot,* released at the tail end of this era, inmates digging an escape hole not only use amphetamines but produce over one hundred gallons of moonshine, causing the entire inmate population to engage in fights and riotous behavior. While such characterizations remain rare at this point, then, depictions of drugs and alcohol are intriguing both because of their vividness and because they focus on the problems the abuses cause the guards rather than with sympathy toward the abuser. That is, while discussions of legal rights cohere toward the new penology, discussions of drug and alcohol usage, which could focus on either penology, are instead bonded to the old.

The Female Inmate

Representations of the female inmate, still rare in the 1960–68 period in mass-mediated publications, remain fairly consistent with those of the last era. The most consistent theme in the representation of female prisoners, a theme that continues in future discussions, concerns their imprisonment for crimes that arise either from poverty or as a result of the scars of sexual, mental, and physical abuse. In brief, women prisoners of all races are represented as naturally "moral," only failing to express this morality when others intervene in their lives, disrupting their natural constitution.

For example, Michael Drury described in *McCall's* her experience teaching writing classes in a women's prison. While acknowledging that her students, because they were self-selected, did not provide an objective representation of the average prisoner, she also noted that the students were generally intelligent and creative although few had any formal education beyond the secondary level (127). In one narrative of her experiences with the students, she described the class's "effeminate" reactions when she brought several dozen daffodils to them one week. After noting the pleasure the prisoners took in an item as basic as flowers, she said, "I am convinced that we can help them only by letting them, to some extent, be the children they were never allowed to be when they were young" (128).

Similarly, when Barbara Deming, an African American, was imprisoned in Birmingham, Alabama, for demonstrating against laws that supported segregation by race, she slowly developed friendships with several of the "regular" prisoners in the "white" ward of the prison. After learning that many of them had drug and alcohol problems, Deming offered an explanation of why they began to partake of these substances and hence were led to a criminal lifestyle: "The briefest conversations with these women revealed the misfortunes that had driven them to drink: family problems, the sudden death of a husband, grave illness. All conspicuously needed help, not punishment" (Deming 437). Offering a similar explanation of her own imprisonment, Dorothy West noted in the *Saturday Evening Post* that "I'm considered to be an excellent bookkeeper, and I never was in trouble until after my husband died of tuberculosis in 1957. In the early 1960s I had problems with bad checks, and then came the hold-up charge" (23). Lawrence Friedman notes that in the nineteenth century, there was a very low number of female prisoners, and he attributes the low number to laws and norms that held husbands and guardians as responsible for the actions of women, not to the commission of fewer crimes by women (211). According to Friedman, when a women stole from a local store, laws held that her husband, rather than the woman herself, would be incarcerated. The cultural norms that prompted such laws shape the discourses of the present: while women do commit crimes, it is always already because of an external force—parental or spousal abuse, the death of her husband, and so on.

In each case, responsibility for criminal behavior is removed in part or in whole from the imprisoned women. Instead, much like the altruistic and redeemable male inmate of the 1950s, she has been taken from a position of morality and thrust into a criminal lifestyle because of her treatment at the hands of others or because of the unfortunate social position into which she was born. The only times when this is not the case is when the female prisoner being represented is imprisoned for social protest and hence does not represent a "normal" prisoner.

Indeed, among the few articles that do explicitly address female prisoners during this period, nearly half concern the imprisonment of women as a result of their involvement with either civil rights protests or protests against U.S. involvement in Vietnam, even though the articles clearly note that protesters do not adequately represent the average prisoner. Hence, even while providing representations of "normal" prisoners, when Gloria Wade Bishop and Barbara Deming separately discussed their imprisonment as a result of work within the civil rights movement and Lillian Rubin discussed her imprisonment as a result of work protesting the Vietnam War, they suggest by their very presence that many of the women in prison are moral crusaders, leading our culture to what they consider higher levels of moral behavior.

In brief, to a great degree, images of imprisoned women during this period are based around either those who have been corrupted by others and hence were led to a life of crime or by those who have chosen, in the cause of "higher" morality, to commit acts that they know will lead to their imprisonment. Regardless of the cause of their imprisonment, such women continue to minister to the needs of others. Generally, then, the representation of the female prisoner continues to posit her as the bearer of the one shared cultural morality, a morality that will find expression in those women who are free from torment and abuse.

Concluding Comments

In order to illumine the ideological depiction of the prisoner of contemporary culture and the influence of this description on contemporary culture, I have highlighted the emergence of general arguments about and characterizations of the prisoner and have noted that these representations work to confine our current conception of the prisoner while simultaneously reflecting the beliefs of the culture from which they emerge. In this second period of discourse, the male prisoner is no longer only a redeemable human being who met with material or social conditions that encouraged a life of crime. While this remains one representation, a second and competing characterization has emerged: a prisoner who is innately irrational and immoral, engaging in violence simply for the sake of violence. His immorality and irrationality are "natural," not to be rehabilitated or changed, only to be repressed through punishment. He cannot be provided with an understanding of the ways in which his actions are immoral; one can only punish him in a desperate attempt to "teach him a lesson." As the era proceeds, he emerges primarily as African-American, and his violent nature manifests itself in extremes. The female prisoner, meanwhile, continues to be reified as redeemable, regardless of ethnicity. Her criminal lifestyle or action is either the result of abuse at the hands of others or of the quest for greater cultural goods. In the solitude of prison, among other women, she is rejuvenated; she rehabilitates herself.

Regardless of the tensions that come to exist between different representations of the male criminal during the period 1960–68, these differences continue to illustrate a belief in one set of cultural norms, one system of values. Under this set of norms, the actions of some prisoners are seen as rational and understandable, requiring treatment and concern; the actions of the others are irrational and immoral, requiring punishment. As subsequent chapters will show, representations of different types of prisoners will prove to be problematic in that they will encourage the pursuit of different forms of discipline for the different dominant characterizations. In effect, the characterizations of the prisoners setting roots in the discourse of the sixties solidify in later eras, becoming rhetorically material constraints on future characterizations of the nature of the prisoner.

5

Rehabilitation, Revolution, and Irrationality, 1969–1974

> What is a convict really like? A convict is often no different than the man who sat next to you on the bus this morning. Convicts are ordinary people with bigger-than-life social problems. . . . Everyone can help destroy the myths surrounding convicts by starting to think of them as human beings with problems. (Torok 10–11)

> [Prisoners of the past] were a conservative lot. . . . They accepted, and must still accept, the authority of prison administrations just because it was authority. . . . [The] new kind of criminal now coming into the prison thinks society has transgressed against him. (B. Jackson, "Prison" 587)

> Many convicts are incorrigible scum whose sole purpose in life closely parallels that of a demented crocodile. They wouldn't lead an honest life if guaranteed a thousand dollars per week and half of God's throne in the hereafter. (Coons 198)

This period, spanning roughly the years 1969 to 1974, is one of rapid transition and change in the portrait of the male prisoner, as well as one of reification and expansion in the representation of the female. During this era, the division between the two dominant depictions of the male prisoner of the most recent era—the redeemable prisoner and the immoral, irrational one—segments once again, creating three public versions of the convict and, consequently, three rival bases for disciplining criminals. The opening quotations, the last two written by prisoners, are crystallizations of these three portraits of the male prisoner. I deal with each in turn before turning to the era's solidification and expansion of the portrait of the female prisoner.

As should by now be obvious, the three representations of this era are rooted in, and constrained by, the historically developing portrait of the male prisoner traced out in previous chapters. I again want to emphasize that such portraits, even when they appear stable, are always already in some degree of transition. On one end, although less prominent than in the past, the prisoner remains a redeemable, bright, and sincere human being, with a desire and ability to rejoin the social body. On the other end, the violent and irredeemable prisoner of the last era is provided with a dual valence and hence represents two different configurations of the prisoner.

In one prong of the division, there is a male prisoner who, while his behavior is admittedly outside of "common" morality, is no longer situated as irrational and immoral. Rather, his behavior is said to constitute a different morality rather than an immorality, a nonrationality rather than an irrationality. He is judged by a separate set of norms; his representation indicates not only the existence of but also the acceptance of cultural diversity by at least one segment of culture. In providing this representation of the prisoner, essayists routinely claimed that many inmates should be neither imprisoned nor rehabilitated because their actions are indeed not "criminal." Rather, such convicts are imprisoned as the result of an unfair and unjust system that ignores the relativity of moral systems and holds the dominant morality to be the correct morality. This representation originates in and features arguments by and about revolutionary African-American inmates such as George Jackson and Huey Newton; it is a persona that garners a considerable amount of interest and attention throughout the period. In this representation, black prisoners are generally depicted as being caught in the grasp of a violent and dictatorial system that treats them according to the norms of the dominant moral system, ignoring subcultural beliefs and cultural diversity. Such representations are the apex of a public "playing out" of DiIulio's new penology; in these representations, concern is given for the life and rights of the prisoner, leaving the guards and wardens with the appearance of brutes who imprison and punish others solely for the sin of difference.

The third representation of the male prisoner reifies the immoral and irrational male inmate of the last era who practices violence for violence's sake, who indeed cannot control his own behavior. Rehabilitation is not an option for this inmate; only in his imprisonment can the culture at large find comfort in protecting itself from his savagery.

The struggle over how prisoners will be presented becomes clear in this era in that many of the same prisoners are represented in one essay as examples of persons imprisoned unfairly simply on the basis of difference and in another as examples of irrational and violent criminals who must remain imprisoned. In the former case, a number of value systems are judged valid; in the latter, only the dominant cultural morality is deemed legitimate. In the first case, the focus is on the rights of the prisoners and is based on the grounds of cultural difference; in the second, the focus is on control and discipline and is based on the grounds of cultural homogeneity. Hence, rather than attempting to articulate respect for cultural diversity, proponents of lengthier prison terms and harsher forms of discipline use this depiction of the prisoner to further their cause.

Because these representations serve as justifications for various forms or systems of punishment, I wish to emphasize that the contours of each must be investigated carefully. This analysis reveals not only something about how prisoners are represented in mass culture but also something about cultural attitudes toward morality and behavior outside of prison. Furthermore, such discourse constrains how new forms of punishment develop, forms dictated by both discursive and material changes. For example, when changes in laws lead to the material condition of overcrowded prisons in the 1980s and 1990s, and these changes lead to the development and utilization of alternative forms of punishment, the representations of prisoners developed historically will necessarily shape and constrain how alternative forms of punishment will be utilized and represented. If the Maria Arnford tale and others like it suggest something problematic about contemporary culture, our understandings of the discursive roots of this one aspect of culture will help enable us to deconstruct and reconstruct the many ways in which we discipline each other.

Representing "White": The Man on the Bus

When Lou Torok noted in *America* that convicts are "often no different than the man who sat next to you on the bus this morning," he was tapping into the most powerful and sustaining representation of the male (Caucasian) prisoner, one that continues to have a great deal of rhetorical force even though the representation of the prisoner is always in a process of transition. This redeemable prisoner is willing to work for the benefit of others, able to recognize and admit his mistakes, and, finally, *with the aid* of prison programs, capable of rehabilitating himself and rejoining the social whole. What is key here is that while the appearance of the redeemable prisoner recurs, his redemption, like that of the treatment-oriented prisoner of the last era, is a function of the tools of the prison system. While the previous era found redeemable prisoners who were self-redemptive and others who required treatment, there is in this period the redeemable inmate who is reliant upon the prison system for the tools by which rehabilitation takes place. The inmate is just like "the man on the bus" *once* the prison system has utilized its mechanisms upon his body and mind.

"Normality," in one form or another, is the dominant description tied to this prisoner. The prominence of overt claims concerning normality suggests that the prisoner's representation is more openly contested than it had been previously. It is only because the prisoner is so effectively and efficiently articulated as abnormal or different in other representations that his normality is so willfully asserted here.

Altruism and Humanity

As noted, altruism remains a dominant characteristic of the redeemable prisoner, with his altruism benefiting both the prison community and the culture at large. Hence, in 1971, *Time* provided an exposition on the multiple Jaycee groups that had been established at prisons nationwide. Beyond pointing to the Jaycee groups, however, *Time* noted that the prisoners' activities for the prison and the "outside" community included providing volunteer services for blood drives for leukemia victims, raising money for children in underdeveloped nations, purchasing fire fighting equipment for a native American reservation, promoting antidrug campaigns, and planting trees in the prison courtyard ("Jaycees" 60). Similarly, *Ebony* described the case of Robert Jenkins, Jr., a prisoner at the Green Haven Correctional Institution in New York, who used the entirety of his free time while imprisoned to transcribe books into Braille for blind readers and to teach other prisoners to do the same ("Braille" 82–85). In New Orleans, a large group of prisoners developed and then lobbied for the establishment and maintenance of a program that allowed small groups of prisoners to travel to local high schools and warn children to stay away from criminal lifestyles, providing their own lives (despite their altruism) as counterexamples of proper behavior (Barnwell 966). Finally, in a *Society* report of the benefits society could accrue from prisoners who serve as subjects in pharmaceutical experiments, criminal justice theorists and critics Michael Mills and Norval Morris contended that while prisoners may have many selfish motives for taking part in such experiments, "The altruism of community service is [one reason], carrying with it for the prisoner the assurance that he is as virtuous as those outside who have banished and rejected him" (64). When compared to most of the "men on the bus" that I have encountered, this representation appears quite virtuous.

This caring attitude carries over into representations of the paroled prisoner. Many articles make note of various programs developed by ex-convicts to keep others out of prison, and discussions of programs developed and maintained by former prisoners that help released inmates to maintain a "legal" lifestyle increase throughout the period. Indeed, a prominent *Newsweek* article began with the scenario of a number of prisoners who, upon their release, found it impossible to find meaningful or lasting work and hence returned to activities that ultimately led them back to the Washington State Penitentiary at Walla Walla. The essay reported that a small group of these inmates convinced Walla Walla's administration to allow the establishment of a factory inside the prison to build furniture that would then be purchased by state agencies. The essay indicated the pride with which the prisoners ran the factory and the multiple benefits gained from the experience. Inmate Gary Butenhoff, for example, said of the program, "Here we can be a credit to society instead of a debit," and others pointed to the factory as an opportunity "to do good" (quoted in "Prisons" 92).

While this altruism is perhaps not of the extreme nature that led Teddy Green in the 1950s to offer his eyes "so that a blind child might see," the same impulse, finally to be of some value, is repeatedly represented. Hence, in a separate *Newsweek* essay, former prisoner John Maher reportedly recognized the difficulty he would face in finding employment once released from prison and thus founded a business conglomerate, the main purpose of which was to help other prisoners establish productive lives "outside." The essay focused on the success of the conglomerate and its growth to include several restaurants and an auto repair business (Kellogg 81). Mike Pittman, a former prisoner and drug addict who was labeled as "impossible to rehabilitate" by one judge, observed that the conglomerate program "gives a person a little bit of self-assurance when you know you can do things for yourself" (quoted in Kellogg 82).

Finally, in 1974, Andress Taylor observed inmates of the Lorton prison in Washington, D.C., who helped establish a program that allowed prisoners to attend college and high school classes while serving out their terms. Not only were inmates represented as academically successful in these classes, but they were also shown as providing support to service programs that aided the local community (172). Hence, the redeemable male prisoner is not only altruistic and able to provide for himself but is also able to integrate his concerns with those of the community at large.

The "Human"

Representations of altruism work hand in hand with narratives and characterizations of the prisoner that emphasize the "human," redeemable essence of inmates. Testimonies from inmates, prison administrators, and commentators work together to provide a depiction of prisoners as most efficiently rehabilitated when treated as one would treat any human being in a similar circumstance. For example, in *Commonweal,* Jim Castelli argued that prisons must abandon all work programs that offer substandard pay to prisoners: "A more flexible, more imaginative work program with equitable pay, and the treatment of inmates like human beings, will do more to reduce recidivism and fight crime than the present convict-for-hire system" (142).

At a national meeting of the State Trial Judge's Association, attendee and reporter Paul Wilson of the *Nation* spent one night in a prison in an attempt to understand the living conditions under which prisoners were forced to live. Upon leaving the morning after, Wilson claimed that his visit gave him certain revelations concerning the effect of prisons on humans, noting that "man, created in the image of God, becomes a number; he is stripped of all symbols of status and individuality" (205). After meeting with convicts and experiencing normal prison conditions, another attendee of a similar conference remarked that "convicts are not a breed apart, not unreachable, not unconcerned human beings" (Goldfarb, "Rapping" 22). His solution to recidivism was that the public at large should learn to treat prisoners as human beings, men "created in the image of God."

Evidence for the popular representation of the male prisoner as essentially human is pervasive throughout the era. For example, law student R. J. Orloski provided a narrative of the personal transformation he experienced in his understanding of the prisoner after visiting a prison as part of a law school project. Orloski and several classmates volunteered to hear the legal complaints of inmates at the New York Maximum Security Prison at Auburn. Orloski recounted the apprehension he felt before his first dealing with prisoners; his fears were fed, he noted, by what others told him to expect. After meeting the prisoners, however, Orloski said that the files "gave way to individual identities. . . . Convicted felons were, after all, human beings with personalities of their own, and they shared that inexplicable desire for freedom that is *embedded in American consciousness*" (153, emphasis added).

Similarly, Arthur Waskow argued in the *Saturday Review* that prisoners are so similar to "the everyday man on the streets" that they should be given their own city to live in rather than prisons, for only in "real human" situations could prisoners learn "real redemption" (20–21). Redemption comes, not from merely removing the criminal from bad circumstances, as was the case in past representations, but from transporting him to good circumstances—the prison offers not only silence for redemption but also the city on the hill for rehabilitation.

Finally, when prisoner Sam Melville (Mad Bomber Sam) was killed in an uprising at Attica, Irving Horowitz, discovering that he had known Melville years earlier when Melville used a different name, offered his memories in *Commonweal.* Horowitz recounted stories of Melville working as a record clerk at Sam Goody's, playing baseball, and singing for friends. In providing these memories, Horowitz gave the deceased and cardboard Melville a human spirit, allowing the reader to understand his actions, to understand that his criminal motives were in all likelihood purely human ones (328–29).

Individual Autonomy versus Program Reliance

This "human" representation of the prisoner provides the basis for reifying and highlighting one of the means for prisoner rehabilitation, namely the move to a reliance on the prison system rather than the self. For example, the *Christian Century* described a prisoner self-help group called "Concept" that met at Parish Prison in New Orleans. The purpose of the group was to allow prisoners to work one-on-one in finding ways to learn to stay "straight," to maintain an acceptable lifestyle once leaving prison. An inmate and Concept participant observed that the program allowed each prisoner to see himself as "a brother, a fellow human being—one who fails but who nevertheless has control over and is responsible for his own destiny" (Barnwell 967). This prisoner's testimony of self-determination will prove to be not only a popular one but also one with lasting discursive implications. Witnessed here is a prisoner who is willing to take full responsibility for his actions, both his rehabilitation and his crimes. Unlike the 1950s male prisoner who had no option but to be rehabilitated, as only one form of behavior was acknowledged as acceptable, the voice of choice and responsibility of this prisoner arises during a moment in which a diversity of moralities, at least on some level, is accepted. As a result, to choose rehabilitation is to *choose* the culture's dominant morality as the one most effective in providing lasting benefits.

While choosing rehabilitation becomes a dominant theme later, here the prisoner faces multiple obstacles on the road to redemption.

For instance, in a rhetorical sense, the forms of discourse of the external rehabilitation programs in the popular press erode the idea that rehabilitation is conceived from within. The autonomy of the individual prisoner is necessarily at risk when constructed in such a manner.

To elaborate, while there is discussion of self-rehabilitation as an idea during this era, it is extremely rare to find characterizations or narratives of prisoners who have indeed rehabilitated themselves without aid from the system. Nevertheless, the characterization of the prisoner as redeemable when given the proper aid of prison programs is far more pervasive. A series of essays in 1974 taking a holistic approach to punishment, for example, proposed generally that prisoners should be given the opportunity to develop their mental and physical faculties if they are going to "graduate" from prison life. Edmund Muth, a prison guard, noted in this series that "there are many hundreds of aspiring writers, musicians, tennis players, and snow mobilers who would welcome the stimulation and comradeship of a closer association with sportsmen and artists in the free community" (28). Similarly, Illinois governor Dan Walker asserted that prisoners need recreation services if they are to be rehabilitated, and he proposed to include artistic, poetic, ethnic, and cultural programs in prisons in order to serve the total inmate (19).[1]

Edward Bunker, a prisoner and successful author of a number of articles about prison conditions, consistently recounted the problems he had in publishing his work and therefore in fully rehabilitating himself. He claimed that if prisons provided more aid for himself and others, many prisoners would be ready to live successful lives outside of prison within a matter of years ("Writer" 205).

Furthermore, the necessity of prison programs in rehabilitating prisoners is illustrated in references to various work programs throughout the period: Prison newspapers are said to allow job training and develop maturity skills that will prove helpful later (Dickson); a prison "writing" club at Terminal Island hints at great results ("Writing"); San Quentin's use of representatives from Bache and Company to teach prisoners how to make investments is hailed as successful training ("Convicts Bone"); and a program in Salisbury, Maryland, that helps inmates learn to read for the blind is declared successful for everyone involved (Whitehill).

One narrative in particular, however, provides keen insight into the tension between the prisoner's ability to rehabilitate the "self" and the need to rely on programs endorsed by the prison. In this rather portentous narrative, a twenty-year-old prisoner who was originally arrested for possession of narcotics was caught attempting to escape from prison and ordered to write a 1,500-word essay entitled, "I am a game-player and have been from day one" ("Justice Within" 54). *Newsweek* reported not only that writing the essay helped the inmate to become self-reflective but also that the prisoner was being held in the "Moral Development Unit" at the State Correctional Institution at Niantic, Connecticut, a unit with the avowed purpose of aiding prisoners in the development of a strong sense of morality. Simultaneously, however, Niantic's supervisor Janet York observed that the unit was designed to help prisoners "express their own personalities" (quoted in "Justice Within" 54–55).

It is worth noting that various programs during this period are described as having been constructed in order to aid the prisoner in assimilating to the outside world once he has served his sentence. Descriptions of these programs are interesting both in terms of the methods of rehabilitation featured in the essays and in terms of the underlying definition of successful assimilation. Once again, the responsibility for change remains separate from the prisoner, lying instead with community and prison programs. For example, *US News and World Report* reported in 1970 that San Quentin offered a number of programs, including college courses, shop classes, and cooperative work release programs, to aid prisoners in the transition from prison to the outside world. Frank Johnson, a forty-four-year-old inmate who had been in and out of prison since he was seventeen, testified to the benefits of such a program after learning silk screening and sign making in the program. Upon his release, Johnson found a job making signs and "today he is married, drives a Cadillac and earns about twelve thousand dollars a year as a salesman and consultant to sign companies" (quoted in "California" 46–47). Not only is Johnson successful, then, but he is successful along very conventional lines of economic prosperity and has met this success as a result of learning during his imprisonment.

Similar programs are widely reported. For example, Daniel Skoler, then staff director of the American Bar Association Commission on Correctional Facilities and Services, argued that prisoners should not be punished so much as, once trained, placed into a program of "community reacceptance, designed to equip offenders for a productive, law-observing role in the society to which virtually all will return" (28). Further, Maryland's Division of Corrections had a "Community Reintegration Project" that helped reacquaint the prisoner and his family and reminded the prisoner how to behave in human interactions (Horn, "On Fitting" 88). Terminal Island, the California prison, allowed selected prisoners to move to a community center two months before their final release to learn how to make friends, get a job, reestablish familial relationships, relearn the skill of making choices, and, in general, "become a functioning human being again"

(Dellinger 89). Finally, Chemical Bank and Chemical New York Corporation hired ex-convicts in New York in order to help them "rehabilitate themselves" (Berkeley 28).[2]

I should stress that when programs of this nature are highlighted, they are almost always represented as unqualified success stories. Hence, Deputy Director of the California Department of Corrections Milton Burdman argued in 1969 that fewer prisoners need to be held in prison when they can be placed in community correction programs: "In excess of 70% of all offenders can be placed immediately in community-based correctional activities," he said, adding that *"only 3 to 5% of prisoners are dangerous"* (71, 75, emphasis added). Similarly, a report in *Time* asserted that prisons should be eliminated because criminals can be rehabilitated through such programs as counseling, community centers, community corrections, and furloughs, hence ending the need for incarceration. The essay noted that programs of this nature in North and South Carolina prisons lowered recidivism rates to 2.0 percent and 6.6 percent from percentages in the 1960s ("Alternatives" 56–57).

Prisoners themselves provide testimony of the virtues of such external rehabilitation programs. For instance, in *Christian Century,* a Carbondale, Illinois, work release prisoner observed, "My confinement behind walls made me free up here [pointing at his head]; I see now where I had confined myself before," he noted (quoted in Marousek 430). In addition, *Life* reported that at Washington's Walla Walla penitentiary, prisoners were given furloughs, allowed to determine their own hair length, allowed to decorate their cells, and generally provided with means to express their individuality. When one inmate involved in the program, Arthur St. Peter, murdered a pawnbroker while out on the prison's "supper program," the other inmates expelled him before the prison administration had a chance to; the prisoners claimed that the current programs were doing so much to rehabilitate them that they would not allow anyone to bring about its termination through abuse (Farrell 34). Not only, then, do administrators and essayists depict prison programs as the leading means of rehabilitation, but the prisoners themselves testify to the programs' virtues. Moreover, while the prisoners are shown as becoming responsible for their own actions, it is at the behest of programs supplied by the prison system.

Minor Themes in the Rhetoric of Rehabilitation

Consistent with calls for rehabilitation programs are calls for other programs that add to the overall representation of the prisoner as a normally functioning human being. For example, Warden Charles Campbell of the Fort Worth, Texas, Federal Correctional Institution, a prison that had recently become "coed," contended that coed prisons show respect for prisoners: "We're just serious about asking residents to take charge of their own lives and to respect themselves and others. . . . It has helped many male residents to adopt a more positive and constructive attitude toward themselves" (quoted in B. Mason 193–96). Thus, recognizing that male prisoners are sexual beings with reasonable heterosexual needs is tied to the idea that rehabilitation is achieved partly by helping prisoners regain their dignity and self-esteem. Prisoners involved in coed programs support its influence on their rehabilitation; in *Newsweek*, one claimed that "what we're dealing with here is rehabilitation in as normal a situation as possible. This is the first time I've had a healthy relationship with a woman" (quoted in "Boys and Girls" 23). In *Time*, convict B. F. Maiz noted, "Sure, it's tormenting sometimes, but it's better than being stuck at an all-male institution. Knowing there's a woman around makes a guy feel good, act good, stay on his toes" (quoted in "Coed Incarceration," 84).

Another theme that becomes linked to rehabilitation during this period is that of the prisoner as a holder of legal rights, a stress that is a clear sign of the public growth and acceptance of the new penology and the key characteristic on which Lawrence Friedman divides the twentieth century. As a legal being, the prisoner is again represented as similar to all human beings, having the same rights as the "man on the bus." This representation of the "legal" inmate takes two directions, both, however, emphasizing the prisoner's status as a normal human being. In the first, the inmate is depicted as a human being with legal rights who has been imprisoned by other human beings. In the second, he is represented as highly intelligent, in that he has the ability to construct legal arguments in his own defense.

Exemplifying the first prong of this argument, *Newsweek* reported in 1971 that prisoners in Virginia had filed a class-action suit against the state on the grounds that they were beaten, held in solitary confinement, chained up, and deprived of medication—illegally and without due process. The suit, filed by inmate Philip J. Hirschkop and later labeled the "Bill of Rights for Inmates," was successful, forcing Virginia to reform its prison policies ("Scandal" 39). At the same time, California prisoners were reported to have created a union and demanded improved pay and better medical facilities. By identifying themselves with labor movements outside of prison, the inmates were able to win several concessions, including safer working conditions (Seidman 6–7).

Significantly, in 1969, a lawsuit was reportedly filed for the first time against drug companies that conducted experiments on prisoners on the grounds that prisoners are never in a position to provide true "informed consent" ("Should Experimentation" 11). While medical experimentation in the past was consistently depicted as providing prisoners with a representation as altruistic, here it represents the prisoner as human, as a person whose legal rights are being ignored. Finally, the Berrigan brothers, two priests who received a good deal of media attention after their imprisonment for various peace movement activities, began to file multiple lawsuits that were meant to define and defend the prisoner's right to free speech (R. Smith 29). One cannot help but see, especially when linked with such activists as the Berrigan brothers, the general tenor of the popular understanding of the 1960s and free speech as playing itself out through these legal actions.

Finally, and on a lighter level, the legal rights argument became so dominant during this era, and prisoners so thoroughly constituted as legal actors, that prisoners in the federal penitentiary in Atlanta, claiming to be members of the "Church of the New Song," took legal action against the penitentiary, charging it with refusal to respect their rights to religious freedom. Members of the church and their leader, the "Bishop of the Earth," based their claim on the penitentiary's refusal to serve each member of the church a meal necessary for church ritual. The meal they demanded would have required seven hundred steaks and ninety-eight bottles of Harvey's Bristol Cream ("New Congregation" 98).

In the second prong of the legal argument, not only is the male prisoner depicted as a legal being, but, because he has the ability to fight legally, he is also represented as possessing above-average intelligence. Hence, San Quentin assistant warden Wayne Bartels said of jailhouse lawyers in *Newsweek:* "These guys are very sharp and they learn quickly when their life depends on it. We've probably got some of the best appeals attorneys in the U.S. locked up here" (quoted in "Death Row: A New" 23). Similarly, Paul Wilson noted in *Nation* that many prisoners took an interest in attending law school upon release from prison after learning to construct legal arguments while incarcerated (200). Finally, because jailhouse lawyers argue their own cases as well as those of other prisoners, they are also singled out as possessing "high moral standards" and as responsible for raising the general level of morality of other prisoners ("Jailhouse Lawyers" 74).

Concluding Observations on the Redeemable Male Prisoner

The first of three major depictions of the male prisoner in the 1969–74 period, then, invests him with the desire and ability to become rehabilitated. More overtly than in the past, he is represented as "one of us," a normal human being faced with abnormal circumstances and problems. While the overall representation is similar to the dominant one of the last two eras, the tendency to point overtly to the prisoner's "normality" suggests that other representations of the prisoner have gained cultural currency and are competing more favorably with the representation of the prisoner as redeemable and as worthy of redemption. That is, one claims rationality only when branded irrational; one claims to be nonviolent only when essentialized as violent.

The redeemable prisoner becomes more commonly represented as Caucasian throughout this period, while African-American male prisoners increasingly become associated with revolutionary discourses. In much the same way that American culture dealt with race in the period immediately following the peak of the civil rights movement and the integration of African Americans into a greater number of arenas traditionally populated by whites, representations of prisoners are now less overtly racist but subtly link together race and behavioral patterns. Hence, as in other discursive domains, the subtle racism of popular representations of the prisoner becomes stronger. Indeed, the cofactoring of race and behavior becomes even more evident as other characterizations of the male prisoner during this era are investigated. The implications of this linkage, in the public perception of prisoners and of free citizens, as well as in the way in which disciplinary procedures are practiced within the prison, should be obvious.

In addition, there is a problematic tension in this period between the belief in the moral autonomy of male prisoners and their need for rehabilitation programs. That is, while there is a belief that this prisoner can and should be responsible for his own actions, there is the simultaneous belief that rehabilitation programs provided by penal institutions are the sole route by which the prisoner can rehabilitate himself. While the prisoner is ultimately responsible for breaking the law, only the state can be responsible for rehabilitating him. Thus, while the culture maintains a belief in the potential and necessity of moving criminals to a normal position, *it also maintains a belief that mechanisms of the state already embody these shared values.* This fact cannot be understated.

Finally, when prisoners like Edward Bunker simultaneously claim that prisoners need rehabilitation programs in order to assimilate into the culture at large and that the values of prisoners often differ from those of the culture in general, he is voicing a theme that prospers in future representations of the prisoner. In effect, even those prisoners who distance themselves from traditional morality define themselves within it. They claim, "I am rehabilitated although I never needed it anyway," or, "While I can have my own values, I choose those of traditional morality." While values may be contingent and diversity respected, prisoners who rehabilitate themselves always choose the culture's dominant morality, a morality to be gained through the employment of rehabilitation programs offered by the state.

Inmate Two: Proud, Black, Oppressed

The second dominant representation of the male prisoner in this period is perhaps not an unexpected one given popular memory of the social events of the late 1960s and early 1970s. Throughout the period, increased media coverage focuses on African-American prisoners or African-American groups with intricate ties to prisons, including the Soledad Brothers, the Black Panthers, and the Nation of Islam (Black Muslims). Furthermore, in general, the "blackness" of prisoners as a whole is often highlighted, regardless of either the topic or prison under discussion, and regardless of the ratio of Caucasian prisoners and prisoners of color held nationwide. However, "blackness" is not this inmate's sole characterization; indeed, his representation is not only as a black male, but also as a human being undeserving of the punishment dealt by an unfair and discriminatory system. He has been punished for practicing a morality different from that of the culture at large rather than for practicing immorality. His punishment is commonly represented as unjustified on the basis of cultural diversity. Indeed, this should not be surprising in that, while this representation occurs in numerous and diverse journals, it is especially prevalent in those magazines associated with leftist politics and attitudes.

The Male Prisoner as African-American

A dominant characteristic of the male prisoner throughout the 1969–74 period is that he is "other than" Caucasian. As Appendix 3 shows, however, this characterization is not verifiable on the basis of an empirical count of prisoners. This inference is made in different ways; while some writers discuss specific behavioral attributes of African-American prisoners, others simply indicate that the majority of prisoners are either black or Hispanic. For example, after "The Family," a New York City theater troupe, went on a tour of prisons, troupe member Kenny Steward observed in *Time* that the reason their group had been such a hit while other theater groups had failed was that they had recognized that "the great majority of prisoners are black and Puerto Rican ghetto citizens" (quoted in "Players" 61). For this reason, he claimed, The Family performed works by playwrights Melvin Van Peebles and Ed Bullins about "where they came from and where they are going to" (quoted in "Players" 61). Similarly, at least in regard to representations of the racial makeup of prisoners, a 1973 *Essence* editorial by Lynn Walker urged black business owners to make a stronger effort to employ black ex-convicts, noting that "close to 80% of young, black, urban males will be arrested at some point in their lives" (20).

References like these are not isolated. The existence of large numbers of African-American prisoners is mentioned (at least briefly) with greater frequency throughout the era. Hence, in a discussion of various classifications of prisons in *Nation* in 1974, it was noted that while Pennsylvania had a black population of 9.4 percent, its Philadelphia County Jail was 95 percent black (Sommer and Sommer 370). Further, authors Robert and Barbara Sommer noted that Illinois's Stateville Penitentiary was 70 percent black and 10 percent Hispanic, Attica 70 percent black and Puerto Rican, and that nearly 100 percent of the guards in both prisons were white (370). Similarly, author Gordon Stewart, in an essay in *Christian Century*, asked, "Who are these prisoners?" and answered himself, noting that "when the tragic killings took place in 1971 at Attica, blacks and Puerto Ricans accounted for nearly 80% of the prison population there, but only one staff member was nonwhite. No staff member was black. The wooden clubs carried by Attica's correctional officers were known as 'nigger sticks' " (290). Nationwide, 60 percent of prisoners were reported to be black and Hispanic, while only 2 percent of the guards fit these categories (B. Jackson, "Prison" 589). While statistics could have been reversed if other prisons had been cited, no such prisons were ever discussed.[3]

Similarly, even when an article's primary concern is the existence of racism in prisons, the prisoner continues to be constituted as primarily black. Hence, Winston Moore, then warden of Cook County (Illinois) Jail, asserted that prison riots are caused by racism because white guards are unable to communicate with black prisoners: "In an institution in which the majority of inmates are urban blacks, you are inviting trouble when you have them guarded by rural redneck types" ("My Cure" 84). Similarly, in a 1973 study revealing that California's Center for the Study of Violent Behavior had been drugging its inmates in order to alter their behavior, Cornish Rogers noted that "a large number of the prisoners at Vacaville are classified as 'Young, black, militants' " (1076).

I am not suggesting that the number of African Americans in

prison relative to the number of Caucasians remained stable during this period; there is evidence that their relative numbers were indeed rising. In 1950, the state and federal prison population was 69 percent Caucasian and 31 percent other ethnicities; in 1975, the composition had changed to 64 percent Caucasian and 36 percent other ethnic makeup (Langan 5). However, the public representation of the prisoner during this period of social unrest and struggles for civil rights is notably African-American. Later, while an even greater proportion of prisoners will be African Americans, the public discussion will not highlight this construction as strongly as it does here. Only in the 1960s is the blackness of the prisoner so overtly highlighted.

Prison Oppression

As noted above, the depiction of the violent and irrational male prisoner from the previous era divides during this period. Both representations resulting from this bifurcation are joined, however, in that both are constituted primarily by African-American prisoners. One of these depictions, which I will discuss later, maintains that the black inmate is violent and irrational by nature, judged under a universal moral system. The representation I will discuss first, however, assumes a different tone, constituting the black prisoner as the victim of an unjust system that classifies his "different" conceptions of morality and justice as immoral and unjust and hence imprisons him "unjustly."

After the riots in the Tombs, San Quentin, and Soledad in 1971, Black Panther Wendell Wade proclaimed in an essay in *Newsweek* that "the prisons are now filling up with political prisoners. Those brothers who were active in opposing the occupation of the black community by the fascist police force and its domination by the exploitative businessman and tyrannical politicians" (quoted in "Prisoner Power" 38). In a very similar statement, George Jackson, writing to *Soledad Brother* editor Greg Armstrong, observed that "all black people, wherever they are, whatever their crimes, even crimes against other blacks, are political prisoners, because the system has dealt with them differently than whites" (111). This prisoner is a political prisoner, innocent of any crime save disagreement with the status quo and the "illegal" operations of the U.S. government. This construction of the prisoner is also pervasive, with the prison riots of the early 1970s, the civil rights movement, and radical black politics combining to provide numerous headlines and articles linking the black prisoner with political victimization.

The media attention given to George Jackson and the Soledad

Brothers during the riotous period of the early seventies provides a clear example of the construction of the male African-American inmate as a political and visionary revolutionary. Jackson had initially been sentenced to prison for seven years after his conviction for robbing seventy dollars from a gas station. Because of indeterminate sentencing policies and his behavior in prison, however, Jackson could have been kept imprisoned for most of the remainder of his life. Indeed, if his case had turned out similar to many others during this period, he likely would have been held much longer than the seven years he did serve. In themselves, neither Jackson's sentence nor crime was distinctive and would have garnered very little public interest. However, after a white guard was killed at Soledad and Jackson and two other black prisoners were charged with the murder, a highly visible public space was created and grew when, during the trial, Jonathan Jackson, George's brother, attempted to break George free by charging the Marin County Courthouse armed. In the brief battle that followed, Jonathan was fatally wounded. Subsequently, George Jackson became an ardent communist theorist, practitioner, and spokesperson, gaining a great deal of press coverage until his death when a guard shot him in an alleged escape attempt.

A majority of the press dealing with the Jackson case revealed at least some degree of sympathy for his position, generally on the grounds that blacks were treated unfairly within American culture. For instance, a *Time* essay entitled "The Shame of the Prisons" describes prisons as being filled with blacks who "see themselves as political victims of a racist society." In the same essay, Jackson described himself as "one irate, resentful nigger—and it's building" (53). Jackson noted that while others may attempt to build racial harmony in prisons, he saw little need to make any move except toward a radicalization of minorities in prisons. He hoped to move them closer to his own stance as a black communist revolutionary, to recognize the existence of different systems and moralities that can serve as models for life (Szulc 11, 16). Elsewhere, Jackson was represented as a prisoner who taught blacks to hold on to their identities amid the growing racial strife within prisons (Pell 48). Further, an essay on the Soledad case in *Nation* placed much of the blame for its outcome on the mistreatment blacks receive in prison and on the presumption that, while most prisoners are black, most guards are white ("Price" 130).

A similar theme is repeated in coverage of other cases of the period. For instance, in an account in *Ramparts* of the way in which Black Panther Bobby Seale had been bound and gagged during his trial and hence not allowed to speak for himself, it was observed that "they [the system] assassinated Malcolm X; they drove Eldridge Cleaver into exile; but Bobby Seale is the first black leader whom they are going to try to murder judicially" ("Comments" 18). The same commentator noted that Judge Julius J. Hoffman, the judge presiding over Seale's hearing, "didn't even investigate; he didn't care. A judge is supposed to at least investigate a person's positions, especially regarding his legal defense" ("Comments" 23). In *Ebony*, Carlyle Douglas noted that the Bobby Seale trial, as unjust and unfair as he considered it, was probably as fair as the criminal system could be, that it was indeed generally more unjust to blacks than in this case (76). Similarly, an *Ebony* discussion of the Bobby Sostre case claimed that Sostre, a "revolutionary African-American" and former Black Muslim, had been unfairly charged with drug sales solely because of his political support for African Americans (Worthy 123). Hence, the Seale and Sostre cases serve as examples of representations of the judicial system's ability and success at unfairly constraining African Americans.

Not only are a majority of male prisoners constituted as black, then, but they are often positioned as having been imprisoned by an unfair judicial process. Hence, black prisoners are portrayed as doubly imprisoned because they are not only physically held within prison walls but also hemmed in by the economic, social, educational, cultural, and ideological walls of culture. In this representation, the hegemony of the dominant culture imprisons the African-American male long before he is placed behind bars.[4]

Not only do prisons unfairly hold African Americans, according to this representation, but African-American criminal behavior is also depicted as partially justified because of the impoverished position that American culture is said to place them in due to discrimination and other factors. That is, the American justice system is unfair because it sends to prison disproportionate numbers of the economically disadvantaged, a group that is high in minority membership (Horn, "Personal" 26). For example, in a 1973 essay focusing on Eddie Sanchez, a prisoner held in the Marion, Illinois, Federal Penitentiary and slated for involuntary involvement in a behavior modification program there, *Psychology Today* argued that Sanchez would never have been put in prison if our judicial system had been fair. The logic of the argument was that Sanchez's life of crime was basically predetermined because both his mother and father were prisoners early in his life, and Sanchez was forced to live in foster homes throughout his childhood. The essay argued that all subjects with such a background should be provided with preventive counseling so that they can learn to avoid actions that will later place them in prison (Horn, "On Fitting" 91). Similarly, an editorialist in *Christianity Today* asserted that unless Christians begin to help the economically impoverished, they should be willing to accept responsibility for the crimes of the impoverished, as the poor have little choice other than crime. That is, if we allow poverty to exist, we are collectively guilty of the crimes that result from it ("Halfway Help" 35). H. G. Moeller, assistant director of the U.S. Bureau of Prisons, noted that he favors furlough, community treatment, and work release programs because many people are simply born into life situations that encourage criminality. Moeller argued that "the general underlying premise for the new directions in corrections is that crime and delinquency are symptoms of failures and disorganization of the community" (83). In such a community, clearly, the impoverished African-American is imprisoned unjustly.

The Effects of Prison

It is the case not only that the African-American prisoner is represented as unjustly imprisoned but also that his imprisonment further encourages criminality due to the exploitative nature of prisons. Regardless of the reason for his initial entry into prison, prison culture will ensure that the African-American male (and other "minority males") will have little choice but to return to a life of crime. As Warden Charles Campbell of the Fort Worth, Texas, Federal Correctional Institution explained in initiating a "coed" prison: "Here we try to reduce the damage created by confinement by having a healthy setting. I don't think there are very many people anymore who can truthfully say that prisons contribute to the criminal justice system in any positive way" (B. Mason 193).

The specter of prison as a graduate school of crime, especially for the minority inmate, is a persistent theme throughout the period. In an essay appropriately entitled "Home at Last: The Prison Habit," Thomas Gaddis estimated that 67 out of 100 prisoners return to prison because they become part of a criminal culture and learn criminal skills while imprisoned (721). The reasons cited for recidivism are many and varied, but it is generally agreed to be the result of dehumanization and the mixing of young prisoners with older ones: a young prisoner "often arrives in chains and becomes a number. His head sheared, he is led to a bare cage dominated by a toilet. In many states, his cellmate may represent any kind of human misbehavior—a docile forger, a vicious killer, an aggressive homosexual" ("Shame" 48–49).

This link is established for readers, not only because of the general cultural zeitgeist pervading discourse in general but also because a majority of male prisoners during this period are represented as prisoners of color. While often no particular ethnic background is noted, the overwhelming impulse in the midst of numerous portrayals of the inmate as African-American is to see the prisoner as African-American unless he is specifically constituted otherwise. That is, arguments and depictions set up backgrounds and contexts for one another. When cultural discourse consistently foregrounds African-American prisoners, readers within that culture begin to make assumptions about the race of individual convicts when race is not mentioned; race becomes enthymematic. Hence, in a period when Richard Nixon publicly declares prisons to be "universities of crime," the cultural pictures of prisoners are painted with black strokes.

Evidence for the link between imprisonment and recidivism is legion, with both prisoners and authorities testifying that the prison system encourages recidivism. One inmate claimed in *Christian Century* that he found prison to be so brutal that in his frustration and rage he had resolved to "stick up the first thing in sight" when he was released (quoted in Shockley and Freeman 1157). Similarly, while arguing for his own innocence, prisoner Edgar Smith claimed that, for others, the conditions of prisons are surely a primary cause of crime ("Pre-posthumous" 112). After attending a workshop in Annapolis, Maryland, in which judges and convicts sought solutions to prison problems, a judge noted that "people in institutions are living in a jungle. If something is not done, we are going to be living in a jungle on the outside, too" ("Jungle Rats" 78). In addition, Bernard Weiner criticized the California Prison at Vacaville in 1972 for claiming that violence was either organic or the result of a conspiracy with social advocates outside the prisons; he argued that, "like prison administration everywhere, it will rarely acknowledge that the prison system itself produces the violence" (434).

This characterization is voiced by those both in and outside of the prison community. Dr. Thomas Szasz, a professor of psychiatry at New York's Upstate Medical Center, argued in 1972 that the rehabilitation program at the Patuxent Institution for Defective Delinquents "is a concentration camp . . . worse than the way they use mental institutions in Russia" (Stanford 71). When Ralph Ginzburg was jailed for publishing *Eros* magazine, a journal of "high culture" erotica, he described his prison experience as dehumanizing and prisons as self-perpetuating institutions: "Every last vestige of a man's individuality and independence is stripped from him" (39). Harris Cailklin, head of the University of Maryland's School of Social Work, noted that prison has debilitating effects on prisoners because it completely takes their decision-making skills away (Horn, "On Fitting" 88). Finally, Fay Stender, a San Francisco lawyer, claimed in *Time* that "we treat everybody in prisons so badly that it isn't surprising that we produce these intense, very romantic, revolutionary people. When people have been caged up as long as they have, the wonder is that we don't see more violence than we really do" ("Organizing" 94).[5]

Furthermore, not only do inhumane and violent conditions create recidivism, some prisoners, as a result of having their identities and decision-making skills stripped from them, are represented as incapable of functioning outside; they learn to enjoy prison and therefore seek reimprisonment. Thus, in one particularly poignant illustration of how prisoners become addicted to prison, the plight of Iowa prisoner Bobby Ferguson was recounted. Robert Ray, then the governor of Iowa, was reported to have received a strange request in a letter from Ferguson at the Fort Madison jail in which Ferguson asked Ray to allow him to remain in prison after his sentence was complete. Ferguson argued that he had neither friends nor family, had no trade, and indeed enjoyed life in prison. The narrative recounted Ferguson's literal birth in a prison hospital, his life in state-run hospitals and schooling programs, and his numerous tenures in prison and juvenile detention centers. Ferguson repeatedly committed crimes each time he was released in order to ensure his reimprisonment. Fort Madison's warden, Lou Brewer, argued against Ferguson's request by noting that many of the prisoners had similar feelings about prison and would make the same request if Ferguson was successful ("Be It"). Not only is the prisoner held under questionable normative standards, then, but he is also there because he has been taught to be.

Riots and the Oppressed African American

Under this representation of the prisoner, riots and disruptive behavior are excused to the degree that such behaviors are represented as having resulted from prison conditions and the frustration that results from "unjust" imprisonment. This argument was given credibility when Philip Zimbardo reported on his famous experiment on prisoner and guard behavior. In the widely reported experiment, Zimbardo took twenty-one students who volunteered for fifteen dollars a day to be placed in a simulated prison and agreed to act out the assigned roles of prisoner or guard. While Zimbardo did place some restrictions on how the experiments would be run, for the most part he allowed the guards to make their own decisions on how best to treat the prisoners. At the end of six days, Zimbardo noted that the "guards" were treating "prisoners" sadistically, and, as a result, the prisoners began to lose control of their mental capabilities. Not only did the prisoners attempt to riot against the conditions of their "prison" on only the second day of the experiment, but three of them collapsed in hysterical fits with one breaking out in a rash when "parole" was denied. The experiment, planned to last for two weeks, had to be stopped at the end of the sixth day because of the psychological discomfort it was giving to the prisoners. Zimbardo concluded that prison conditions encourage both guards and inmates to live out already fashioned roles, regardless of their personal orientations (Faber). Reflecting on his experiment later, Zimbardo claimed that "individual behavior is largely under the control of social forces and environmental contingencies rather than personality traits" (6). In effect, he provided a justification for riotous behavior by asserting that riots emerge "from within every man and woman who refuses to let the system turn them into an object, a number, a thing, or a nothing" (8). Regardless of the validity of the experiment or Zimbardo's claims, his discourse, reported on discursively and pictorially in such highly visible publications as *Life,* justified riotous behavior and hence provided a clear public model for this understanding of riots.

Zimbardo's assertions are confirmed throughout the era in comments made by inmates and prison administrators alike. For instance, an Attica inmate argued that the riots at Attica were caused by monotony and "the numerous ways you are made to feel you are finished as a man. . . . The only time cons begin to get radical is when they feel their backs are against the wall" (quoted in Coons 92). Furthermore, Huey Newton argued that riots are inevitable as long as prisons continue to dehumanize prisoners by giving them numbers, classifying them according to the results of exams with racist biases, paying low wages, and cutting off their communication with the outside world (30–34). Prison riots represent not the "misbehavior" of prisoners but the "need to be more responsive to the needs of prisoners, particularly black prisoners" ("Library" 20). Prisons are indicted on the grounds of censorship, poor health care (B. Jackson, "Prison" 586), and bad food (Torok 14). In an essay blaming the riots at Attica on poor health care, a narrative is included of a man who suffered a stroke in prison and was then forced to sit on a wooden bench so that he would not soil his bed. Another man, charged in a car accident, had to wait three days to find out that he had broken his back ("Treatment" 35). Finally, Winston Moore, who earlier had claimed the ratio of white guards to black prisoners was a major cause of prison unrest, noted that "if we stop to analyze Attica and all the other prison eruptions, we find that the cause in each was racism—pure and simple white racism aimed at blacks" ("My Cure" 86). Riots, then, are caused by racism and other injustices in this representation of the prisoner, not by prisoners who are essentially violent or disruptive. In effect, the solution to these riots is the demand for the new penology, the demand that more attention be paid to the needs and rights of "human" prisoners.

A particular narrative that was retold on several occasions in various publications illustrates the alleged problems with prisoner treatment by guards and its potential to lead to riotous behavior. The scene for the narrative is a 1969 protest against the Vietnam War in Berkeley, California. According to various accounts, hundreds of people who were near the protest, whether involved or not, were arrested and taken to the Santa Rita Prison in Alameda County. Those arrested were forced to sit on their knees in place for several hours outside the prison building with their faces on the ground; they were not given phone privileges and were threatened repeatedly throughout the night. Guards continually walked among the crowd shouting at all of the prisoners, beating some of them and prodding them with sticks. One of those arrested observed that a person seated near him "identified himself as a diabetic and was cruelly beaten" (quoted in Ritter 52). The prisoners were made to stay awake throughout the night, awaiting release proceedings that did not begin until the following day. Early in the morning, a guard reportedly entered and yelled, "I had a good night's sleep, and I feel like killing" (Ritter 104). Alameda sheriff Frank Madigan blamed the problem on the combination of the type of protest and the type of guards who had been hired: "We have a bunch of young deputies back from Viet Nam who tend to treat prisoners like Viet Cong" (Scheer 51). Each of the narrators of the event comments upon it, however, as another example of why prisoners can be expected to riot and why holding them in prison is not a feasible solution.[6]

Behavior Modification

The theory of behavior modification, the use of severe rewards and punishment (for example, sensory deprivation, brainwashing techniques, spying) to change the behavior of prisoners, is a final aspect of discipline that is significant in understanding this representation of the prisoner. Much like the treatment model, the stories and opinions concerning behavior modification do not in themselves represent prisoners as being harmed by such procedures. However, unlike the discussions of the treatment model, a number of investigative reports, like Jessica Mitford's below, frame these procedures in such a way that the harmful consequences of behavior modification are associated with the effects of imprisonment in general. Again, imprisonment is depicted as working to dehumanize inmates and hence ensuring their recidivism. And again, the focus is on the rights of prisoners rather than on prison control by the administration.

Jessica Mitford was active during this period with her attempt to publicize the problems of behavior modification programs and the ways in which prisons and social conditions are guilty of producing criminals. Mitford pointed to the case of Dr. Edward Schein, associate professor of psychology at MIT, who argued that prisoners should be brainwashed: "I would like you to think of brainwashing not in terms of politics, ethics, and morals, but in terms of the deliberate changing of human behavior and attitudes by a group of men who have relatively complete control over the environment in which the captive population lives" (quoted in Mitford, "Torture" 18). Similarly, Mitford noted that Martin Groder of the U.S. Department of Justice advanced a plan that included the separation of prisoners from family and friends and placed them among members of a "thought-reform" team, a group of already "modified" prisoners who help others change their aberrant ways of thinking: "It is also driven into [the prisoner] that society, in the guise of its authorities, is looking out for his best interests and will help if he will only permit it to do so" (Mitford, "Torture" 24). Finally, James V. McConnell, professor of psychology at the University of Michigan, suggested that sensory deprivation, drugs, hypnosis, and manipulation be used to gain "almost absolute control over an individual's behavior" (quoted in Mitford, "Torture" 24). The prisoner cannot be held at fault, Mitford argued, if this is the way supposedly enlightened people are treating him. That is, prison programs may claim to show prisoners that society is looking out for their best interests, but these programs provide them with norms that encourage their return to prison, that encourage a treatment of others as inhuman. Mitford's essays, I would note, were being published in the same period that Watergate was being unraveled and Vietnam was continuing to come under fire. As a nation becomes disillusioned with what its government can be trusted to do, the light of discontent also falls upon prison systems.

Among narratives that construct this disillusionment is the story of a California prisoner who was a long-term participant in a behavior modification program. When this prisoner's son came to visit, the prisoner unexpectedly grabbed the boy and slammed him into a wall until the boy died. Cornish Rogers, investigating the case, charged that the prisoner killed his son while under the influence of drugs prescribed as part of the behavioral modification program. The program had been endorsed by then-Governor Ronald Reagan and the California prison system under the premise that people commit criminal acts due to malfunctioning thought processes that could be amended in part through medication (Rogers 1076). Similarly, Eddie

Sanchez, a prisoner at Marion, Illinois, who was forced into a behavior modification program against his wishes, charged in *The Nation* that he was often given drugs and after a long period of time in the program suffered from "stimulus deprivation psychosis," a condition experienced by those kept away from any sensory input. Sanchez reported such experiences as watching people who were part of the program being beaten or forced to defecate on themselves while chained to their beds (Steinman 590–92).

A separate Jessica Mitford essay in 1973 described a number of behavior modification programs nationwide. At the Connecticut Prison at Somers, a sex offender was given electric shocks while looking at pictures of nude children; at the Iowa State Penitentiary, inmates who swore were given apomorphine, a drug that made them vomit for fifteen minutes; in Michigan, convicts were forced to go through a series of debilitating stunts if they hoped to escape extreme punishments. Mitford's essay concluded that these programs only reinforce criminal behavior ("Experiments" 64).

In similar fashion, a legal suit was brought against the Marion, Illinois, Federal Penitentiary during this period, charging it with the creation of programs that "make robots of [the inmates] for the greater convenience of the guards" ("Crime Cures" 230). Finally, in a *Nation* report on the Butner, North Carolina, prison complex designed for behavior modification programs, Martin Groder was blamed for using a program in which prisoners were subject to verbal attack by a group of colleagues and were forced to defend themselves or give in to a new image (Pinsky 294).

In sum, then, behavior modification programs are for the most part critiqued in the public realm for their assumption that, as Caleb Foote of the Law and Society Center in Berkeley claimed, the prisoner is "sick and therefore in need of treatment that will cure" him (quoted in Shockley 497). This represents quite a turn from the accepting attitude taken toward such programs in past representations. Such a reaction illustrates the growing belief that prisoners are mentally and morally sound, although different from the norm, and that prisons are the cause of many social problems associated with criminal behavior. While the criminal may arrive at the prison with individual problems and with an individual morality, prison administrators and behavior modification programs judge him on grounds that allow him to ignore his humanity and individual morality.

Concluding Observations on the Oppressed Prisoner

This construction of the prisoner, a predominantly African-American, revolutionary, and "guiltless" prisoner, reflects a number of changes in the cultural articulation of the prisoner and of punishment. One of the more obvious and striking conclusions to be drawn from this representation of the male prisoner of color is that he is constituted as holding values that differ from those of the dominant culture. One can surmise that the heightened awareness and discussion of prisoners of color, during both this and the following period, results from the media exposure of people of color in general through the civil rights movement. Compared to the representation I will discuss next, this construction is the more sympathetic, suggesting that African Americans are unjustly arrested and sentenced and unjustly treated once imprisoned because of the moral diversity they represent.

Perhaps more important, this depiction of the prisoner reflects the growing strength not only of the belief that African Americans hold different morals but also that cultural and normative differences should be respected, even if those differences have been constructed by the prison environment. Such a transition is clearly a part of the larger cultural move to focus on "individuals" rather than on "institutions." As such, it is also a part of the move to the new penology.

Unlike the African-American male prisoner of the next section, this one is represented as having values different from, but not necessarily better or worse than, those of traditional morality. This belief will later blossom publicly into the theme of just deserts, an attempt to punish prisoners in a way equivalent to the crimes they have committed without tying rehabilitation programs to the punishment. Only in such a way can culture continue to enforce agreed-upon laws without overtly endorsing and enforcing a particular morality.

Similarly, this construction of the prisoner continues to reveal a faith in the ability of social and prison conditions to affect the behavior of individual prisoners. That is, just as the "redeemable" and "irrational" inmates can be negatively influenced by prison conditions, the oppressed prisoner is also shown to be affected by such prison conditions. However, in this construction, prison conditions encourage prisoners to take actions that reflect their cultural and moral diversity rather than their immorality.

Both this representation of the prisoner and the one of the redeemable inmate share a basic assumption that prisoners can return to a normal, moral position, although the latter representation posits this morality as the only legitimate one. However, the discourse of the redeemable prisoner describes the prisoner as altruistic and helpful to others. The prisoner described in this section, however much his morality may be constructed as simply different from the dominant morality, is described as behaving violently. That is, while both types of prisoner are nominally said to operate within acceptable moralities, only the prisoner of color is described as primarily violent, and only the prisoner of color will signify violence by his mere presence in future discussions of the prisoner. Difference may be nominally accepted, but it is again accepted within the frame of racial stereotypes.

Inmate Three: Black, Incorrigible and Irrational

The third quotation beginning this chapter was written by a former Attica inmate (or "inmate graduate," as the *New York Times Magazine* labeled him) who was asked to provide an assessment of the average prisoner. His essay, representing the prisoner as incorrigible and irrational, must be supplemented to provide a fuller sketch of this representation of the prisoner. To that end, in an essay advocating the isolation of violent criminals in order to keep them from having contact with others, Minnesota's Commissioner of Corrections David Fogel said, "There are some people—like the man who tells me, 'If you let me out of this cell, I'll tear your throat open, Mr. Fogel'—whom I tend to believe must be held" ("Lock" 11). The quotation representing the voice of the prisoner is highlighted separately from the article and is accompanied by a photo. When one reads the article, attention is drawn to the photograph—a picture of an African-American male standing behind bars, apparently mouthing those very words: "I'll tear your throat out." While the printed text of the article itself provides no evidence or reason to suggest that the quotation need be linked with an African American, the connection is made through the location of text and picture, thus marking violence and incorrigibility as the domain of the African-American prisoner ("Lock" 11).

Not only, then, is this representation one of incorrigibility, but it is simultaneously that of a black male inmate. While some of the characteristics of this prisoner overlap with those in the depiction covered previously, the primary difference, a key one, is that this prisoner is constructed as personally responsible for his actions and, further, generally unable to rejoin the social order. That is, while the misbehavior of the second representation can be explained as the result of cultural or societal influences or of the practices of a different morality, and while the first prisoner, generally white, can be redeemed within the culture's shared morality, the second type of inmate is represented as fully responsible for his behavior. He is a free agent who chooses to violate the norms of moral behavior. Moreover, even though he chooses a life of immorality, he is paralyzed by his irrationality and incapable of rehabilitation; society's only answer is to punish him and keep him separate from the populace at large.

The African American

While the general depiction of the prisoner as black shares characteristics with the previous depiction, here the African American is drawn in much bolder strokes, with a stronger link maintained between African Americanism and violent, irrational, and immoral behavior, even when the representations apparently are meant to be sympathetic. For instance, an editorial in *Christianity Today* encouraged Christians to begin taking their crusades into prisons, noting that most prisoners have "six characteristics: they are black; have not finished high school; have few job skills; come from ghetto areas; have drug problems; and are products of broken homes" (Doyle 45). Similarly, in her exposé of behavior modification programs, Jessica Mitford quoted Robert E. Doran, who studied the Maximum Psychiatric Diagnostic Unit of the California prison system, as noting in regard to prison radicals: "They are younger and darker than the prison population as a whole: 61 percent are under thirty . . . 60 to 70 percent are black or Chicano" ("Torture" 16).

A number of claims specifically link black prisoners and violence. For example, in 1971, Victor Taylor discussed the effect heroin had had on the black community and noted that in Philadelphia, 92.7 percent of all murderers, 86 percent of rapists, 93.4 percent of burglars, and 83 percent of all perpetrators of aggravated assaults were black (691). Similarly, Mills and Morris describe the prisoners in Stateville Penitentiary in Illinois as "very much of the 1970s: young, mostly black, urban, violent, and prone to riot" (60). Furthermore, in an investigation of minimum security prisons primarily designed to hold white-collar nonviolent criminals, *Newsweek,* while not dealing specifically with African-American prisoners, made race a determining factor in the behavior of prisoners, noting that the only people who attempt to escape these prisons are "Mexicans detained for illegal entry into the U.S." ("Good Life" 55). Finally, in a discussion of the need for progressive prison reform in California, Raymond Procuner, chief of the prison system, said that a large proportion of the problems in prisons can be pinpointed as arising from the new black prisoner's unjustified view of himself as the victim of a racist society. Procuner asked, "Who is in prison today? They are mostly losers, mostly poor, and mostly black" (quoted in S. Alexander 35).

While a black prisoner is again the subject of articulation, he is now one who is inherently violent and the cause of a disproportionate number of social and prison problems. Furthermore, this black prisoner is not created by an unfair or racist society but is a human being who began with the same benefits and choices of all human beings but has freely chosen to lead a life that brings danger to others. While he may claim to be a victim of racism or the holder of a "different" morality, he is instead, in this articulation, using the claim of racism to justify his irrational and immoral behaviors. In that he seems unable to control his behavior, he needs to be punished rather than rehabilitated.

Violent Behavior

It will become clear that here we are not seeing two unconnected visions of this prisoner, one depicting him as black and the other as a perpetrator of violent crimes; rather, in this articulation, the links are explicit. More than the direct links, however, when racial tension is claimed to be the cause of prison violence, as it is here, and when the rhetorical field prefigures African Americans as violent, a strong implicit link is established between problems of violence and the African American as perpetrator. *Time* reported, for example, that in California prisons, "Racial tension is so bad that some prisoners wear thick magazines strapped to their backs to ward off knife blades" ("Shame" 50). Simultaneously, riots in the prison at Pontiac, Illinois, in 1973 were attributed to gangs that generally maintain memberships based on race. However, the only gangs discussed in the *Time* essay were the Black P. Stone Nation, the Black Disciples, and the Vice Lords, all constituted by either black or Hispanic memberships ("Gang's" 39). The following year, in another *Time* investigation of gangs, it was reported that racial tension between gangs was responsible for 450 stabbings in prisons from 1971 to 1973 ("Organizing" 93–94).

Even when other issues, such as overcrowding, are suggested as possible causes of violent outbreaks, a racist slant is taken. Indeed, it is in just such an essay that the photo of the black prisoner discussed earlier was linked to the claim, "If you let me out of this cell, I'll tear your throat open" ("Lock" 11). Even when the linguistic argument has little to say about violence along racial lines, the nonlinguistic arguments implicate black males as violent offenders.

In general, the potential for violence is prefigured in representations of prisoners. Hence, in a discussion of a three-day-long Christian crusade at the Kentucky State Prison at Eddyville, an inmate noted that before the crusade, tensions had been mounting quickly because "There hadn't been a killing in more than a month" (quoted in Doyle 44). Similarly, in a *Newsweek* discussion of prison problems, Californians were said to be calling for prison reform because "For a decade California's prisons have been rocked with increasing violence—hundreds of stabbings and homicides in recent years" (S. Alexander 35). The 1969 riot at San Quentin was described by Robert Minton and Stephen Rice, teachers and counselors at San Quentin, as exhibiting just "the sort of behavior the public has been taught to expect from convicts" (18). In a *Life* exposé, inmate Harold (Kayo) Konigsberg of the United States Medical Center for Federal Prisoners in Springfield (Missouri) was shown to have gained unprecedented privileges and concessions from the prison administration through his use of lawsuits, bribes, and intimidation. The portrait of Konigsberg illustrates the degree to which violent behavior benefits the prisoner: "He can be rational one minute, beyond control the next. In conversation, he is alternatively abusive and slyly threatening. 'Tell me,' he might ask a guard, 'How are your children?' " (quoted in Walsh 44)

In addition to descriptions made by nonprisoners of the violent nature of prisoners, prisoners themselves once again testify to this representation. In an account of an Annapolis, Maryland, experiment in which prisoners met with prison officials and judges to go through role-playing exercises and workshops, violence is represented as natural to prison life and beyond anyone's control but the prisoners themselves. During the workshop, different narratives were read aloud to prisoners, judges, and prison officials. Each group then provided its understanding of the story and how it would have played itself out in prison, in the hopes that each of the three groups would learn something about the way the other two groups perceived prison life. After the reading of a fictional narrative in which a white inmate, who had been threatened physically and sexually by black inmates, went to prison officials who promised to protect him and prosecute the blacks, the prisoners at the workshop were reported to have yelled, "Man, you can't give him no protection. He'll have boiling coffee thrown at him even if you lock him up in solitary," and, "There's a million ways to get to him. We'd be in contact with him and that would be that" (quoted in Hammer 60–62).

The report on this workshop is interesting on a number of counts. Not only does the fictional narrative represent African-American inmates as rapists and white inmates as passive victims, but when read to a group of inmates, they are reported to have objected only when the prison administrators and judges make the assumption that the prisoners could be stopped from carrying out their violent acts; the prisoners were reportedly silent throughout the description itself, ignoring their own representation as specifically violent in terms of race. They apparently ignore the rape or the racist configuration and question only whether the victim could be protected from future violence.

Again, the difference between this major representation of the prisoner and the previous one lies in the causes of violence. Both are violent and both primarily African-American, but this prisoner is represented as either "essentially" violent or as choosing to be so, while the previous type was violent either as the result of oppressive social conditions or as a result of constraints on the practice of his own morality. Hence, the major problem with this prisoner is his essence as "an incorrigible scum" (Coons 198). Donn Pearce, former prisoner and author of *Cool Hand Luke,* depicts this prisoner in the following terms: "Up they come: cripples, lunatics, fairies, killers, thieves, cheats, beggars, drunks, addicts, and rapists; sauntering, shuffling, prancing up from their cages and their tombs, smiling, scowling, and sulking" (216).

More directly, Albert Nussbaum, director of the American Bar Association Commission on Correctional Facilities and Services Staff, argued in 1971 that rehabilitation must be seen as a myth, not because men cannot change, but because rehabilitation attempts to take a person back to a higher state of behavior. Most prisoners, he claimed, have never chosen to live their lives in a manner that would be considered acceptable (674). As a result, their rehabilitation would only be a rehabilitation to a condition below what we accept culturally. Finally, in an essay that attempted to explore the degree of responsibility criminals should admit for their crimes, Fordham University law professor Robert Byrn argued in *America* that while there are small social factors involved in how prisoners behave, we need "a re-recognition that the offender's conduct is immoral"; we must attempt "to educate the offender to social productivity, as well as to an awareness of moral guilt and personal responsibility" (40–41).

The Incomplete Human Being

I should again emphasize that whether the male prisoner is represented as essentially irrational and violent or as choosing this lifestyle, his behavior is not seen as representing cultural or moral relativity. In this representation, such behaviors only serve to depict the inmate as an "incomplete human being," as failing to reach the sole standard of humanity. For example, during this period Chief Justice Warren Burger of the U.S. Supreme Court described prisoners as "disorganized and inadequate human being(s) who cannot cope with life" (322). Similarly, Robert Taggart, executive director of the National

Manpower Policy Task Force, noted that in the world of work many prisoners are "losers" who can only hold jobs in the lowest status occupations because they either cannot or do not have the drive to work toward higher goals (17). In both essays, it is implied that prisoners either hold their positions by choice or by their inherent constitution as "losers" with little chance of changing.

Once again, convict testimony provides confirmation for this representation, as prisoners often testify to their incomplete and irrational nature. For instance, when Rahway State Prison inmates were asked to provide a positive image of the prisoner, many noted the demise of the "real con," a prisoner who helped those who are less fortunate in prison, who was friendly, respected, and trusted. Most prisoners are now just the opposite, they claimed; they are never to be trusted and impossible to reform.

Rape

One further attribute of this prisoner is found in the strengthening link between the African-American prisoner and the role of homosexual rapist, as well as the strengthening link between the Caucasian inmate and the role of victim. In a 1974 study of homosexuality in institutions for juvenile delinquents, sociologists Clemens Bartollas, Stuart Miller, and Simon Dinitz claimed that a large number of those in the institution were committed to the sexual exploitation of other prisoners. They dubbed these sexual exploiters the "booty bandits" and noted that they "are older, black youths from the ghetto who avoid emotional involvement with their victims and merely use them for their own physical release. Indignant about their own exploitation at the hands of 'white society,' they quickly become sexual exploiters in this institution, usually exploiting passive whites" (203). The authors further stereotyped the black rapist by noting that rapists generally choose white victims and avoid black ones in order to show "loyalty to the brothers" and to avoid fights, as blacks are assumed to be generally better fighters (208). Returning again to the Annapolis, Maryland, meeting of prisoners, lawyers, prison officials, and judges, one of the scenarios created to facilitate discussion of supposedly real prison problems underlines this link. In the scenario, after arriving in prison, a white prisoner is confronted with sexual advances by several black inmates. While pondering what action he should take, he is offered protection by a single black prisoner who, in turn for the protection, will receive sexual favors from the white inmate. The black inmate argues that this protection is beneficial to the white inmate because he will only have to participate in sexual relations with one man rather than with all of the advancing prisoners and will not have to suffer severe physical beatings (Hammer 57–60). Again, the narrative itself, with its racist codings, met no reported objection by prisoners or others.

Less overtly, Huey Newton aids in the creation of this representation by noting that in San Luis Obispo's California Men's Colony, the population is not only mostly composed of black prisoners but that over 80 percent of them are involved in homosexual activities. Such behavior, he asserted, is encouraged by the guards and administration of the prison, who determined that if prisoners engage in sexual relations, they will have little time to worry about other problems in the prison and will commit fewer violent acts (31).

There is, then, a strengthening link between the representation of the prisoner as black and as a rapist. White inmates, on the other hand, are never or rarely shown as participating in sexual activities of their own volition. Rather, they are in a constant struggle against the advances and coercion of their black counterparts. While homosexuality as a consensual—albeit aberrant—type of behavior was acknowledged in the fifties, the eras following the fifties discuss sexual behavior in the prison almost solely in terms of violence. It was possible in the 1950s to envision a homosexual Caucasian in need of reform; from that point on, however, the only sex discussed is not only coercive but coercive along racial lines—there is no homosexuality, only rape. Moreover, the rapist cannot be redeemed, only punished.

Drug Use

One final characteristic that develops more fully in this era (and specifically in this representation of the prisoner) is drug use. The discussion of drug use broadens and is solidly tied to the depiction of the prisoner as one to be blamed for his own problems, one who is black, violent, and irredeemable. Given the social conditions of the period, it hardly seems surprising that drug use is indicated as a problem within prisons. In a *Time* profile of the poor conditions in Arkansas prisons, for example, prisoners were blamed for a portion of these problems, given their consumption of drugs while imprisoned: "They sniff glue and gobble smuggled pills. Some mornings, two hundred men are too stoned to work" ("Shame" 49–50). Citings of such evidence are pervasive. When New York governor Nelson Rockefeller began to campaign for life prison terms for all drug pushers, investigations of the types of prisoners who were currently imprisoned were begun. The reports that followed indicated that many of the problems associated with overcrowded prisons were the result of the influx of former drug users who had committed crimes that placed them in prison ("Lock" 11). Furthermore, in *American Scholar,* Victor Taylor noted that many blacks were in prison due to their alarming use of heroin and that this was one of the causes of overcrowding (691).

The argument is so pervasive that it arrives dressed in unusual ways. Hence, in a slight twist on this theme, one narrative appears to celebrate the fact that many inmates are now drug users. When Washington State's Walla Walla prison began allowing privileges for its inmates, including individual cell decoration and individual choices regarding hair length, Warden Booby Rhay noted in *Life* that "one thing that is making all this possible is that we've got so many people inside today who are kids, dopers, and druggers" (Farrell 36).

Concluding Observations on the Irrational Inmate

This representation of the male prisoner, framed as primarily African-American and with violent and abusive tendencies, is judged according to (and hence supports) the dominant cultural morality. That is, his behaviors and activities are condemned under the same set of norms and values that praise the actions and behavior of the altruistic and redeemable inmate. Both depictions reflect the existence of a single system of judgment.

Again, race has become a stronger distinguishing factor between the redeemable and irredeemable prisoners. Although we also witness the added liberal construction of the African-American inmate as innocent by virtue of different moral standards or by virtue of unfair imprisonment, the representation of him as violent and irrational simultaneously persists. While connections grow between this prisoner, violence, and rape, the moral universe by which he is judged remains. As I noted in the last section, the existence of this stereotype creates a well-worn path by which different prisoners may be judged by the culture at large; it maintains a cultural and rhetorical racism that not only affects prisoners but the perceptions of all members of the culture toward each other and their own sense of self. Furthermore, while this incorrigible prisoner and the one labeled as oppressed are constructed in vastly different ways in terms of responsibility, they both are constructed as behaving violently, while the redeemable and generally Caucasian inmate behaves humanely, with altruistic motives.

The Female Inmate

During this period, the representation of the female inmate continues to be largely consistent with its historical representations. She is once again positioned along the lines of the gendered roles of motherhood and protector of cultural morality. Indeed, the imprisonment of females proves problematic in that it implies that the reproduction of both the species and of morality may end. Representations continue to focus on the general nature of women as moral beings who have been maligned by past abuses, generally abuses within the woman's family. In general, the crimes that have placed women into prison are explicitly shown to have resulted from dysfunctional living situations that prevented the female prisoners from following the normal path of development. Once removed from abusive situations through imprisonment, however, women rediscover their basic morality and their essential nature as "caring" nurturers. The belief in an essential and traditional morality of women proves so strong that even behaviors such as homosexuality that one would expect to see illustrated in a negative light by being linked to immorality are instead represented positively by being linked to such behaviors as "human caring." Moreover, the influx of women imprisoned for political work, such as strikes in favor of improved working conditions for farm workers and teachers, shapes the overall portrait of the female prisoner, painting her as primarily an intelligent and working member of the social order. While aberrations to this portrait do exist, and while movie titles might continue to stress the "reform school girl" persona of highly sexed beings who turn to lesbianism in the absence of men, the general discursive representation focuses on the reproductive roles of women both within and outside of prison.

Moral Reproduction in Prison

The female inmates of this era are represented as having been moved toward a life of criminal behavior because of the abusive behavior of their families, both those into which they are born and those into which they move socially. This general portrait of the female inmate is so common as to have become an underlying assumption in most representations of female prisoners. Indeed, in 1972 the *Ladies Home Journal* held a writing contest for female prisoners in which the periodical's editors asked female inmates throughout the nation to explain "what forces in our society had led these girls and women to break the law" by writing articles specifically on the topic of "What Parents Can Do to Keep Their Daughters Out of Trouble" ("Women in Prison" 58). The bias of the question posited the women as unassuming pawns to various social forces, forces that can lead them toward or away from lives of crime. The journal published the essays of the top three winners, and each of the winning essays presented a brief biography of the author, including the reasons for her criminal lifestyle. The stories are remarkable in that they parallel one another and place the general burden for their criminality on their mistreatment at the hands of family members, generally members of their immediate family. For instance, first prize winner Jo Anne A. Moore implied that the only possible reason for a criminal lifestyle is parental conflict: "Each of us has a different excuse for being in prison. For some, it is parents who were too strict—or too lenient. For others, it might be a promiscuous parent, or a parent involved in illegal activities. For still others, as in my own case, an alcoholic parent" (58). Similarly, second prize winner Andrea Charlene Kaszycki claimed that she ended up in prison because every authority figure she encountered passively encouraged her to take drugs. As she noted, "I once went to apply for a job when I was 'tripping' on LSD. The prospective employer knew this. Yet I got the job" (62). When she did get jobs, very little changed: "One employer, who knew I was addicted to heroin, gave me 'sick leave' to recover from hepatitis. When I did recover, he took me back. . . . I was still an addict, and he knew it" (62). In each case, an authority figure could have taken action to force her to improve her lifestyle; in each case, he or she did nothing. Women, it is implied, need to be told how to behave or their actions are not their responsibility.

In a lengthy examination of female prisoners in *Ramparts*, it was argued that female prisoners adopted criminal lifestyles either because their roles in society were so unfair as to lead them to take frustrated actions in an attempt to find equality, or because they were sexually, emotionally, or economically abused as children. Hence, one prisoner interviewed for the article noted, "I was in two foster homes before I got married. . . . They put us in there mainly because my father was drinking, and they thought he couldn't take care of us" (Burkhart 23). Kitsi Burkhart, the article's author, further asserted that "most of the women in prison have come from families on welfare. They're poor" (23). Again, social circumstances, rather than individual agency, have moved women from an essential state of morality to a life of crime and immorality.

While mistreatment at the hands of others might lead women to criminal lives, their imprisonment entails removing them from an abusive situation and allowing for their rehabilitation, their rediscovery of "natural morality." Hence, a 1970 *Ebony* feature entitled

"A New Life for Women Inmates" began with a discussion of the similarities between the Oakdale State Reformatory for Women in Dwight, Illinois, and any college campus. The story observed that prisoners of the Oakdale "campus" take courses in such specialty areas as beauty counseling, dental hygiene, clothing design, and body dynamics. Each of the inmates interviewed for the essay praised the institution's influence in shaping their lives. The words chosen by the inmates to express this gratitude are surprisingly similar to those of Maria Arnford. One inmate said, for instance, "I still want to get out of here, but it's because I want to try out some of the things I've learned here. *It's too bad I had to come here to learn how to live*" (105, emphasis added). Another noted that "I've learned to like myself [in prison] and that's all I needed to do in the first place" (109).

In a similar fashion, when striking teacher Betty Rufalo found herself imprisoned with "regular" criminals, she was surprised at how much the prison system helped some of the women by simply getting them away from people who would abuse them or supply them with drugs. She quoted one inmate as saying of prison life, "I hate it, but I need it. Life is hectic on the streets" (quoted in Gallagher 59). As Rufalo observed, the prison serves as a home, or at least as a respite from abuse. And, as with the cases above, prison teaches the inmates how to live; it provides the space necessary for the growth of moral authority.

In effect, each female finds a home in prison, complete with guardians, that allows her to express her "essential morality." Hence, we find Margaret Morrissey, the director of the Oakdale reformatory, described as "a den mother," metaphorically transforming the prisoners into scouts, to be raised and disciplined by prison guardians ("New Life" 109). The sole difference between these testimonies and those we will see in the next era (from both male and female prisoners) is that rehabilitation and participation in prison programs is represented as required in this era and optional later. Here, the state is praised for what it must do; later, it will be praised for what human subjects assert that they have chosen to allow it to do.

Perhaps the strongest case for the strength of these assumptions about the female inmate lies in the representation of behaviors that, when practiced by male inmates, are judged to be immoral. For example, while homosexuality in male prisons loses its sense of sexuality in giving way to discussions of power dynamics and rape, with female inmates, it loses its sense of sexuality in giving way to discussions of caring and human contact. Hence, when Rufalo, a woman described in *Redbook* as "a wife, mother, elementary-school teacher, union official—-and concerned citizen," was arrested for illegally striking and then imprisoned at the Essex County Penitentiary in

Caldwell, New Jersey, she spent a great deal of her time observing the intricacies of prison life. Amongst her numerous observations were the following on lesbianism: "I began to understand . . . about homosexuality in prison. It's just two girls taking care of each other. There was never an opportunity for anything but touching, fondling, combing each other's hair. Everyone needs someone to take care of them, and when you're in prison and there are only girls around, then girls take care of you. Once I sat down on a bench and a girl's leg touched mine. And you know what? I liked it. A human body touching me, warm and nice. If I'd been outside, I'd have moved away. But in there, I needed that contact" (Gallagher 164). Rufalo not only removes sexual relations from lesbianism ("there was never an opportunity for anything but touching"), but she also transforms the behavior into something everyone "needs." One is led to assume that, if she had been imprisoned longer than her thirty-two days, a natural consequence of Rufalo's caring for others would have been to partake of lesbian behavior.

Even when it is situated negatively, homosexuality among women is explained as part of the overall scheme of prison life, understandable within the parameters of imprisonment. Hence, one prisoner claimed in *Ramparts* that while homosexuality may be "corrupting and wrong, . . . at least it gives you something to look forward to in here. Like you can think, 'I'm going to work tomorrow and I can see her' " (Burkhart 26). Although different in part from Rufalo's response, in spirit, there is this similarity: Lesbianism does not parallel the representation of rape in men's prisons. Instead, it is represented as always consensual—at best, an extension of caring for one another; at worst, a way to pass time.

Not only does the sexuality of women in all-female prisons become an extension of their common human ethic of caring, but it is also represented as having a calming influence over males when both males and females are held together in "coed" prisons. In 1973, the federal government and several state governments opened a small number of mixed-gender prisons. Predictably, such prisons drew press coverage that seemed to focus only on the potential for sexual relations between inmates. Despite the plurality of representations of male prisoners evident elsewhere, coed prisons were depicted as havens for responsibility and positive transformation. In *Newsweek*'s coverage of the prisons, it was observed that the prisons had not led to the "feared orgies" or a "country club atmosphere," but instead that "correctional authorities who run the experimental programs are discovering that coed prisons can actually help to rehabilitate some inmates" ("Boys" 23). In *Ebony,* Warden Charles Campbell of the coed Federal Correction Institution at Forth Worth, Texas, noted that "we're just serious about asking residents to take charge of their own lives and to respect themselves and others. We have a commitment on the part of our staff and residents to work together to develop a setting where our programs can work" (B. Mason 193).

Representatives of the coed facilities stress that sexual contact between prisoners is not allowed and that this lack of sexual behavior allows inmates to realize that they have, as Campbell notes, "a primal need for each other that's quite apart from sex" (quoted in "Boys" 23). While the prisons are meant to be beneficial to all, then, the central thesis of each discussion of the prisons is on how the presence of women affects the men. While the coed experience might have "a feminizing aspect on women," it also changes the behavior of the male prisoners (B. Mason 194). As convict B. F. Maiz noted of his experiences in the coed facility: "Knowing there's women around makes a guy feel good, act good, stay on his toes. And nothing beats having a woman around to talk to or to touch or just look at. Even if we didn't have the program, the fact that there is no homosexuality or intimidation to deal with is enough to make it a viable experiment worth trying" (quoted in B. Mason 196). While a valuable experience for both genders, the female prisoners, consistently recognized as promoters of morality, make the males "feel and act good" by their presence and cause a cessation of homosexual behaviors. Indeed, while lesbianism may be an act of intimacy when women are alone, when grouped with men, the "natural" order manifests itself and homosexual behavior reportedly ceases for both genders.

Finally, the representation of the female prisoner as having a high moral purpose and as essentially redeemable is only enhanced as the number of representations of female political prisoners grows. Although they are clearly a minority, the fact that women who are arrested for protesting for stronger education and better working conditions are being represented as prisoners means that the general population of prisons naturally shares elements of this representation. Hence, *Ramparts* noted that "a relatively new 'minority' in prisons is women imprisoned for their involvement in anti-war and anti-establishment political actions—burning draft files or destroying federal property" (Burkhart 27). Again, *Redbook* featured the story of Betty Rufalo and her imprisonment for striking in order to lower the size of classrooms and improve facilities for schoolchildren (Gallagher). During this period, *America* reported on the "moral solidarity" of women imprisoned for their support of farm workers striking under Cesar Chavez for better and safer working conditions and noted the fasting and Gandhi-inspired behavior of the prisoners (Von Gottfried). In each case, women are imprisoned for higher principles, right or wrong, not for selfish motives. Tied together with other inmates, each shares in this brushstroke of moral behavior.

Reproduction and Moral Influence

The reproductive capabilities of women and their culturally recognized role of maintaining a moral influence within the home also transform the representation of female prisoners. Repeatedly, authors observe that many, if not most, imprisoned females are mothers who wish to be reunited with their children. For instance, Kitsi Burkhart reported that "approximately 80 percent of the women behind bars have children whom they support. Thus the system finances not only the incarceration of mothers deemed for the most part non-violent, but creates its own welfare recipients" (23). Burkhart provided numerous stories of various women imprisoned while their children were put into foster homes and noted that the inmates were concerned because they blame their own experiences with foster homes for their imprisonment. She suggested that only by joining their children could the women assure the safety and morality of their children; prison keeps women from their child-rearing responsibilities.

Substantiating this claim, Burkhart reported that when one prisoner was not released on parole when expected, the prisoner's "daughter got rebellious and ran away" (24). Imprisoned teacher Betty Rufalo was repeatedly pointed to as a "wife and mother" whose moral stances would be transferred to her children (Gallagher). Furthermore, in the *Ladies Home Journal* contest in which prisoners were asked to suggest how parents could keep their children from criminal lifestyles, prisoner Wanda Boyle asserted that, as the mother of five children, she planned "on following my thoughts through on this subject and only hope and pray that I can keep all my children from experiencing what I have" (Boyle 68). Only outside of prison can she teach them moral stability; only outside of prison can she find fulfillment.

Similarly, after numerous women were arrested while striking in support of their "farm worker" husbands, the only concern that any of them are reported to have expressed is that their children be taken care of during their imprisonment. One noted that "I do not do this for myself, but for my children," even while she expressed guilt for being away from them (Von Gottfried 264). In each case, as bearers of the species, they are also bearers of our shared cultural morality. That is, as women, they are not only naturally mothers, but naturally mothers who can and must reproduce cultural morals.

In short, female inmates, regardless of race, continue to be seen as moral agents, in need of and capable of rehabilitation. While their lives have been sidetracked by the abusive treatment of others, prison allows them to learn a skill, to learn how to live. Removed from abusive situations, women can reassert themselves as caring human beings. Furthermore, their reasons for imprisonment, as represented by the notable inclusion of political prisoners, provide them with a higher sense of morality than their male counterparts. Hence, as the guardian of our morality and as the reproducer of the species, the female inmate is able to relearn her proper role through imprisonment and required rehabilitation programs; she has a calming influence over males and is able to rehabilitate herself in order to better play her role as mother upon release. Her role, both in and out of the penitentiary, is that of the maintainer of cultural morality, the protector of the species.

Concluding Comments

Thus far, I have shown that the male prisoner of the 1950s was represented as a primarily white prisoner who riots and violates prison rules primarily because poor prison conditions and a lack of rehabilitation programs encourage him to do so. Very few voices give credence to the belief that the prisoner should be faulted for his acts unless he is provided with help to remove himself from his social and mental conditions. As reports begin to illustrate the apparent failure of rehabilitation programs and as riots begin to occur more frequently in the 1960s, two depictions come to the fore. The first of these represents the male prisoner in a fashion similar to that of the 1950s, a prisoner who is primarily "human" and generally Caucasian, needing only help and understanding in order to escape the mental fetters that place him in prison. The second male prisoner of the 1960s, one increasingly depicted as African-American, is constructed as violent, tending toward rape, and generally irredeemable; he needs and deserves punishment. Race becomes a method by which to distinguish between two cultural depictions of the prisoner. However, the fact that each is judged in terms of a shared and homogeneous value system reflects the existence of a strong belief in that set of values. Once these arguments find popular support, as evidenced by their frequent use, they become the foundations on which future constructions of prisoners are constrained and enabled.

Finally, in the era studied in this chapter, I have attempted to outline three prominent characterizations of the male prisoner. While I have already commented on the implications of each of the constructions of the prisoner of this era, I want to highlight here two of the emergent themes that will prove dominant in contemporary discourses. In the era under study here, we find conflict over distinct moral systems. While the redeemable and irrational prisoners continue to exist and reflect the existence and stability of a common morality, the existence of another prisoner, one who is accepted as operating under a different moral system and imprisoned either because of this difference or because of the racism of the system, threatens the dominance of traditional values. That is, because the prisoner is represented in a sympathetic tone that situates his imprisonment as politically motivated and depicts him as innocent of (or at least not responsible for) moral crimes, there is an evident debate in the overarching values within the culture. Two of the prisoner types, judged in terms of the status quo value system, reveal the continuing strength of that system. The other, judged outside of the system, represents the existence of a cultural challenge to that system.

Even this moderately sympathetic presentation of the nonwhite prisoner, however, hinting at respect for cultural diversity as it does, continues to stereotype him as violent. While the first and third representations are constructed under the auspices of a commonly shared morality that favors the redeemable and primarily Caucasian prisoner, both of the constructions of the nonwhite prisoner emphasize his violent nature rather than suggesting themes of altruism or possibilities for rehabilitation.

The female prisoner, regardless of race, continues to be depicted as the bearer of cultural moral values as she has been fairly consistently throughout the period of study. Her imprisonment is represented as resulting from conditions outside of her control (for example, poverty or abuse). Given a fair set of living conditions, her essence as reproducer of values and mother of the species will reassert itself. In this era, her role in prison has been a calming one; her destiny, however, is out of prison, with the children she leaves behind and to whom she must return.

Finally, I wish to note the growth of the ideology of moral autonomy and the contradictions represented by it. The discussions of each of the prisoners reveal a growing cultural belief that the individual should take responsibility for both crimes and rehabilitation. At the same time, there is a tendency to discuss male rehabilitation only in terms of programs designed and implemented by institutions and not in terms of what the prisoner can do for himself. There is an emerging cultural belief that prisoners need to take responsibility for their own lives and the simultaneous implication that they can do so only by relying on programs facilitated by the state. The implications of this tendency will loom large.

6

The Meaning of Just Deserts

Valuing Our Discipline, 1975–1993

> I can imagine the black men's mute rage as they sat in their chains and watched. What they saw probably shocked them less than it does the average reader of this magazine. In the cage and the ghetto one quickly becomes acclimated to lethal violence. If you have been in and out of prisons since the age of sixteen, as Harris was, you learn at an early age that power makes right and killing doesn't shake the heavens or necessarily bring retribution or the wrath of God. (Bunker, "Lynching" 699)

> [John Erwin, Head of the Pace Institute, a program dedicated to helping rehabilitate male prisoners through teaching them to read]: I've learned one thing in this jail. Anybody from any culture at any time can understand the power of love. That's all my staff and I give. Our job is to keep chipping away until we free some angels in there. (quoted in Yancey 28)

> The typical [female] offender . . . is a young mother. In general, she is slightly better educated and less violent than her male counterpart. Many inmates were victims themselves—of poverty, physical violence or sexual abuse. Though most poor people are obviously law abiding, some analysts say more women have taken to crime to support their families as economic conditions have worsened. (Salholz et al. 51)

Taken from contemporary journals, this set of discourses from 1975 to 1993 proves particularly interesting in highlighting and providing insight into the relationships between prisoners and the culture at large, between prisoner and punisher, between culture and moral authority. The period is of interest not only because it brings us to the present, to those assumptions under which Maria Arnford's statements must be understood, but also because this is the period that both John Irwin (230–40) and Larry Sullivan (211) claim as the beginning of the "just deserts" era of punishment.

Promoted by liberals and conservatives alike, the concept of "just deserts" represents a popular philosophy of criminal justice that holds that criminals should be given only their due, nothing more and nothing less. That is, every criminal activity is posited as entailing a specific measure of punishment, and the distribution of that punishment is the sole responsibility of the criminal justice system in its relationship to criminals. Other considerations, such as rehabilitation or training, cannot be required but may be offered on a voluntary basis. While prisoners should be provided with clean cells that allow them to maintain a sense of humanity, and while rehabilitation programs should be available for those prisoners who volunteer to take part in them, undergoing the prescribed punishment is the only necessary concern of criminal justice.

Indeed, as James Jacobs notes in his study of the Stateville Penitentiary, it was during this period that David Brierton took over the wardenship of Stateville and ushered in an era of "just deserts" at that institution. Brierton saw no need to speak out in favor of, or against, rehabilitation; instead, he demanded only "a safe, clean, program-oriented institution that functions smoothly on a day to day basis and that is not in violation of code provisions, Administrative Regulations, or court orders" (103–4). Similarly, in *Life Sentences*, a collection of essays written and published by prisoners in the Louisiana State Penitentiary, prisoner Wilbert Rideau notes that former warden Ross Maggio had noted during this period that his goal was to "create an atmosphere here that will allow any man who wants to improve himself the opportunity to do so" (Rideau and Wikberg 182). Moreover, Pete Earley notes in his popular work *The Hot House* that with the retirement of James V. Bennett as the director of the Bureau of Prisons and the eventual succession of Norman Carlson, prison systems made a move from the medical model of rehabilitation to a more pragmatic administration. Indeed, in late 1975 and early 1976, Carlson and the bureau officially abandoned the medical model that would heal "sick" inmates and took on the prison as a place where men were held and given the opportunity, if they chose it, to cure themselves (48–50). Each of these moves represents a similar orientation—a move to just deserts that was meant to negate differences in the treatment of prisoners, stop the coercion that leads to ineffective rehabilitation, and put an end to the injustice that is dealt the victims of crime when punishment is not carried out.

Rhetorically, the growth of "just deserts" as a philosophy of punishment is engaging, first off, because it must be put into play with regard to all prisoners. Hence, just deserts must take into account each of the three very different depictions of the prisoner traced out in the previous chapter, a task that is understandably difficult when the historically anchored representations of the prisoner are understood and recognized. As the two representative quotations that begin this chapter illustrate, the promise of consistent treatment of diverse prisoners for the same offenses is not to be easily kept, discursively or otherwise. That is, the bricks and mortar that are culture, in their resistance to change, do not allow us to overlook easily the differences we have created between different types of prisoners. Consequently, this chapter deals inadvertently with the strength of rhetoric, the influence of past constructions of the prisoner on the definitions and activities of the present, the ability of past representations to act as material constraints shaping contemporary discourses, and the effect of these past representations on "real" bodies.

In the first of the three quotations that begin the chapter, author and prisoner Edward Bunker comments on several male African-American inmates who were witnesses when another African-American prisoner, Vinson Harris, was apparently killed by a deputy as he was being transferred from Talladega, Alabama, to Butner, North Carolina. In order to silence Harris, who the deputy claimed had been causing trouble by verbally harassing him, the deputy placed duct tape over Harris's face. Provided with insufficient air holes and thus unable to breathe freely, Harris died of asphyxiation in the transport vehicle in front of the other prisoners, who were chained together and unable to rescue him. Although originally scheduled to serve their sentences in the same prison, the black prisoners who witnessed the event were placed in separate institutions.

In the essay from which this quotation is drawn, Bunker is evidently attempting to sympathize with the plight of African-American prisoners. Simultaneously, however, he represents each of them as familiar with the ghetto and the cage, acclimated to lethal violence, and living with a worldview in which "might makes right" and killing does not bring the wrath of God. In his attack on the system that killed Harris, Bunker himself ironically acts as part of the discursive system that already works to silence African-American prisoners as redeemable in that he represents the African-American inmates to be as violent and as irredeemable as the very system he critiques. Indeed, that such a representation of African Americans appears in a critique of the way in which African Americans are treated illustrates just how strong a force past representations have on present considerations.

The second quotation is offered by John Erwin, a former repeat offender who had been raised in foster homes and orphanages. During one stretch of time out of prison, Erwin was befriended by a man who taught him the value of unrequited and undeserved love. Learning that his new friend found strength in Christianity, Erwin converted, later becoming a Protestant minister. Furthermore, in an attempt to help others avoid his former recidivist lifestyle, he established the Pace Institute, a company that attempts to help prisoners rehabilitate themselves by providing them with access to reading materials and reading courses. When Erwin's claim to teach people of all cultures and backgrounds is combined with the fact that he focuses only on white prisoners as the beneficiaries of his program, a familiar theme emerges. While the implementations of just deserts attempts to rid the criminal justice system of bias and discrimination in punishment or rehabilitation, the strength of past arguments pulls against Erwin's claim and other similar ones. That is, while he might aspire to treat all people with love, to "free the angels in everyone," he is represented as only aiding a specific group. While Bunker's critique of prison systems represents African Americans in line with their historical representation as violent, Erwin's elaboration of his rehabilitation program makes it appear that only Caucasian prisoners are amenable to change.

The third quotation is taken from a 1990 *Newsweek* essay that attempts to draw out some of the reasons why an increasing number of women have been imprisoned in recent years. The authors provide a quintessential delineation of the representation of the female inmate, one consistent with past representations. She is again a mother, the bearer of the species. Again, her imprisonment and the corruption of her morality result from external influences, here "poverty, physical violence, or sexual abuse" (Salholz et al. 51). Again, her crimes are not violent ones and are indeed justifiable in part, not only because her morality was corrupted by external forces but also because her crime was committed for "moral" purposes (here, to support her family). Again, despite an underlying "seamy" representation of women in such B-films as *Reform School Girls,* the female prisoner's representation in print constructs an argument that sees eventual release from incarceration as the only "moral" option. The female needs to be reunited with her progeny, to reenact the role of sustainer of moral and physical life.

The weight of past representations of prisoners, the force of rhetoric, is the essence of this chapter. In the previous era, there were three different dominant versions of the male inmate (the redeemable prisoner, the violent but victimized minority, and the violent, victimizing minority) and one dominant representation of the female. From roughly 1975 on, the philosophy of just deserts, a philosophy that by definition attempts to collapse all previous depictions of the prisoner into one, to treat prisoners alike regardless of differences, grows radically. While the phrase "just deserts" is not always used, there is certainly an overall cultural move from a marginal acceptance of cultural diversity to one that is no longer concerned overtly with beliefs, but only with behavior. As Constance Holden notes in *Science* at the beginning of this era, the idea of "just deserts" leads to the creation of policies that treat all prisoners equitably for similar crimes; its call is to give the prisoner what he or she deserves in terms of punishment and then allow him or her the means of rehabilitation if this is what he or she chooses (Holden, "Prisons" 815). However, while just deserts or the discourse supporting the concept might be espoused by policymakers and editorialists, the force of past depictions of prisoners determines how just deserts will be carried out as policy. In effect, while just deserts may claim to focus only on the behavior of individuals, in practice, the focus is on their attitudes and values and those of the culture at large.

I will suggest below that the idea of just deserts appears to be implemented to a large degree in line with the representations of the prisoner that carry over from previous eras. Hence, the meaning of just deserts is defined along the axes of race and gender. Because African-American males have been represented as irrational and violent whether the blame lies with society, the prison system, or the individual prisoner, they are unqualified rhetorically for rehabilitation programs and alternatives to incarceration, alternatives that require trustworthiness and rationality. It matters little that the past brought us two different representations of the male African-American prisoner, only one of whom is ultimately responsible for his violent behavior. Both are constructed as violent, and it is this violence that constructs them as unworthy of trust. Caucasian male inmates, on the other hand, portrayed as not only redeemable but also as inherently moving toward that rehabilitated state, are more likely candidates for these programs.

Just deserts also work along the axis of gender. Constituted as reproducers of both species and morality, female inmates are "always already" on the road to rehabilitation; their just deserts are not paid in terms of unsanitary prison conditions or brutal fights but in separation from their children. Their representation features them as women first and as convicts second. As a consequence of their constituted essence as moral beings, they are more likely to be represented as being eligible for alternative programs and thus are more likely to be represented as involved in rehabilitation programs. This representation is true for female inmates in general, regardless of race.

In practice, then, just deserts may have different meanings for different representations of criminals. Despite the stated intent of just deserts' policies, given the same crimes, two prisoners may be represented as encountering two different forms of punishment. Hence, in narratives concerning alternative forms of punishment, if the punishment is to be represented as both supplying just deserts and allowing for the rehabilitation of prisoners, only particular "types" of prisoners will fit the role needed for the particular punishment. Cultural expectations require this to be so.

The implications of these differences go beyond the obviously important one of the treatment of prisoners on the basis of race or gender, however. Indeed, these differences are not my primary concern. Again, this study is an exposition of the discipline of discipline, a study of how mass-mediated discussions of punishment influence the relationships of individuals with the culture at large and the multitude of existing disciplinary procedures partaken of on a daily basis. Hence, while I will trace out the various ways in which different criminals are shown to be either eligible or ineligible for various programs, I also wish to claim that the tensions inherent in the growth of alternatives to incarceration create a noteworthy relationship between the "law-abiding" individuals who make up the general culture and the forms of discipline it encourages, implicating everything from limiting the types of food people eat to learning new ways to discipline children.

As I will show later, those who undergo alternative systems of punishment (e.g., boot camp, electronic monitoring systems) must be punished under the dictates of just deserts; being rhetorically tied to rehabilitation, however, they are also generally represented *as having chosen* rehabilitation as one element of their punishment. Hence, the public arguments concerning their punishment places this brand of criminal in a quagmire in which they must acknowledge that they are suffering mentally and/or physically at the hands of the state's disciplinary procedures while they simultaneously must represent themselves as having chosen to be rehabilitated *and* grateful for the consequences of this choice. Hence, a Maria Arnford publicly announces that our state and cultural forms of punishment benefit the individual who undergoes their procedures. She invites us to approach the definitions provided by state and cultural institutions as ones we should encourage—indeed invite—into our own lives.

In order to make this argument clear before proceeding to texts that support it, I would like to provide a brief narrative of the influence of the just deserts argument and its relationship with both material and symbolic forces. First, as both Sullivan and Irwin note, it is the arguments for just deserts, accompanied by increasing interest in longer sentences for those convicted of crimes involving illegal drugs, that place a greater number of persons behind bars for lengthier periods of time (Irwin 175–81; L. Sullivan 113–14). These sentencing policies in turn lead to a nationwide prison overcrowding problem. Overcrowding itself, then, becomes both a material problem (that is, lack of space to house prisoners) and a discursive one (the cause of violence and riots as prisoners are forced to live in inhumane conditions).

Second, the discursive growth and maturation of the prisoner as a legal being encourage prisoners to file legal complaints against government bodies for their substandard or insufficient maintenance of overcrowded prisoners. That is, in part because prisoners have been argued into the constitutive position of "legal beings" deserving of humane forms of punishment, they are enabled to bring lawsuits protesting inhumane treatment. Legal victories then force federal and state agencies to take several possible actions: release prisoners, build new cells, and/or develop alternative forms of punishment. While all of these alternates are utilized, the cry for just deserts makes the release of prisoners a less feasible response. However, the development of alternative forms of punishment (such as electronic monitoring, furloughs, boot camp), the more expedient and economical of the two remaining solutions, itself arrives with several rhetorical dilemmas.

First, there is the issue of race. Inmates who are constructed as irrational and violent are considered ineligible for many of the alternative programs, at least as these programs and inmates are represented publicly; hence, only Caucasian male prisoners have social constitutions that make them safe candidates for these alternatives. A policy of just deserts, therefore, is necessarily defined along lines of race.

Second is the issue of gender. Because women in general have been discursively and culturally articulated as the purveyors of cultural morality, they most easily fit the discursive mold making them eligible for alternative forms of punishment. They are trustworthy and "naturally" designed to rediscover their "natural" morality. A more powerful factor than race, gender defines women as ideal candidates for alternative forms of punishment, regardless of race.

Third, and perhaps more important, the clash of the material need for new forms of punishment, the discursive need for just deserts, and the discursive creation of those prisoners who are eligible to take part in the programs as redeemable create a potent rhetorical situation. Those who undergo alternative forms of punishment must be punished in order to provide just deserts, but they also must be rehabilitated, brought back to the norm, as this is a characteristic of their prefigured construction. Furthermore, they must *choose* to be redeemed, as this too is one element of the general discourse of just deserts and rehabilitation programs. As a result of the intermingling of these arguments, the criminals taking part in alternatives must illustrate the punitive nature of their punishment *and* its welcomed ability to move them to correct behaviors. In effect, this criminal will invite each of us to see state discipline as necessarily positive, as a necessary good even when it hurts. The African-American male leaves prison tinged with the stigma of a violent and irrational nature; the Caucasian male prisoner and the female prisoner in general emerge prefigured as redeemable and hence represent the punishment imparted by the state as not only fair, but productive; not only tough, but helpful.

Just Deserts

The general philosophy or orientation toward criminal justice and punishment loosely collected under the title "just deserts" sets the conditions under which this era of discipline develops. In his history of the prison reform movement, Larry Sullivan notes that the concept of just deserts grew out of the discourse of works such as the American Friends Service Committee's *Struggle for Justice,* a general call for viewing prisoners as morally autonomous, as responsible for their actions in the commission of crime, and hence, as responsible for bearing the community's definition of just deserts for the crime (Sullivan 111). A just deserts model of punishment holds that, regardless of prisoner attributes (race, gender, socioeconomic background), the punishment must fit the crime, no more and no less. Furthermore, a just deserts model asserts that the prisoner should not be forced to take part in rehabilitation programs because participation in such programs will not necessarily enhance his or her chances at early release. Instead, if we are to respect the individual's right to determine his or her own life and moral system, to take ultimate responsibility for action, the choice to take on rehabilitation programs must ultimately be a free one. In short, the criminal must serve the sentence imposed by the community; all else, including rehabilitation, must be voluntary.

One factor that tends to make the rise of the just deserts model successful is the historical drop in society's faith in the viability of rehabilitation programs. Historian Edward Cuddy blatantly asserted in a 1977 issue of *Progressive* that " 'rehabilitation' is a tarnished word today in the current literature on prison reform—an endless chronicle of failure" (54). Similarly, in a *Newsweek* essay investigating the purpose of punishment, sociologist Robert Martinson claimed that rehabilitation is infeasible: "With few exceptions the rehabilitation efforts that have been reported so far have no effect on recidivism" (quoted in Howard, Lubenow, and Lesher 36). In addition, when John Whitley, warden of the Louisiana State Penitentiary, was interviewed in 1992 in *Time,* he recounted the changes in his own beliefs about prisoners over time: " 'As a starry-eyed corrections rookie,' Whitley admits, 'I was going to save them all.' Twenty-two years later, he thinks it's a 'complete farce' to speak of rehabilitating inmates; they must do that for themselves. 'All we can do,' he says, 'is provide the opportunity' " (Smolowe, "Bringing" 60). Even when traditional rehabilitation programs are described during this period, they are given a "punishment" orientation. For example, in an essay written by former prisoner Nick DiSpoldo, we find halfway houses depicted as places of punishment rather than rehabilitation: "You know what a halfway house is? It's a bed move, man, that's all it is, 'cause you are really still in prison. You just do your time on the streets instead of in the slammer" ("Halfway" 320). Furthermore, before his current notoriety as the prophet of active euthanasia, Dr. Jack Kevorkian argued that the most heinous of criminals should not only be put to death but also forced to donate their organs to those in need. If just deserts are to be served, we must have not only death but repayment. As *Newsweek* reported, Kevorkian asserted, " 'We need organs, and these men owe a debt to society' " ("Death-Row Murderers" 49).

In the language of just deserts, the prescription for the treatment of the criminal lies in a balance: weight of crime must equal weight of punishment and rehabilitation must be of secondary importance, tied to the desires of the prisoner rather than the demands of the institution. While it is not the case that rehabilitation is completely ignored in the cultural quest for just deserts, it does become the subordinate thesis.

As noted earlier, the just deserts attitude brings with it the representation of the prisoner as responsible for his or her actions. Hence, when the Texas Department of Corrections was being sued for inhumane treatment of prisoners, Chief Defense Counsel Ed Idar, Jr., argued in *Newsweek* that "we are dealing with the dregs of society. We make no bones about hard work and discipline" (quoted in Bonventre and Marbach 74). Six years later, Warden Frank Blackburn of Louisiana's death row made a similar observation in *US News and World Report,* noting that no comforts should be provided to his inmates because "a man has got to try hard to get in here. We have high entrance standards" (quoted in Chaze 68). Jonathon Rubinstein observed in the *New Yorker* that "the guiding principle is to make felons responsible for their own lives" (82). Furthermore, in an essay on poor health care conditions in prisons, social critic George Anderson observed that poor health care conditions exist because people "feel that prisoners are bad people whose sufferings and privations are deserved" ("D. C. Jail" 354). It is the responsibility and burden of the criminal to accept the standards of punishment dictated for the crime; punishment is deserved—one must take responsibility for one's action.

When the behavior modification–oriented Patuxent Institute in Maryland switched to a system that allowed prisoners to take part in modification programs on a strictly voluntary basis, it exemplified one of the most common movements of this era in corrections. While prison policies continued to favor rehabilitation, they increasingly made participation in rehabilitation programs voluntary. If just deserts were to be the model for punishment, rehabilitation could not be forced as it was not included in what was due for the crime. Thus, in an essay describing Patuxent's transformation, it was observed that the new belief at Patuxent was that prisoners must learn to take responsibility for their crimes but not necessarily change future behavior. The prisoners at Patuxent were described as "impulsive, emotionally volatile, showing poor judgment, denying . . . guilt, and manifesting a defiant attitude. Perhaps the main thing that characterizes Patuxent patients is that they are 'losers' in crime," that they cannot admit their guilt (Holden, "Patuxent" 667).

The need for the prisoner to admit responsibility may have reached its rhetorical apex when University of Miami law professor Bruce Winick argued in *Psychology Today* that many criminals found to be mentally incompetent to stand trial can and should be forced to take medication that will allow their competence, even if only temporarily. That is, if criminals can be provided with drugs that allow them to become competent for the period of a trial, such actions should be not only approved but enforced. Winick supported this argument by drawing a parallel between a criminal who needs medication to be considered sane and a diabetic who can only be considered healthy while taking insulin. For Winick, the importance of this argument is that it allows criminals to admit responsibility for their behavior (Horn, "A Rule" 29). Not only, then, is there a move toward just deserts, but the move to just deserts also implies that the prisoner must learn to take responsibility for crime.

Finally, it is during this period that the Federal Penitentiary in Marion, Illinois, was widely reported to have become the modern equivalent of Alcatraz, a maximum security prison from which escape would be impossible. Discussions of the Marion facility emphasized both just deserts and the necessity of having prisoners take responsibility for their actions. Marion became a highly secured prison when, after a riot in which several people including guards were killed, actions were taken to restrict temporarily all prison movement. The condition became permanent as the Bureau of Prisons recognized the need for such a facility on a permanent basis. The philosophy directing the Marion facility is in effect an exaggeration of the philosophy of prisons throughout the country during this period. As Michael Satchell reported in *US News and World Report*, "Its philosophy is to psychologically emasculate a man, strip down his ego, crush his macho insolence and force him to conform to the strictest rules ever implemented in modern American penology" (23). As if on cue with just deserts' demand for responsibility, Randy Gometz, an inmate at the prison who had murdered a guard during a previous riot, admitted his responsibility for the murder and acknowledged the need for a facility like Marion. Gometz noted, "What should society do for me? I'm a criminal, I don't profess to be anything else. Let me out and I'll do it again. I deserve to be in here" (quoted in Satchell 23). In effect, the philosophy of this facility and of the era in general is one of holding inmates for a length of time that will allow the inmate to "pay for the crime" and acknowledge responsibility.[1]

As I proceed, it will become evident that the overall attitude of the just deserts model creates rhetorical binds later in the discourse of punishment. Below, I will illustrate that as violence and drug use within prisons become high profile media topics, blame for each will be placed on overcrowding in prisons, a condition that has resulted indirectly from policies invoked in the name of just deserts. As a result, just deserts in practice will need to be rethought; as more people are sentenced to punishment outside of incarceration in order to ease overcrowding, these alternative forms of punishment will have to be translated rhetorically into the discourse of just deserts.

Violence

Newsweek staff writer Aric Press, in an essay seeking to determine when riots would again arise in prisons, commented that "every day, somewhere, an inmate beats or is beaten, rapes or is raped, stabs or is stabbed" (Press et al., "When Will" 68). This statement reflects a dominant depiction of the prisoner of this era. Not only is there violence "every day," but it is savage and reciprocal; prisoners rape or are raped, stab or are stabbed, on a daily basis.

The violence of inmates is characteristically represented as animalistic and senseless, arising from warped personalities. For example, after Clifford Irving's imprisonment for having faked the biography of Howard Hughes, he wrote an essay for *Playboy* describing his experiences. In it, Irving provided "matter of fact" narratives of two confrontations that he witnessed, each arising from seemingly trivial conflicts. In the first, a prisoner was brutally beaten for not having said "Excuse me" after having brushed up against another prisoner. In the second, while waiting in line for food, Irving witnessed one prisoner steal another's doughnut and say, "Fuck you, bubblehead." The second inmate immediately drew a knife and stabbed the first prisoner in the stomach, retrieved the doughnut and said, "You a bubble belly, bubblehead," sitting down in order to eat the doughnut while the stabbed prisoner lay injured at his feet (170). Later, when sent to Leavenworth for having been caught drinking beer while imprisoned, Irving noted that he witnessed a prisoner kill two inmates and wound two more. When asked the reason for the killings, the prisoner said, "Well, . . . they was standing right there" (187). For the male prisoner, such violence arises without cause, without provocation, and without rational thought; moreover, it arises daily.

The Federal Penitentiary at Marion, Illinois, becomes a magnet for discussions of the violent behavior of prisoners throughout this era. A 1990 *Newsweek* essay concerning Marion notes that it houses the most dangerous prisoners of the federal prison system and that some 98 percent of them have a history of violent behavior (Dickey 66). The central narrative of the essay focuses on Marion's transformation from one of many federal prisons to the premiere "locked-down," maximum-security prison, a transformation that grew more out of circumstance than design: "From February 1980 to October 1983, nine inmates were killed and two guards were murdered. There were 10 riots, 57 assaults, 33 attacks on staff" (Dickey 67).

After one of these riots, the institution was put into a permanent lock-down status, under which the prisoners remain in their cells twenty-three hours a day. Even in the hour that each is allowed out to exercise, he remains shackled. However, even with the lock-down, Marion is represented as the scene of several killings because of inmates who are described as routinely violent. Moreover, not only are the inmates described as violent, but the guards at Marion are reported to discuss the prisoners in terms that paint every move that an inmate makes as potentially violent. For instance, Danny Hilliard, an officer in one of the most secure portions of the prison, asserted, "Some inmates, you look in their eyes, and you know they're thinking about cutting your throat, but if you start looking at them like wild animals, you're going to have problems" (Dickey 68). Even while claiming to see the inmates as something more than "wild animals," Hilliard's statement reflects a common impulse to see the very looks of the inmates as signifiers of an inhuman form of violent behavior.

If this representation of the male prisoner as naturally violent only arose in discussions concerning maximum security prisons like Marion, it would be difficult to see the average inmate as being represented as violent. The representation is pervasive and graphic, however, describing prisoners of all levels of culture. A widely reported incident in Boise, Idaho, illustrates the pervasiveness of such violence as well as the seeming irrationality of prisoners, even juvenile ones. The narrative centers on Chris Peterman, a seventeen-year-old who had accumulated seventy-three dollars in traffic fines. While his parents could afford to pay the fines, they agreed with their son that his spending the weekend in jail would help him to learn to take responsibility for his actions. After two days in the prison and after having written his parents to say that he thought he was well-liked by other inmates, Peterman was found in the prison showers, beaten, burned, and kicked to death by five other juveniles, a group that had murdered another inmate one week earlier (Abramson 42; Sarah Hall 36–37).

In another case, after a number of riots and fights at the Texas Eastham Unit, guards began to utilize "building tenders," armed prisoners trusted by the guards and feared by other inmates, in order to control the rest of the prison population. However, as noted in *Newsweek,* as time passed, "inmates turned on inmates. Between January 1984 and September 1985, 52 prisoners were fatally shivved [stabbed] and mangled throughout the 27-unit system; six died at Eastham" (Press, "Inside" 48). The report is interesting beyond its representation of violent prisoners, however, as it represents a basic change in the way violence itself was discussed. Press noted that "by 1985, the prison zeitgeist had changed: from violence as an instrument of control, it has moved to violence as a matter of course" ("Inside" 56). Violence, then, becomes increasingly pervasive and is less often justified as the result of cultural racism as this period proceeds.

While this case does not need overstatement, a review of the discourse of this era shows a significant increase in mass-mediated reports of prison violence. In 1981, *Time* reported that San Quentin witnessed seven murders and fifty-four stabbings, giving its inmates a one-in-three-thousand chance of being killed in any given year ("What Are" 38–41). *US News and World Report* observed that over 70 percent of California prisoners reportedly had histories of violent behavior ("Jobs" 60). *Flying* noted that a private airline that flies transferred prisoners from one facility to another had hired extra security as prisoners were known to kick guards, attempt to set planes afire, and tear up airplane seats (Baxter 44).

The violent environment of prison makes the prison itself a dangerous place to send criminals. Regarding this violence, the *Nation* reported that after prisoner James Beanwalker escaped from a prison in

Arkansas and settled in California, successfully operating a leather goods shop for a number of years, he was arrested on a minor charge and discovered to be a prison escapee. A debate then ensued over whether Beanwalker should be returned to the Arkansas prison, a place described by a federal court as "a dark and evil world . . . inherently dangerous," or left to lead a productive life ("Into the Fire" 260). Finally, in the Indiana State Prison at Michigan City, a man who taught in a rehabilitation/education program claimed that "tension and stress are constant realities, and violence is never far from the surface" (quoted in Gribben 657). In his description of this violence, the teacher reported having witnessed a gruesome stabbing outside of his classroom (Gribben 657).

Violence, simply stated, is constructed as a norm of prison behavior and begins to include inmates of all ethnicities in this period. The era's films further the representation. In *Attica,* the film account of the 1971 riots at Attica that is mostly critical of the prison administration, not only are the prisoners represented as rioting, they are also portrayed as irrationally violent. In one scene, *New York Times* reporter Tom Wicker, requested by the prisoners to be an observer who would report on their activities, is driven to the prison by a law officer. When Wicker tells the officer that he plans on reasoning with the inmates, the officer replies, "Those are mean dudes in there—murderers, rapists, armed robbers. What do you think they're going to do with those hostages? Yes sir," he says cynically, "reason with them . . . reason with 1,2C0 rioting cons" (*Attica*). Even in HBO's 1993 retelling of the Attica story, *Against the Wall,* others besides the anomalous character Jamaal X are seen as demanding the killing of snitches and guards. Moreover, the prisoners end up killing one of their fellow inmates who had too much lust for murdering during the riot.

In another film of the period, 1978's *Scared Straight,* the renowned graphic documentary shown nationally on network television, an account is given of a program in New Jersey in which juvenile delinquents are taken into the Rahway State Prison to meet "lifers" and get an understanding of what prison life would be like. From the opening shot of a prisoner saying, "When I wake up in the morning, I think maybe I'll have to kill someone today," to the shot of a prisoner noting that "three guys will slide in your cell and do bodily harm by sticking a dick in your asshole," to the closing shots of "rehabilitated" youth leaving the prison, the message is clear: prison is a violent place where murder and rape are a daily occurrence.[2]

Not only do reporters discuss the violent nature of criminals, but, and perhaps of more significance, prisoners themselves testify to their own violent nature. The *Scared Straight* documentary is only one of many examples. In the *New York Times Magazine,* a prisoner in the Indiana State Prison at Michigan City declared, "You don't know when you walk out of your cell if you're gonna get knifed. . . . I sleep with my eyes open now. I don't even close my eyes when I shampoo" (quoted in Lieber 35). When one inmate stole the Kool-Aid of inmate Robert "Bonzai" Vickers in an Arizona prison, Vickers stabbed the thief ten times, going on to carve his nickname on the dead body. Later, when an inmate expressed lust at a picture of his niece, Vickers threw a molotov cocktail in the prisoner's cell, killing him. When asked by *Newsweek* if he would continue such behavior, Vickers was affirmative: "Until the system kills me. . . . Death don't mean nothin' to me, not mine, not yours" (quoted in Press and Friendly 88–90). In a report on the rising rate of violence in overcrowded prisons, *Time* noted that almost every prisoner had a number of weapons; one prisoner noted, "In here, not having a knife is a death sentence" (Magnuson 16–17).

Finally, the discourse of the "violent prisoner" also appears on the governmental level. *US News and World Report* suggested that prison violence is so pervasive that it is exceedingly difficult for any politicians, even liberal ones, to ignore calls for capital punishment and more overall intense punishment for all prisoners. As a result, Atlanta mayor Andrew Young claimed that he had seen so many friends brutalized by crime that he had begun to believe that "the state has got to have the right to put mad dogs to death" (Roberts and Gest 25). In addition, Democratic strategist Ray Strother asserted that as no one can trust the state's ability to keep violent criminals behind bars, all political candidates must pursue a line of discourse that encourages more fully punishing the prisoner, providing true "just deserts" (Roberts and Gest 25).

Drug Use

The perceived problem with the inmate of this era is not only one of violence but also (and often concurrently) one of drug abuse. Prisoners are either represented as having committed crimes because of the influence of drugs or as utilizing drugs while imprisoned. Among those discourses that attribute criminal activity to drug use, we find criminal justice critic Norval Morris noting that "President Ford suggested that 50% of city-street crime is attributable to crime by addicts. I think that's a gross exaggeration. But suppose you make it 20%. That's still an appalling amount of crime. I simply care more about that than I do the addicts, and I think it is crazy for us to continue to push them to crime" (61). Furthermore, in a study of parolees in Pennsylvania in 1977, the composite picture was of young people whose main social interest lay in drinking heavily (Panik and Mobley 29). In a 1987 study of elderly prisoners, sociologist, prison reformer, and author Sol Chaneles noted that "80% have led an actively abusive life involving drugs, alcohol, and hallucinogens" (49). The poor health of prisoners and the high rate of heart disease and AIDS during this period are often attributed to intravenous drug usage (G. Anderson, "Sick" 124–34). Moreover, Carole Decuir, a foster grandparent for inmates, noted in *Aging,* "If they could keep these kids off drugs, they wouldn't commit these crimes" (quoted in C. Carlson 23). *Esquire* also reported during this period that "drugs are now the most significant single factor in the crimes that lead to imprisonment" (Farbar 154). Finally, in a *Futurist* article voicing support for home monitoring as an alternative to punishment, psychologist Charles Brown argued that "whether you are a career criminal or commit crime as an avocation, you are likely to get yourself in the appropriate frame of mind by drinking or using drugs" (27).

In addition to the testimony of psychologists and criminal justice theorists, prisoners themselves testify to the connection between drug use and criminal behavior. In a lengthy *Sports Illustrated* essay that suggested that a large number of prisoners could have been professional athletes had they not become addicted to drugs and alcohol, Leroy Fowler, an inmate of Montgomery Correctional Institution in Georgia, reflected on his turn away from sports in attempting to understand where he "went wrong." He recalled that "there's a lot of alcoholism in my family, and my grandfather put a capful of liquor in my hand when I was six or seven. I believe if I had sought professional help for my drinking, I'd be in the major leagues" (quoted in Telander 83–87).

When the Arthur Kill Correctional Facility's drug treatment program, run by former prisoner and heroin addict Arthur Cash, was threatened with elimination due to budget constraints in New York, several prisoners were asked to provide their feelings about the program. Albert Nelson, a prisoner at Arthur Kill, said, "I used drugs for 20 years and never stopped to look at what I did until I got here. I knew drugs were bad. . . . But I still chose to do drugs" (quoted in Corn 660). Similarly, inmates on death row interviewed for an *Esquire* essay repeatedly blamed the cause of their crimes on their abuse of drugs and alcohol (R. Friedman 86). As a whole, then, prison administrators and prisoners alike understand drug use to be highly correlated with criminal behavior.

In addition to the citation of drug use as an underlying cause of crime, prisoners also are constructed as utilizing drugs even while imprisoned. For example, Tommy Ray Mason, a convicted murderer in the Louisiana State Penitentiary, claimed that some prisoners "are pill heads. They have become dependent on drugs, which ease their imagined aches and pains" (6). Edward Bunker, a well-published former prisoner, reported in *The Nation* that it was easy to maintain a drug habit in prison because so many of the other inmates also have narcotics addictions, creating a market for a variety of drugs ("Fasting" 628). John Coleman, a reporter who went undercover in South Carolina's Wateree River Correctional Institution, noted in *Psychology Today* that "the use of drugs isn't covert at Wateree. A few men in bunks near me shared their grass quite openly. . . . One man gave himself a shot in the arm without once looking around to see who was watching. Another, a young white, sat on his upper bunk every evening sniffing his way far over the prison walls" (Coleman 14). Further, former president Jimmy Carter's nephew, William Spann, in Soledad Prison for robbery, claimed in an interview in *Newsweek* that he had acquired a heroin habit in prison and was able to satisfy it covertly every day during his imprisonment (Keerdoja, Gayle, and Donosky 12). Finally, former inmate Clifford Irving discussed the ease with which he was able to purchase alcohol and prostitutes while imprisoned in Allentown. A fellow prisoner told him that "booze is made inside—yeast from the bakery, alcohol from the medical department. And they got drugs too. They steal the drugs meant for other inmates" (170). Hence, the prisoner finds himself in prison as a result of drugs, and prison is itself a location in which addictions are continued or initiated.

Simultaneous with the centering of the philosophy of just deserts, then, is a crystallization of the representation of the prisoner, at least the male prisoner, as a routine user or abuser of drugs and a purveyor of violence. Different from past representations, this articulation of the prisoner arises with little regard to race (outside of the fact the dominant representation of the male prisoner is African-American). The link constructed between violence and drug abuse becomes more complex and appears somewhat justified, however, as violence and drug use are often blamed on the effects of overcrowded prisons, and overcrowded prisons are linked to policies encouraged by the just deserts orientation. That is, when prisoners are given "just" sentences (whether through the War on Drugs or mandatory sentences for violent crimes) more convicts remain in prison for longer periods of time. And as convicts learn to use the legal system to their advantage, they are represented as forcing legislators and disciplinary systems to develop new forms of punishment and hence change the disciplinary landscape.

Overcrowding and Legal Issues

Again, while the male prisoner of this period is represented as violent and as a user of illegal drugs, much of the blame for these behaviors is further shown to be rooted in overcrowded prison facilities. Unlike the 1950s, however, when overcrowded cells deflected blame from prisoners for their consequent actions, in this era, the call for just deserts continues to be articulated. That is, while it is acknowledged that the prisoner's violence is a response to the prison environment, the prisoner's transgressions are not forgiven. As becomes clear, the problem of overcrowding provides space for arguments that posit normal discipline (that is, incarceration) as cruel and unusual. Hence, overcrowding, spurred on by the principles and policies of just deserts, forces the cultivation of means for achieving just deserts in ways other than imprisonment. Regardless, however—and as Robert Friedman has noted—it is during this period that prisoners are for the first time represented as holding the capabilities and the *rights* to argue against inhumane conditions.

As with the problems of violence and drug abuse, overcrowding is addressed by observers and prisoners alike in popular media. In an examination of the causes of riots at Attica and at the New Mexico prison, David Savold asserted in *Science 84* that "in both cases, overcrowded conditions in the prisons were largely blamed for the violence" (80). When the Washington, D.C., jail had an average of 2,400 inmates in its building designed for one thousand prisoners, George Anderson observed in *America* that "medical, food, and social services were not being met. It came as a surprise to few when a series of disturbances erupted in the third week of July" ("D. C. Jail" 354). In a *Senior Scholastic* essay entitled "Our Overcrowded Prisons," Michigan's governor Milliken observed that while no one would point to overcrowding as the only cause of prison riots, it is surely the central factor in their occurrence (O'Gorman 16). And as early as 1978, *US News and World Report* stated that the past five years had witnessed an increase in the nation's prison population from 204,000 to 278,000. While this increase is significant on its own, the magazine went on to note: "The result: more and more penitentiaries have become powder kegs that foster violence, racial tension, sexual assault and unrest. It was overcrowding, exacerbated by the summer heat, that was blamed in large part for the inmate riot at the Pontiac Correctional Center in Illinois. . . . Overcrowding may have also helped trigger a riot of the Georgia State Prison" ("Crisis Builds" 32).

In further examples, as far back as 1976, the *New Republic* noted that the state of Florida had built 4,200 new cells, yet remained 5,000 short; as a result, the state was placing tents in an open field to house its prisoners. In South Carolina, where 825 prisoners were living in 448 one-man cells, Commissioner Leeke noted that the conditions were inhumane and at the root of a large number of problems with prisoners: "Living within a few feet of someone he hasn't chosen to live with is what makes an inmate talk about going crazy" (quoted in Astrachan, "Standing" 12). This argument is repeated throughout the period. Not only are prisons violent domiciles, but the blame for this condition can be traced to overcrowded conditions that are in turn tied to the "war on drugs" and just deserts sentencing.[3]

Physical abuse of prisoners at the hands of guards is another commonly noted problem that results from overcrowded prisons. In a discussion of the riots at Attica, Scott Christianson, former director of the State Facilities Unit of New York, claimed that riots will continue, first, because prisoners are given drugs in an attempt to make them behave and, second, because prisoners are often mistreated by guards. He recalled that the most recent riot experienced in New York prisons began when several guards began to ride on the back of a prisoner because the prisoner had refused to submit to a rectal examination in full view of other inmates (587–88). Additionally, Phillip Zimbardo, in a follow-up to his celebrated experiment on the behavior of guards and inmates, argued that prisons utilizing solitary confinement "violate the psychological integrity of the individual, undermining his self-esteem . . . and seriously impairing his capacity for meaningful interpersonal relations. The physical features of the adjustment center all combine to create an ecology of dehumanization" ("Corporal" 146).

The conditions of prisons and the problems bred by overcrowding and mistreatment, then, teach prisoners how to (mis)behave. Rape is one example of the behaviors represented as learned in prison. Tom Cahill, the executive director of People Organized to Stop Rape of Imprisoned Persons, provides the story of Stephen Donaldson, a Quaker who was initially imprisoned for his attendance at a peace protest. While only briefly imprisoned, Donaldson was raped sixty times when placed in a cell with far more men than it was designed to hold. In his account of Donaldson's turmoil, Cahill claims that these rapes left Donaldson emotionally disturbed. As a result, he began to commit a series of crimes after release, subconsciously seeking to return to prison, to be raped each time. Indeed, Cahill notes that Donaldson learned to replicate this behavior on his own: "Imprisoned in the late 1970s, shortly after a suicide attempt, bright, gentle, spiritual Donaldson . . . took a punk himself, raping a lonely, frightened teenager" (Cahill 33). Rape—indeed all prison behavior—becomes a normal sequence of events and begins to be manifested in prisoners regardless of race. It is in this "normality" that prisoners find comfort and hence learn to continue certain behavi[illegible] San Quentin prisoner noted in *Commonweal* of his relative [illegible] in prison, "I know what's expected of me. I can get along" (Stout [illegible]

It is noteworthy that the Federal Penitentiary at Marion, Illinois, becomes increasingly articulated as the paradigm of a secure prison and is simultaneously blamed for breeding violence. As noted earlier, the Marion penitentiary gained the reputation of being the "New Alcatraz" after two guards were killed in a prison riot, and prison administrators decided to increase security at the prison. Michael McConnell noted in the *Progressive* that in attempting to quell the riots, guards in full riot gear removed prisoners from their cells, and beat the inmates with a three-foot-long club with embedded steel blades and kicked them in the groin until they passed out. Prisoners were repeatedly beaten; at times guards would force their fingers into the anuses of particular prisoners, ostensibly searching for hacksaw blades (16–17).

Since that riot, prisoners have frequently charged the facility with mistreatment. One inmate sued the prison on the grounds that he was being silenced without justification by being placed in the Central Control Unit, a section of the facility used to house especially difficult prisoners. Federal judge James Foreman agreed in ruling that the Central Control Unit had been used "to silence prison critics. It has been used to silence religious leaders. It has been used to silence economic and philosophical dissidents" (Nowlen 25). Another inmate at the facility, Roberto Del-Cid, said, "Your [the prisoner's] mail may be thrown at you through your cell door. A cup of coffee may be put in your cell so that the coffee pours over the edge and dirties your floor, or guards may make some comment to you about your wife cheating on you. . . . You hurt so much that any little thing can make you go like that" (quoted in Nowlen 27–28). After Joseph Cannon, former warden of Stateville Penitentiary in Illinois, toured the facility at Marion, he asserted that violence would certainly reestablish itself at Marion because the prisoners are dehumanized: "I have never seen procedures so extreme and so seemingly designed to degrade and aggravate the prisoners" (quoted in "Crimes" 12). As examples of such treatment, he noted unwarranted beatings, forced rectal examinations, and denial of all religious freedom ("Crimes" 12).

Because it serves as a prominent example of prisons during this period, Marion illustrates one of the rhetorical problems that the just deserts argument faces. While the concept of just deserts does not call for the rehabilitation of prisoners, neither does it call for dehumanizing treatment. Overcrowded conditions and the historical mistreatment of prisoners by guards problematize the just deserts philosophy as it is practiced. Just deserts cannot be achieved in practice

sons create an environment in which the pun-
e crime. It is just this point that is being made
against a number of prisons.

constructions of the prisoner that was emergent
ecomes dominant here is that of the legal inmate.
are overcrowding and the resulting inhumane con-
via mass media outlets, but there is a simultaneous
ne representation of the prisoner as someone with le-
s expected to pursue legal action to assure the validity
of ju . Examples of this legal inmate appear throughout the period. For instance, as Jason Newman of Georgetown University reported in *Time,* inmates at the prison complex in Lorton, Virginia, were encouraged to take courses on law in order to "understand the legal system and know it's there to help them, so they can use it and not abuse it" (quoted in "Teaching Law" 57). Further, in a *Newsweek* essay on the causes of prison riots, Aric Press claimed that inmates are now demanding their rights as legal beings: "The inmates themselves appeared different. They were younger, more aggressive, openly rebellious and insistent upon their rights even if it meant creating new ones" ("When Will" 70). In addition, prisoner and author Nick DiSpoldo noted in *America* that prisoners have a responsibility to themselves to learn law. As he argued, the Supreme Court, in *Coffin v. Reichard,* asserted that "the prisoner retains all the rights of an ordinary citizen except those expressly, or by necessary implication, taken from him by law" ("Prisoners" 270).

While prisoners do of course lose some of their cases (for example, their arguments for longer visitation and phone rights at the Marion facility), a range of victories is also represented. For example, *Jet* reported in 1985 that one "jailhouse lawyer" in Chicago was awarded $100,000 in damages and mental anguish after guards took away her property and unjustly beat her ("Court Upholds" 12). Further, a prisoner in Pennsylvania successfully won the right for increased visitation and exercise rights ("Pennsylvania Death" 32). In the Texas Eastham Unit described earlier, the process of removing "building tenders" and providing less oppressive conditions in general was the result of a suit brought by prisoner David Ruiz. Reported in *Newsweek,* Ruiz's lawsuit provides a prominent narrative of the prisoner's ability to pursue legal rights. The narrative begins with Ruiz submitting a writ against the conditions at the prison. When Ruiz initially took the writ to the prison warden, *Newsweek* reported that "the warden said 'I'm going to tell you what I think about inmates' rights. . . . This.' And he tore it in half" (Press, "Inside" 50). However, Ruiz continued to pursue legal action and was eventually able to advance his claims of legal rights for himself and the other inmates of the prison.

Showing both the humanity of the prisoner as well as his knowledge of legal issues is the somewhat humorous story of jailhouse lawyer and prisoner Jerry Rosenberg, an inmate at the Auburn Correctional Facility in upstate New York. While imprisoned on death row, Rosenberg suffered a heart attack, and his doctors pronounced him technically dead. As reported in *People,* after surviving, Rosenberg sued the prison for his release on the grounds that his "technical" death was full payment for the death sentence he had received. When attorney Kenneth Goldman argued for the state that death is irreversible, Rosenberg returned, "If it was irreversible, I wouldn't be here arguing this case" ("Back" 71). In short, the prisoner is able to constitute himself as a legal being with the right to sue for proper treatment.

There exists, then, a growing number of arguments with historical antecedents working together and providing a problematic depiction of prisoners and punishment. To generalize: The concept of just deserts as a philosophy of punishment, as originally constituted, has a resulting material outcome of overcrowded prisons. These overcrowded conditions are in turn constructed as the major cause of violence and prisoner abuse among all male prisoners, regardless of race. The violence and mistreatment then encourage the representation of the male prisoner as a legal being with the right to argue that just deserts cannot be achieved in overcrowded prisons. For example, from Ohio's Lucasville Prison, prisoners Kelly Chapman and Richard Jaworski sued the prison for "one man, one cell" rights. As a report in *Business Week* noted in 1981, the large number of legal cases being initiated by prisoners led not only to the building of new facilities but also to the development of alternatives to incarceration ("New Jails" 80).

It is in the development of alternatives to incarceration that the historical force of rhetoric proves problematic in numerous ways. As I illustrate below, the representations of prisoners developed historically and traced out here in previous chapters not only constrain how alternatives to punishment and discipline in general are put into practice but also create a rhetorical scenario in which "criminal" and "citizen" alike are encouraged to view the disciplinary procedures of the state as worthy of both praise and imitation. In effect, the complex mix of various representations of prisoners and punishment not only shapes how prisoners are represented as being disciplined along lines of race and gender but also leads to a situation in which "redeemable" prisoners represent their redemption as a matter of choice and encourage the culture at large to imitate that choice, to practice the morality endorsed by the dominant cultural ideology.

The Rhetorical Constraints of Arguments by Race: The Black Inmate

While the concept of just deserts was developing as a dominant cultural philosophy, the pull of the past dictated the parameters of how the practice of just deserts would be represented. That is, just as the gradual growth in the representation of the "legal" inmate both magnifies the impression that overcrowding is the root of many problems and assures that the prisoner could be seen as relatively autonomous, and just as overcrowding provides the impetus for the development of new forms of punishment, the historical representation of prisoners along the lines of race and gender in the last two eras influences how the practice of just deserts will be articulated in the present and future. The historical constructions of the prisoner from the past will not relinquish their hold on the present easily, and as a result prisoners are represented as receiving different punishments according to the characteristics that are tied to both the prisoner's race or gender and the demands of the particular form of punishment.

Hence, because alternative systems of punishment, such as electronic monitoring or work release, require specific personality traits (for example, trustworthiness, rationality), Caucasian male inmates (and as we shall see) female inmates in general are more easily articulated as likely participants in such programs. That is, because Caucasian males have traditionally been represented as trustworthy and redeemable, their representations more easily fit discussions of alternatives to incarceration. Even though they have been represented along with African Americans as violent in this era, their violence is not part of their nature historically; indeed, their violence now stems from prison overcrowding. In the absence of overcrowding, the historical representation of Caucasian males articulates them as behaving in a potentially redeemable manner, while that of the African-American male and other "raced" inmates articulates them as violent and irrational regardless of conditions. Society is prefigured to believe in the possibility of the white prisoner's rehabilitation. As a result, African-American and other "raced" inmates are less likely to be *represented* as chosen for alternative forms of punishment, regardless of the actual numbers.

Before investigating the public representations of the ethnic make-up of prisoners of this era and of how those prisoners are treated, it may prove useful to look at the numerical composition of the prison. In 1975, 64 percent of state and federal male inmates were white and 36 percent were of other ethnic backgrounds (Langan 5). By 1985, the ratio was closer to fifty-fifty (Langan 5). However, the representations of the prisoner's ethnicity differ from the statistical ratios. Here, throughout the period, the dominant representation of prisoners in general is that they are African-American and then that they are irredeemable.

In the midst of a *Time*-sponsored discussion of the Bernard Goetz case with inmates at Virginia's Lorton Prison, the following observations concerning the demographics of the Lorton prisoners were made: "At no time are more than five of the approximately 1,200 inmates whites"; "They are from the slums of southeast Washington and were convicted mostly of murder and robbery" ("Views" 23). Elsewhere, the Lorton Prison is described as holding men, women, and youth who "are black, uneducated, and from the poorest sections of Washington" (G. Anderson, "D. C. Jail," 353). Likewise, in a 1986 *Sporting Magazine* discussion of the sports played in prisons, it was reported that the inmates at the Green Haven Correctional Facility in New York are 95 percent black and Hispanic and basically live to play basketball (Rosen 30). Such claims are not isolated: The *New York Times Magazine* remarked that "blacks are being placed in prison at a rate that is about nine times greater than whites" (Lieber 28); *Newsweek* noted that the majority of condemned prisoners are black (Footlick, Boyd, and Camp 105); prisoners in both Graterford, Pennsylvania, and the Clinton Correctional Facility in Dannemora, New York, were reported in *Sports Illustrated* to be primarily black and Puerto Rican (Telander 108); and *Newsweek* also claimed that prisoners at Mississippi's State Penitentiary at Parchman are primarily black (Boyd and Minor 105).

Although I do not wish to ignore the simultaneous and fairly widespread critique of racism within prisons, I do wish to note that such critiques inadvertently reinforce the notion that a majority of crimes are committed by people of color. A rather celebrated case that occurs in this period, referred to in one of the epigraphs that begin this chapter, involves the transfer of black prisoner Vinson Harris from Talladega, Alabama, to Butner, North Carolina. While the specific narrative varies in its telling, the basic plot lines are consistent. Along with several other prisoners who were being moved from one prison facility to another, Harris was placed in the back of a van with two guards, both white. At times, Harris is said to have spoken with disrespect to guard Gerry Dale. Tiring of Harris, Dale reportedly turned to him and said, "This is Alabama, nigger, and we're going to teach you to keep your mouth shut" ("Justice Department"). Dale proceeded to wrap Harris's head with an ace bandage, taping it down with duct tape. Because the duct tape was put on tightly, Harris was unable to breathe and died of asphyxiation before the van's arrival at the Butner facility (see "Justice Department"; Bunker, "Lynching"; Carroll). The first of the two quotations at the beginning of the chapter represents the other prisoners' reaction to Harris's death and highlights the prevalent notion that black felons are more inured to violence than are whites. Further, because the van was described as being filled with black prisoners who had learned in the ghetto that "power makes right," the reification of blacks as prisoners is also implied (Bunker, "Lynching" 699).

Other articles provide clearer clues that recognition of racism in disciplinary institutions is significant throughout the period. For example, in a 1976 *Nation* discussion of the possibility of a new Attica uprising, several of Attica's guards were rumored to be Ku Klux Klan officials, and a corrections officer at the predominantly black Eastern State Correctional Facility was reputed to be the grand dragon of the KKK of New York State (Christianson 586). Moreover, the death penalty is consistently pointed to as a racist prison policy in action because African Americans are more likely than whites to receive a death sentence when convicted of murder ("Black Men"; Kenney; Johnson; "New York Gov."; Pawelek; Smolowe, "Race"). A number of other reports also point to the ratio of white guards to black prisoners and to the existence of racist groups within the prison.[5] Again, while these essays point to a problem with racism in prisons, they also rearticulate the prisoner as primarily black, and these representations also illustrate the idea that, rather than waiting for the wheels of justice to turn, blacks, raised in a racist culture, turn to violence to voice their concerns. Witness the following observation made in *The New Republic:* "As almost everyone positioned between the far right and the far left by now understands, the huge disproportion of black convicts is a product not of a deeply flawed criminal justice system but of a deeply rooted social pathology. It is a pathology spawned by centuries of slavery, a subsequent century of officially sanctioned discrimination, further decades of residual bias and even some well meaning but misguided paternalism" ("One in Four" 6). Even here, although the causes of black criminality can be tied to long-standing social and institutional racism, the prisoner remains black.

Other examples only serve to stress this point. In an *Esquire* essay on the life of former Black Panther and George Jackson confidante Johnny Spain, author Chip Brown observed that Spain was first imprisoned when, after many encounters with racism, he committed a murder. After befriending Jackson and joining the Black Panthers, Spain was accused of aiding in Jackson's escape attempt and of murdering several guards. However, after Spain began to make contact with his natural mother, a white woman who gave him up for adoption after being ostracized by her Jackson, Mississippi, community, Spain repented of his actions in prison and removed himself from radical black politics (Chip Brown). Changed in constitution from black to white, Spain becomes redeemable, less radical, more rational.

Finally, in *Attica,* the film reproduction of the infamous uprising at that prison, the riot's roots are clearly shown to lie in the prisoners' collective grief and subsequent protest over the death of George Jackson. Even though there is racial solidarity during the riot, it is based on a reaction to racism and begins when an African-American inmate shoves a Caucasian guard. In each case, violence and irrationality are linked to race. Even when the prisoner is reacting to racism, violence must be dealt with through just deserts. That is, even "noble" violence is violence in the case of the African American; white racism does not excuse it.

While the representation of the violent and irrational inmate of color often occurs simply because most prisoners are depicted simultaneously as minorities and as violent, it is also the case that African-American and Hispanic inmates are depicted as naturally violent, regardless of prison facility inadequacies. The utilization of Willie Horton as a national symbol of the violent black inmate during George Bush's 1988 presidential campaign is exemplary of this type of discourse. Horton's violence is not seen to be the result of overcrowding; rather, it is because Horton was released on furlough before he had paid his just deserts that he behaved violently. When Massachusetts representative Larry Giordano noted that "people in our society are saying, 'We don't want people like Horton out on the street,' " he was representing prisoners such as Horton as violent and black, and arguing that such prisoners must be imprisoned in order to provide just deserts; alternatives to incarceration are unacceptable (quoted in Starr 63).

The joint articulation of African-American inmates and rape continues to flourish throughout this period. In Tom Cahill's 1985 essay on rape in prison, he provided the narrative, mentioned above, of Stephen Donaldson, a Quaker activist then teaching Indian Buddhism at Columbia University. Donaldson was arrested during a "pray-in" at the White House and, refusing to post ten dollars bond on the grounds that bail discriminates against the poor, he was imprisoned. After two nights in prison, he ended up torn and bleeding in a hospital after his fellow inmates raped him sixty times in two days. Donaldson claimed that the wing he was placed in had 200 prisoners, 199 of whom were black (Cahill 32–33). In an ironic fashion, then, while attempting to provide a critique of the problems with the prison system, Cahill's account of Donaldson's rape serves to reify the links between race and rape.

In another example, Winston E. Moore, executive director of the Cook County Department of Corrections, provided the narrative of a rape in his prison. He noted that one white and four black inmates raped an eighteen-year-old prisoner on that prisoner's entry into the prison ("How to" 83). Clifford Irving's narrative of his prison stay mentions both homosexuality and rape and both references are made in regard to black prisoners. His roommate was "Geraldine," a transsexual and homosexual black man who dressed as a woman each night and sought out sexual partners (170). Irving shared the following entry from his prison journal: "Christmas Day: A rape this morning, about 2 a.m. A new kid arrived last week and some black dudes have been propositioning him. The kid complained to a hack but wouldn't name names so this morning they dragged him outside the dorm, stuffed a yellow towel in his mouth and raped him" (170–72). Two popular books published in the 1990s on prisons, *Life Sentences* (Rideau and Wikberg 92–93) and *The Hot House* (Earley) address the rape of white prisoners by blacks or represent black prisoners as rapists in general. In *The Hot House,* prisoner Carl Bowles, who is attempting to help out a new inmate at Leavenworth, notes, "Oh, we got to protect this poor kid! Why, he's white and he doesn't want anything to do with the niggers and he is afraid they are going to take him and fuck him" (3). In a discussion of gangs at Leavenworth, Earley notes that "DC Blacks" make up 10 percent of the prisoner population and that they "were especially notorious as locker-knockers—petty thieves who ransacked the personal lockers of other inmates—and for pressuring new inmates for sex" (91). Additionally, Bernard Farbar related a tale of his prison tenure in *Esquire* in which he heard a black inmate threaten another prisoner, "Your shit on my dick or your blood on my blade" (149–50).

I refer to these narratives not to indicate that rape is never discussed outside of the specific depiction of a black prisoner committing the rape. However, during the entire period of this study, the white male prisoner is never specifically mentioned in the "popular essays" as a rapist or homosexual outside of Moore's observation above that one white inmate joined four black ones in the rape of a new prisoner. While rape is mentioned repeatedly in essays about the prisoner, the racial identity of the rapist is black, if it is mentioned at all. As a result, when race is not mentioned, the only guide readers have to discern the race of the rapist are other essays that have depicted him as black.[6] Again, homosexuality is not the focus; rape and violence are.

Other examples only serve to reify this point. I point to Winston Moore who, after depicting the rapist as a black male, claimed that prisoners rape because they "equate violence with sexuality" (Moore, "How to" 84). Furthermore, after his tenure in prison, G. Gordon Liddy attempted to explain why blacks and whites take different attitudes toward homosexuality in prison: "Within the homosexual class, there exists among blacks a further distinction: generally speaking, blacks do not condemn one of their race who takes the male part in a homosexual relationship. Among whites, however, the rule is: 'Don't make no difference which end of the dick you're on—You're still a faggot' " ("Serving Time" 222). The black prisoner, according to Liddy, is able to maintain his male identity if he is a rapist and does not engage in any "true" homosexual behavior, while the white inmate can take no part in homosexual behavior if he wishes to maintain his identity as a heterosexual male. Liddy's argument implies that the white prisoner would see rape as the practice of a homosexual act while the black inmate sees rape as an act of violence and not as an affront to his sexuality.

In a general sense, male African-American prisoners (and, to a degree, other nonwhite male prisoners) are constrained by their past representations. Although arguments for just deserts may suggest that punishment should be based on what is due for the particular crime and on that alone, overcrowded prisons and the development of alternative punishments combine with the historical and rhetorical construction of the black inmate as dangerous and violent to suggest that he is unqualified to take part in alternative programs. There are, then, hints of a clash of ideological arguments, a clash brought on by changing material conditions. While theories of discipline bound by the philosophy of just deserts represent the prisoner as homogeneous and hence treated similarly, the rhetorical configuration of inmates on the grounds of race leads to just deserts being represented differently for different inmates. The African-American male will more often than not be represented as imprisoned while the Caucasian will be allowed other forms of discipline, again, at least in representation.

The representations suggest problematic positions for both: the African-American male prisoner, while represented as violent and irrational, is consequently rarely depicted as bowing to the dominant order and hence is better positioned to critique that order. On the other hand, the white male criminal (and, as I will argue, the female criminal), framed as "on the whole" redeemable and trustworthy, is positioned as fit for alternatives to incarceration, but only at the cost of a loss in relative autonomy: this prisoner is represented as bowing to the dominant cultural ideology, the cultural sense of right and wrong, existence and nonexistence; this representation encourages others to do the same.

White Prisoners and the Redeemable Persona: The Move to Alternatives

As I noted above, one of the dominant articulations of this period ties together the overcrowded condition of prisons with violent behavior by all inmates, including Caucasian males. However, when historical meanings are part of the overall representation, as indeed they must be, the overall configuration changes. That is, while overcrowding is shown as encouraging all prisoners to behave violently, for African Americans this is only an extension of the behavior they have always been represented as enacting. For male Caucasians, overcrowding is represented as acting to encourage them to behave in ways that run counter to their "natural behavior." In addition to this logic, however, Caucasian males are also represented throughout the period as redeemable. While it would be absurd to claim that all redeemable male prisoners are represented as white or that all white prisoners are represented as redeemable, it is the case that given that 50 percent of prisoners are white, there is an unusually high positive correlation between Caucasian males and their positioning as redeemable. This relationship is articulated either because the examples of redeemable inmates are specifically identified as being Caucasian males (or females in general) or because the pictorial representations of prisoners accompanying articles concerning redemption are of Caucasian males (or females in general, as I will discuss below).

In general, however, discussions of rehabilitation are rare throughout the period when compared to representations of the prisoner as violent. Furthermore, representations of redeemable black males occur even less frequently. The few African Americans (and the number is indeed small) who do accompany discussions of prison rehabilitation are either pointed to overtly as rare cases, or are marginalized as a simple result of being surrounded by the large number of articles that represent potential for rehabilitation as an attribute of white males and violence as an attribute of blacks.

Interestingly, the literature on potentially redeemable inmates remains fairly consistently tied to Caucasian males despite the overall theme of just deserts. The major difference in the meaning of rehabilitation in this period is that, due to the demands of just deserts, rehabilitation programs are illustrated as a matter of choice for the individual rather than as a requirement. In effect, because a policy of just deserts forces the inmate to choose rehabilitation rather than to undergo it as a condition of release, those prisoners who are rehabilitated are represented as more self-made than they had been in the past. Narratives concerning rehabilitation become human interest stories that characterize the prisoner as an individual who has overcome great obstacles in an attempt to improve himself. When rehabilitation is framed as an option, each time a prisoner chooses to rehabilitate him- or herself, he or she appears to be choosing a contingent lifestyle as the best possible lifestyle.

Below, I focus specifically on this era's narratives of rehabilitation. My focus is on both depictions of individual Caucasian men who are self-rehabilitated and on discussions of rehabilitation that provide photographs only of Caucasian males as evidence that rehabilitation programs are successful. When an essay describing prisoner redemption is accompanied by a photo of a Caucasian male, the reader is left with little to assume except that such prisoners are redeemable. This is especially true when the claim is accompanied by a lack of photographs of prisoners of other ethnicities.

The evidence of such representations is diverse and widespread. The articulation of the redeemable white male is often more direct than the implied relationship between story and picture. For example, it is during this era that Eddie Bunker began to receive a great deal of attention for his attempts to win parole from Terminal Island. Having served most of his sentence, Bunker had also written numerous articles for national publications and had two novels published by major presses. In an open letter in *The Nation* in 1976, Bunker wrote to U.S. Bureau of Prisons director Norman Carlson, citing a number of achievements and suggesting that these achievements served as illustrations of his fully rehabilitated state. In fact, Bunker argued, if immediately released, he would be able to be employed, first, to serve as an assistant to Dustin Hoffman on a movie being made from his first book and second, to go on a publicity tour for his second book. Being released from prison would provide Bunker with a better chance at redeeming himself than would remaining imprisoned. His prison tenure, he claimed, had already been long enough to provide just deserts; more time in prison would only affect his person negatively ("Open" 657).

Similarly, Dannie Martin of Lompoc Prison, another prisoner who wrote numerous articles for national publications, was moved from one prison to another because, he claimed, prison officials wanted to silence his critique of prison conditions (Zuckerman 66). Martin claimed a willingness to serve his time in prison but wished to have the freedom to choose his personal activities, such as writing, in order to hasten his self-rehabilitation. In effect, he too holds fast to the theme of just deserts while simultaneously suggesting that he be left to make his own choices, to design his own transformation. Furthermore, Martin observed that the public's understanding of the prisoner is misguided and makes "a careful distinction between the kind of sociopath who fits the stereotypical vision of convicts—of which he says you won't find more than twenty or thirty out of a thousand prisoners—and prisoners like himself, 'human beings, people with feelings' " (quoted in DiLeo 81). Not only is Martin redeemable and white, then, but he wants to be seen not as an aberration but as representing the true nature of the convict.

In another example, a *Family Health* article titled "The Good/Hood Samaritan" featured Bill Wallace, a former prisoner who served a six-year sentence for armed robbery. Wallace was described as having a troubled family background, with little promise or chance for a successful life. Upon release from prison, however, Wallace was hired by a Boston dairy firm for the sole purpose of driving up and down the streets of Boston with enough all-purpose tools to help anyone in distress. In an interview, Wallace pointed out that he had paid his "just due" by serving his full sentence in prison and was now ready for a career helping others (Russell and Nevard 38). Not only, then, has Wallace received his just deserts, but he has been able to rehabilitate himself despite the hindrance of a family background that was not conducive to success. While the focus on a troubled background or family life often suggests the inability for redemption in the case of African-American inmates, here it represents the heroic struggle of the Caucasian prisoner against his own background.

The theme of rehabilitation is similarly tied to the ability of prisoners to take advantage of educational opportunities while imprisoned. For example, Hank Mosiello, convicted for first degree murder and imprisoned in Trenton, New Jersey, was described in *Time* as a person who, while continuing to claim his innocence, had the wherewithal to earn both B.S. and M.S. degrees from Columbia, take correspondence courses in law, and begin a paralegal service while in prison. Moreover, Mosiello was said to have brought together a number of other jailhouse lawyers to create a service providing legal aid to all prisoners and to have created outreach by being interviewed on local radio stations ("Beating" 75).

In another case, Attica inmate Jerry Rosenberg was described in *People* as a jailhouse lawyer with a degree from Chicago's Blackstone College and coursework in criminal justice from Boston College. Lawyer William Kunstler observed that "Jerry has a quick, alert, shrewd mind, and he can talk to his clients in terms no one else would understand" (quoted in McCall 88). Similarly, Nick DiSpoldo wrote in *America* that prisoners have the ability to learn the law and should do so in order to understand both their responsibility for past behaviors and ways to operate within legal limits upon their release from prison. While at first it may take the novice jailhouse lawyer weeks to read a few pages of legalese, he noted, they are intelligent enough to catch on quickly ("Prisoners" 271).

Finally, *People* also provided the narrative of Hank Arsenault, a former death row inmate at the Massachusetts State Prison who, after receiving a reprieve of his sentence, took an interest in psychology. In 1978, he was eleven credits shy of a Ph.D. in child psychology and was working by lecturing to over 130,000 young people a year about drug use (Jennes 55–56). In each of the essays dealing with education, then, prisoners are characterized as able to accept blame for their crimes and to rise above their guilt, to become self-educated, to help others, and to benefit society.

In addition to indicating the acceptance of guilt by white male prisoners, stories of their backgrounds often indicate that their move to a "straight life" is *restorative rather than transitory.* Rehabilitation returns them to their natural state rather than to something new. Hence, David Herman described himself as a former circuit tennis player who had shown potential on the junior circuit. Having been raised in an affluent family, Herman was "popular at parties, received complimentary tickets to the U.S. Open, and generally enjoyed the life of a tennis brat" (Coan 20). However, as part of that life, Herman developed a drug habit that required him to use and sell drugs in order to pay for his habit. Caught and imprisoned, Herman recognized the pitfalls of his past and established a tennis club in prison in order to help keep other inmates occupied and in better physical shape. His playing ability even provided a morale booster to the other inmates when, during his imprisonment, prison administrators invited a tennis pro to play him. When Herman won the match, the morale of the inmates rose significantly.

In another narrative concerning talented inmates in *People,* a group of prisoners at the Maryland Correctional Institution in Norfolk, Maryland, who wrote and then performed a play reenacting the Watergate tapes was featured. The picture accompanying the article illustrated that the group was entirely Caucasian. Led by former actor Mark Frechette, the group was described as "professional" in their performance. Inmate John Walsh, who played John Ehrlichman in the production, noted, "Frechette is unreal. With all the other things you have to think about in prison, it was amazing how Mark got us into our parts" ("In Prison" 23).

In both of the aforementioned narratives, white inmates reveal their potential to become self-redeemed by their participation in what have traditionally been seen as respectable enterprises: Herman in the traditionally upper-middle-class and upper-class sport of tennis and Frechette in the relatively respectable world of the stage. Herman and Frechette originate from these backgrounds and avocations, fall into a criminal lifestyle, and are subsequently able to rehabilitate themselves by returning to their respective backgrounds.

In a perhaps more obvious example of the redemptive potential of Caucasian males, *People* describes the patients of Emilee "Auntie Em" Wilson, a psychiatrist who treats convicted rapists at the medical facility at the California Prison at Vacaville. The prisoners in this program, at least the ones pictured in the article, were white and were all convicted rapists. While this is a rare example of white prisoners being presented prominently as guilty of a crime such as rape, almost all of them were said to have been rehabilitated by Wilson as a result of enrollment in this voluntary program. Indeed, Wilson noted that only one of the one hundred rapists she had treated has been reconvicted of rape. One of her patients affirmed, "I've been fighting a private war with women. If I had had someone like doc when I was younger, maybe it would have been different" (quoted in Junger 62). While prison rapists are often represented as African-American, here we find Caucasian inmates who, while guilty of heterosexual rape, are able to take advantage of voluntary prison programs in order to rehabilitate themselves.

The textual linkage between white males and the redeemable persona is so widespread as to be seemingly inescapable. For instance, numerous representations reveal the white male prisoner as exhibiting normal human emotions and actions, behaving in ways any human being would. These observations are noteworthy in that they appear to be limited to white prisoners. Hence, in 1981, *People* provided the narrative of Tommy Trantino, a prisoner serving a sentence for the murder of a police officer. During his trial, Trantino became friends with his lawyer's wife. After developing a close friendship, the two fell in love and made plans to wed during one of his furloughs (Bricker). The story is interesting in that it focuses on the "normal" emotions exhibited by Trantino. In another article linking white males with the potential for rehabilitation, author Peter Carlson recounted in *The Nation* a visit with his arguably innocent friend John Kerrigan on death row. Carlson claimed that Kerrigan "is more than a symbol of a horrible institution. He is a human being" (774); he described Kerrigan as looking "like a tired grandfather" and "a monk" with a friendly and caring disposition (775).

Finally, *Psychology Today* provided a study of the case of Gary Gilmore that highlighted Gilmore's "human" emotions. After Gilmore refused to appeal his death sentence and hence became the object of national news, he received a large volume of mail from individuals throughout the nation. In reporting the results of a study of these letters, author Toni Gerber noted that Gilmore answered several of the letters, claiming that they gave his life "significance in the face of death" (33). Further, the 1982 film detailing the Gilmore case, *The Executioner's Song,* provides the same complex portrait of Gilmore. While he is clearly represented as violent and irrational, he is also depicted as possessing human emotions, with a love for his girlfriend that transcends his actions. In each case, a Caucasian male is provided with a humanity that is generally denied black prisoners and other prisoners of color. In the overall representation of the prisoner, such differences accumulate and have wide-ranging implications.

The linkage between redemption and the Caucasian male is also made on the basis of the close proximity of narratives, illustrations, and photographs. Often narratives of redemptive criminals are accompanied by photos of prisoners who are not necessarily described in the narrative. However, the placement of the picture alongside the narrative links the characteristics of each, including racial characteristics, together.[7] When narratives of redemption are articulated with pictures of prisoners, the link is almost exclusively with Caucasian males.

For instance, in *US News and World Report,* former prisoner Bruce Cape provided a narrative of his imprisonment and self-redemption. Cape explained that he made multiple trips into and out of the "circle of prison" before deciding on his own to remove himself from the criminal lifestyle by attending computer programming courses, acquiring a programming job upon his release, and launching a successful career. Cape ended his essay with a message for other prisoners: "My message is always the same: I made it. So can you" (Cape 46). While no mention is made of his ethnicity, the article is accompanied by a single drawing that leaves little question as to his ethnicity; the drawing is of a white male walking away from a prison, his face looking outward, as if toward a more promising future. The words describing the prisoner do not signify ethnicity but are accompanied by drawings that do. Without the drawing, Cape is a redeemable prisoner; with the drawing, he is a redeemable white prisoner.

Similar cases are widespread. For example, when articles on religious worship in prison (Cowley 84) or on prisoners who are responsible enough to hold down jobs while they are imprisoned ("Jobs") are accompanied by pictures of exclusively or almost exclusively white prisoners, an association concerning the constitution of the redeemable prisoner is being made. In an essay that predicts the direction of electronic surveillance as a means of rehabilitation, three drawings are used to illustrate three different levels of electronic surveillance.

Each picture is of a Caucasian, trustworthy enough to be placed under such surveillance (Winkler 34–37). Such a link holds true even when the written message ignores the issue of race. In such cases, pictures and words work interdependently to form an image of the white male prisoner even when the text itself argues for the equality called for by just deserts. This argument is strengthened by the fact that the majority of irredeemable prisoners are depicted as black. If most prisoners are black, and white prisoners are pictorially featured in an article about rehabilitation, the link between race and potential for rehabilitation is strengthened.

In another example, a pictorial "essay" on the 130 people on death row in Texas's Ellis Unit in 1979, the notation under a picture of inmate Doyle Boulware claims that he taught himself German, translated books in his cell, and built his own postage scale while imprisoned. In this same set of essays is a touching tale of inmate Billy McMahon and his family, a unit that has continued to work as a "loving family" despite McMahon's imprisonment. With each narrative, the only two Caucasians in the essay are represented in a redeemable and human fashion (Jackson and Christian 55–57). Again, while the pictures are not specifically labeled in either essay, their being positioned next to the text leads the reader to assume a link between words and picture, between text and simulacrum.

In a similar fashion, San Quentin prisoner Richard Rigwood, who learned to grind lenses for eyeglasses while in prison, said in *Scholastic Update* that "it's the first time I've had a good trade I could make a living at" (quoted in Cohen 10). Here again, the picture above the quotation is of a white prisoner working, presumably grinding lenses. Furthermore, a 1987 *US News and World Report* essay featured a number of successful voluntary rehabilitation programs, including the use of New York prisoners to answer licensing questions over the phone, Iowa inmates to do telemarketing, and Virginia inmates to take part in various reading programs. Each of the pictures accompanying these essays indicates that the vast majority of inmates taking part in the various programs are white (Gest, "Teaching"). Similarly, in a discussion of the Texas prison system's use of the Birkman exam, a battery of psychological tests that matches prisoners with jobs, a picture of a white prisoner is accompanied by a description of a thirty-one-year-old inmate who works in a machine operator's capacity. The prisoner's supervisor notes that the inmate "is the most dependable worker in the department" ("Matching" 106). Again, in each case, words and images effectively combine to create an overall image of the redeemable white male and, by negation, to reinforce the image of the savage, untrustworthy, and irredeemable minority.

Thus far, then, despite the philosophical move to, and public justification of, a supposedly unbiased system of just deserts punishment, the historical and rhetorical strength of the different representations of the prisoner that emerged historically continues to maintain rhetorical influence in the present. In particular, there is the reified depiction of the white male prisoner as redeemable and his crimes somewhat justifiable, while minority inmates, primarily African-American inmates, continue to be held by the "bricks and mortar" of their earlier depiction as violent and irredeemable. The implications for how each inmate is represented are perhaps obvious. Regardless of how individual African Americans attempt to justify their crimes in public, the cultural definition encourages that African-Americans be represented as imprisoned in the pursuit of just deserts. Past representations of violence and trustworthiness are the determining factors in how just deserts will be incurred in present representations.

In sum, while just deserts would prescribe that all prisoners be disciplined in ways equivalent to their crime, rhetorical and historical forces make the mix far more complex. These representations include different standard depictions and possibilities not only by race but also, as I will illustrate, by gender. Material constraints and changes conspire with rhetorical constructions to make modifications in just deserts policies necessary. Material changes, such as overcrowded prisons, the War on Drugs, and the resulting creation of alternatives to punishment, all work together in changing this definition of just deserts and in influencing the treatment of prisoners. Because alternatives to incarceration often require some degree of trustworthiness, nonwhite male inmates are to a degree rhetorically and publicly disqualified from these programs while white male inmates are almost universally qualified.

Following an analysis of the representation of the female inmate, I will turn to an analysis of the rise of alternatives to incarceration and will argue that, because of the stress on just deserts, all prisoners, indeed all members of our culture, are placed in a perilous situation with regard to public discipline.

Mother and Moral Guidepost: Constraints by Gender

As the third of the quotations that begin this chapter indicates, the female inmate of the 1976–1992 era is "always already" depicted as on the way to redemption. Indeed, her corruption and crime are encouraged by external sources; as in the past, prison provides the opportunity for the female inmate to rediscover her essence as a moral being. Indeed, alternatives to incarceration appear natural in the case of female prisoners as such alternatives allow them to return to their natural condition: to be reunited with their children, to teach cultural morals to the next generation. While I wish to note again that alternatives to this representation of female prisoners do exist, the description here delineates what is clearly the most common representation. In turn, I will discuss three aspects of this dominant representation: the roots of female crime, the female inmate's positioning as mother, and the female inmate's ultimately redeemable nature.

As in past representations, prior abuse of the female inmate is highlighted as the root of her criminal behavior. While it may in fact be the case that all (sexually, emotionally, or economically) abused children are more likely to commit crimes later in life, in the case of women, this route is almost universally stressed in public narratives. Women's crimes indeed become partially justified in that they arise as the result of external forces. For example, in a *Children Today* essay entitled "Moms in Jail" that focuses on a parenting class taught in the Nassau County (New York) Correctional Facility, authors Alane Fagin and Arlene Reid noted that "there is a wide body of empirical evidence that strongly suggests the relationship between child abuse and other social problems. . . . These women reveal similar experiences: abuse, abandonment, domestic violence, destructive adult relationships, teen pregnancy, and an incomplete education" (13). Similarly, *America*'s George Anderson claimed that many women become criminals as a result of their having been abused as children ("Criminal" 341).

This representation is evident in descriptions of individual female inmates as well as female inmates in general. Hence, a *People* essay on Terry Jean Moore's legal battle to allow her to keep her infant daughter with her in prison reported that Moore's life of crime had its roots in the fact that "her parents were separated when she was an infant, forcing Terry to spend her first seven years in and out of foster homes" (Hinson 64). A *Nation* essay on the sexual abuse of women in prison observed that Carol Ann Wilds, a prisoner suing the Indiana Women's Prison on the grounds that she was abused by guards, was sexually abused by her step-grandfather and then forced to be a prostitute by her husband. These abuses are pointed to not only as leading to her criminal lifestyle but also as making her vulnerable to the numerous sexual advances of prison guards (Jones 456–57). In the *New York Times Magazine*, Jean Harris points out that the parenting classes taught at the Bedford Hills Correctional Facility serve the purpose of keeping mothers from abusing their children in the same way that they were abused: "It is far easier to teach the new mother than the one with seven children who has long since fallen into the customs of her own childhood—frequent smacks to the head and shouted expletives. Allison is deaf in one ear and partly deaf in the other from smacks to her head by her alcoholic mother. But who is taking care of her two children while Allison is in prison? Her mother" ("Babies" 26).

In the general depiction of the female criminal, her abuse as a child only acts as a prerequisite for criminal behavior. The behavior itself is generally shown as being triggered by difficult economic circumstances that lead women to commit crimes in support of their families or to find a release from domestic stress through the use of drugs. Thus, even in crime, the women's behavior appears either somewhat heroic or somewhat justifiable. For example, in *Scholastic Update,* Maura Christopher attempted to explain why women commit crimes and noted that "more women are single heads of households. They have kids and they need money. A large number of these single mothers are uneducated and unskilled, so more of them are committing crimes to support their families. . . . Statistics back up this theory" (8). Similarly, Jean Harris, convicted murderer of the "Scarsdale Diet Doctor," stated in her *McCall's* article "Life in Prison" that female crime has an economic base: "If you were to think of an average female inmate in America's prisons today, she would be about 27 years old . . . and the mother of two children, of whom she is the sole support" (73). Hence, not only do external conditions move females away from a naturally moral lifestyle, but their crimes are often committed only in support of their own families.

If not committed in order to aid their families, their crime is often that of drug abuse; addiction is depicted as accompanying the stress of attempting to raise a family on a poverty-level income. Hence, Jean Harris also noted that many women turn to drugs and alcohol when they find themselves single heads of households and are frightened by the responsibility this position brings ("Life" 73). Similar linkages between parenting and drug and alcohol abuse appear in sources as divergent as *Ms.* (Kort), *America* (Kelly), *Children Today* (Fagin and Reid), and the *Progressive* (Huie).

Tied closely with this representation of crimes as being related to the attempts of women to deal with raising a family is the more general representation of female prisoners as mothers. Not only, then, are women shown to commit somewhat justifiable crimes as a result of their backgrounds and economic hardships, but their primary function as human beings is framed with regard to their perceived role as the perpetuators of the human species. While many of the male prisoners are also parents, any discussion of their progeny and of how their progeny deal with having an imprisoned parent is for the most part negligible. With female inmates, on the other hand, motherhood is clearly a key articulation. Even a cursory survey of essay titles reveals this concern: "Jailhouse Mothering" (Slade), "Kids of Women Prisoners Must Bear Emotional Scars," "Pregnant in Prison" (Stein and Mistiaen), "Moms in Jail" (Fagin and Reid), "Serving Time, Family Style" (Paumier), and "My Baby Was Born in Prison" (Freeman).

Discussions of imprisoned mothers work on both general and specific levels. General discussions of imprisoned mothers simply note the magnitude of the problem; in the specific cases, we find female inmates fighting for the right to remain with their children, to help raise them as normal human beings who will not gravitate toward a life of crime. On a general level, then, notation is often made of the large number of mothers imprisoned. *Psychology Today* reported in 1978 that "about 12,000 mothers are currently imprisoned in federal, state, and local facilities in the United States" (Slade 35). *The Progressive* noted in 1988 that three to four thousand women in prison at any given point are pregnant (Stein and Mistiaen 18). In addition, *US News and World Report* pointed out that the total number of children left behind when women are imprisoned is close to 54,000 (Creighton 22), and Jean Harris observed that "on the average, between 70–80% of the inmates in a women's prison are mothers" (Harris, "Life" 74–75).

Imprisoned, then, women are constituted more as mothers than as criminals, more as human beings than criminals. As an anonymous writer for *US News and World Report* asserted, "By and large, they don't adhere to the convicts' code. Women are human beings first, only secondarily are they in prison, in their own eyes. Men see themselves as convicts first and men second" ("What Life" 79). Indeed, prison sentences raise cultural problems for women to the degree that the general articulation of femininity is tied to mothering; imprisonment forcibly separates mothers from children. It is in this sense that imprisonment is represented as more difficult for women than men: "While women convicts generally face fewer physical hardships and less violence than men, experts agree that separation from children and family is harder on female prisoners" ("What Life" 79).

The widely reported case of prisoner Terry Jean Moore illustrates the way individual cases of prison mothers represent the influence of motherhood in changing the female prisoner, in reminding her of her values. Convicted for armed robbery and given a seven-and-a-half-year sentence at the Florida Correctional Institute at Lowell, Moore became pregnant in prison after sexual involvement with a prison guard who was later dismissed from his duties. While observers note that Moore had a very troubled life until her imprisonment, the stress in each representation is on how giving birth to a child and fighting to keep the child in prison changed Moore's life. In effect, having a child allowed Moore to understand "moral" behavior. As she herself claimed, "When I held my child in my arms and nursed her, I think for the first time, I really grew up. I've made a lot of mistakes. I know I shouldn't have taken the money, I know I shouldn't have got pregnant without being married first, but now that my baby is here, I'm going to be a good mother. Up to now, I've just had myself to take care of. But now I have this helpless baby, and that makes a difference" (Freeman 130). Indeed, Moore noted in *People* that having a child provided her with a stronger spiritual dimension, that "God will guide me through these doors" (Hinson 63).

With Moore as a representative, we find the female inmate moralized by motherhood. Not only, then, can the crimes committed by women be traced back to their abuse at the hands of others and the responsibilities that accompany parenthood, but simply having a family constitutes women as moral exemplars, providing them with a need and route for redemption. As inmates Yvonne Acevedo and Dorothy Polan of the Bedford Hills State Prison in New York stated in *US News and World Report:* "We're not breeding criminals here. We breed love. It's kids that grew up like me who are the criminals" (quoted in Creighton 23). Indeed, in the third and final aspect of this representation, female prisoners are shown to have the ability to rehabilitate themselves in order to ready themselves for a return to their position as mothers and moral exemplars.

Even without children, though, female inmates are portrayed as more easily rehabilitated than their male counterparts. Again, for example, a report on coed prisons reported that the presence of women creates a safer environment, that "there tends to be much less violence and more desire to participate in work and education programs" as a result of their influence (Press et al., "When Prisons" 66). Michelle Kort recalled in *Ms.* that women at the California Institute for Women at Chino Valley strongly pursued the implementation of an exercise program designed to keep them drug-free. They even threatened a sexual discrimination suit when their gym was almost taken away while the men's prison continued to have access to weight training equipment (32). Further, the establishment of chapters of the National Organization for Women in various prisons is represented as helping female prisoners transform themselves. As one inmate declared, "I feel more sure of myself now; like I don't have to be so dependent and isolated" (quoted in Felder 21; see also G. Allen).

Furthermore, many observers of female prisoners during this period suggest that the greatest percentage of them are drug offenders who are already morally straight and need more medical help than punishment. As inmate Kathy Kelly of the Lexington, Kentucky, Federal Prison claimed of the women imprisoned there, "I met women who truly regret their offenses, long for their children and who need medical attention, not incarceration, to help them overcome their drug habits" (230). The high profile of Jean Harris and her discussions of prison life provide a similar representation of female inmates: not only does she work with prison mothers and write books while imprisoned, but she also vehemently advocates rehabilitation as a philosophy (Harris, "Inside Story" 24; Sanz 75–78; Jacoby 60).

In sum, the female prisoner of this period, while once again given cursory representation at best, is almost essentialized as an always already redeemable person. Born into conditions that lead to her corruption, she either strays into a life of drug addiction because of domestic stress or commits crimes in an attempt to aid her family. In either case, the conditions for a criminal lifestyle are rooted in her mistreatment at the hands of others and are depicted as at least partially justifiable. In either case, motherhood and the removal of the female from an abusive environment work together to restore her humanity and morality. In effect, this era is remarkably consistent with past representations of female inmates: women's task is to maintain the species and cultural morality. In prison, she is able to recover her essence, and hence she desires and deserves release in order to assure that the next generation will learn the proper boundaries of social order.

The Binds of Alternatives to Incarceration

> [Jeffrey Stafford, a Florida criminal sentenced to wear an electronic monitoring device]: "It would never enter my mind to tamper with the anklet. This is a nice apartment. I haven't had my own bed for a long time" (quoted in "Spiderman's" 93).

In many ways, this simple observation makes obvious the potential rhetorical and cultural problems that arrive with the use of electronic home monitoring and other alternative forms of punishment. Because these alternatives are initiated under the philosophical and cultural canopy of just deserts, they necessarily must be represented as providing a harsh enough punishment to fit any given crime and hence bring just deserts. As a result, Stafford's apparent glee with this punishment should seem somewhat misplaced, somehow "unjust" when compared with what most would consider harsher punishment. In effect, there is a tension between the prisoner's presentation of alternatives as preferable to imprisonment and the simultaneous presentation of all alternatives as equally severe as imprisonment. It is the working out of this tension that moves us back toward the Maria Arnford story and similar ones. Further, it is in the working out of this tension that the demarcating lines of race and gender in popular culture take their toll in the representation of the disciplining of the prisoner.

The pressures from the clashing discourses and material constraints, the "bricks and mortar," create a double bind in the discussion of prisoners and punishment. First, as I have noted, African-American and other "minority" male convicts are publicly represented as violent and irrational; hence, imprisonment becomes the only form of discipline that can be represented as just deserts. Second, Caucasian male prisoners, as well as female prisoners in general, are represented as trustworthy enough for the various alternatives to incarceration. However, because they are preconstructed as redeemable and because of the historical necessity for prisoners to agree to rehabilitation, they are implicitly encouraged to position themselves as in complete agreement with cultural norms and morals as well as their own punishment. They must, then, simultaneously testify to the harshness of the punishment dealt by disciplinary procedures in providing a sense of just deserts and testify to their personal redemption in keeping within the bounds of their culturally defined position.

It is important that this implication not be understated. To put it another way, the intermingling of the material conditions that bring about alternatives to incarceration (such as technological advances, overcrowding via mandatory prison sentences) with the historical categorization of inmates by race and gender brings with it implications not only for the representation of criminals but also for the general culture's relationship to the dominant ideology. Hence, because female and Caucasian male inmates are depicted as trustworthy enough to undergo alternative disciplinary procedures *and* because this depiction takes place in a period of just deserts in which rehabilitation becomes a matter of choice on the part of the criminal rather than a matter of force, the public statements of inmates in praise of the procedures that have given them redemption act implicitly as arguments that all members of the culture should welcome the discipline provided by the dominant cultural ideology. When disciplinary authorities are configured as "parents," doling out punishment with loving concern, and when criminals voluntarily redeem themselves under this authoritarian gaze, the prisoners who voice agreement with their punishment provide a general example of the importance of following the prescriptions of morals and laws in a productive life; they position each of us as children who should seek guidance from the state. After all, their own redemption comes only when they quit resisting and choose the route of rehabilitation made possible through their discipline. When Maria Arnford praises her punishment, she is a mother and moral guide, bowing to the disciplining guidance of a stronger force.

In sum, then, the construction of punishment and prisoners with regard to alternative punishments is problematic on two grounds: first, in its different delineations of punishment on the basis of the race and gender of the criminal, and second, in its celebration of cultural discipline. As I hinted earlier, the difference between violent and nonviolent criminals often acts as the public justification for the choice of imprisonment or an alternative form of justice. In attempting to find solutions to prison overcrowding, officials suggest in public that only certain criminals should be imprisoned, while other nonviolent ones may experience their just deserts in some manner other than incarceration (Lacayo "Considering" 60–61; Lacayo "Our" 28–31). Hence, Donald Murray, legal representative of the National Association of Counties, testified in 1990 that certain criminals "are not dangerous. There are a lot of community options that need to be developed for prisoners who present no threat to the community" (J. Morris, "Municipal" 29). As one might guess, with rare exceptions, only white male convicts or female convicts are represented in public discourse as benefiting from alternatives. Indeed, in each of the following examples, the articles either directly concern or provide pictures of white male prisoners or female prisoners in general (although here, too, they are generally white). In effect, nonviolence and redemption become equated with white men and women in general; irrationality, violence, and an incapacity for rehabilitation are equated with men of color.

The inequity of this system, or at least its representation along the lines of class, does not go entirely without comment. At times, as in this line from a *New York Times* editorial, media voices decry the inequity of the system: "When a nonviolent middle class white offender comes up for sentencing, judges and the public readily accept the idea that an alternative, like community service, is a good idea. . . . Why can't the same thing be true for many of the poor thieves and burglars who fill our prison warehouses?" (Crittenden). Simultaneously, however, the pervasiveness of the racial division can be seen when, in arguing against the use of electronic home monitoring, *Progressive* editorialist Keenen Peck indirectly reinforces the stereotypes that justify its current usage: "The poor and the minority defendant is usually one who has committed a violent crime, is without means, and has little or no recognition in his community. As a result, the middle class defendant gets alternative sentencing or part-time imprisonment, usually without incarceration, and the poor and the minority defendant gets a heavy jail term with incarceration" (28). While critics point out the inconsistencies in how alternative sentencing is utilized, then, the material conditions of overcrowded prisons coupled with and supported by just deserts policies and "get-tough" campaigns such as the War on Drugs create a rhetorical and material bind in which alternatives are necessary. Again, however, because only white males and females in general have been represented as nonviolent, trustworthy, and redeemable, they alone can be represented as taking part in the alternative systems.

As states and the federal government began to deal with the inclusion of alternative forms of punishment, numerous methods were developed and discussed publicly. For example, then Arkansas governor Bill Clinton suggested a number of alternatives, including home monitoring of nonviolent criminals, community service work in exchange for time spent in prison, education and rehabilitation programs, and finally a military-style boot camp for first-time offenders (Weintraub). In an engaging and yet frightening look into the future of electronic surveillance of convicts, Colorado parole officer Max Winkler imagines a third generation of electronic monitors that will be combined with behavior altering drugs. In a sidebar next to a picture of a man who is evidently drinking alcohol while looking at children on a playground is the following description: "Electronic monitors and behavior-altering drugs are implanted in the offender's arm. A microprocessor relays the offender's physiological data to a central monitoring station, alerting authorities to the onset of undesirable behavior. Here, an offender with a history of pedophilia is not only consuming alcohol, but loitering in a restricted area—outside of a school playground. Law-enforcement personnel transmit a signal to release a sedative from the implant, keeping the offender immobilized until authorities arrive" (36). As alternative systems like these are introduced, one of the primary rhetorical challenges facing authorities concerns the severity of the discipline they provide. That is, if the alternatives are to provide just deserts for the crime committed, the punishment must be equal to that which would have been administered by a prison term if the alternative were not available.

In their evident recognition of the political necessity of framing alternatives to incarceration as fulfilling the requirements of just deserts, institutions responsible for offering alternative forms of punishment provide labels that highlight the punishment end of the punishment-rehabilitation spectrum. Hence, as Ted Gest observed in *US News and World Report,* labels such as the "Community Penalty Program" are given to such systems in order to downplay any potential notion that alternatives are an "easy ride" for criminals ("Personalized" 75). Similarly, Herbert Heltuer, director of the National Center for Alternatives, observed in *Time* that his main problem in getting people to accept alternatives is a rhetorical one: "We're all against crime," he affirmed, "but we need to convince people that there are other ways to get justice" (quoted in Lacayo, "Considering" 61). Indeed, the public's perception of prison as the only acceptable form of punishment is labeled in *American City and County* as dangerous: "Punishment begins with any denial of freedom; it doesn't have to include incarceration in a jail or prison" (Quinn 78).

This rhetorical problem develops in part because a number of sentenced criminals who have undergone electronic home monitoring point to their preference for it over incarceration. In addition to the attitude of Jeffrey Stafford, whose observation began this section, thirty-two-year-old Gloria Pena, who was provided an electronic home monitoring system after she was caught using cocaine while on parole, observed in *Rolling Stone* that home monitoring "kept me at home, *where I'm supposed to be.* It's better than being in jail" (quoted in R. Sullivan 51; emphasis added). Marvin Trigueros, who was provided with an electronic monitoring bracelet after his conviction for aggravated assault, said in *Psychology Today,* "It just tells when I'm home. I feel like I'm being watched but it's not like my privacy is being invaded" (Krajick 72). Finally, after reviewing court cases in which convicted criminals were allowed the option of prison terms or the use of electronic bracelets, author Dee Reid noted that prisoners generally choose electronic bracelets over jail (13). These claims and similar ones by convicted criminals and other observers of disciplinary procedures create a rhetorical bind for the criminal justice system: if the punishment dealt out by alternative systems is to be seen as "just," criminals should not choose them so happily.

On the other hand, the opposite impulse—to represent the alternative forms of punishment as indeed harsh disciplinary procedures—is more prominent. Here, alternatives to incarceration are depicted as in fact more disciplinary than their prison-term counterparts. Hence, observers such as *US News and World Report*'s Ted Gest claim that "many suspects actually prefer incarceration when the alternative is living at home with such strictures as random drug tests and constant electronic monitoring" ("Personalized" 76). Furthermore, John DiIulio of The Brookings Institution argued that house arrest systems "are no picnic for the offender" ("Punishing" 4).

Additionally, those who critique alternative forms of punishment on the grounds that they are too invasive of the private sphere also inadvertently raise the value of the procedures as a form of rigorous punishment. For example, editorialist Keenen Peck argued in *The Progressive* in 1988 that electronic home monitoring allows the state to "monitor its citizens in the last bastion of privacy, the home. . . . The beeper . . . further erodes the sphere of the self" (26). With this claim Peck highlights the representation of alternatives to incarceration as fierce punishment and thus inadvertently makes them more acceptable as just deserts. Similarly, Joseph Vitek, director of the Department of Corrections for Douglas County, Nebraska, claimed in *Time* that electronic home monitoring "smacks of a police state" (quoted in "Spiderman's" 93), and Ari Kirpivaara of the American Civil Liberties Union argued that "it opens doors for allowing TV cameras and listening devices to monitor probationers in their homes," another sign of its police-state-like nature (quoted in Reid 14). These arguments work to establish *1984*-like horrors of alternatives while arguing against their employment. In short, while posited as critiques of electronic monitoring, such arguments represent alternatives in such a way that they are a more readily acceptable option in the pursuit of just deserts.

Warnings about the invasiveness of electronic home monitoring are further bolstered by the attitude of modern behaviorists, who create an even more daunting picture in their praise of various alternatives. In "Drugging Inmates: God in Pill Form," a 1979 essay directed against the use of alternative systems of punishment, the claims of behaviorist James V. McConnell are utilized as examples of how far alternatives can be taken. McConnell is quoted in the essay as noting:

> The day has come when we can combine sensory deprivation with drugs, hypnosis, and astute manipulation of reward and punishment to gain almost absolute control over an individual's behavior. It should be possible, then, to achieve a very rigid and highly effective type of brainwashing that would allow us to make dramatic changes in a person's behavior and personality. We should reshape society so that we all would be trained from birth to want to do what society wants to do. . . . No one owns his own personality. You had no say about what kind of personality you acquired, and there's no reason to believe you should have the right to refuse to acquire a new personality if your old one is anti-social. (quoted in Fleming 44)

Moreover, in a 1993 *Futurist* essay on electronic monitoring, Colorado parole officer Max Winkler comments that even though such technologies might be used exploitatively and "could conceivably contribute to the ultimate totalitarian society," their use is worth the risk as it makes convicted offenders productive citizens (36). Hence, the countering of the claim that alternative systems of incarceration are too soft on criminals creates a horrifying portrait in which no action goes unnoticed, in which it is never too early or late to begin such discipline.

The combination of the representation of alternative forms of punishment with the historical categorization of the criminal by race and gender creates a fascinating pastiche. Posited as bringing about just deserts but also requiring trustworthy and redeemable prisoners, alternative forms of punishment subtly reaffirm the validity of the social whole's definition of morality and correct behavior through the testimony of those who undergo these disciplinary procedures. Thus, Maria Arnford speaks of the parent she never had, while others similarly represent their punishment as being directed by a harsh parental surveyor of all actions, a parent who in the end helps them once again to shape their "selves" into productive and healthy citizens. As I noted in the previous chapter, while prisoners are often represented as self-redeemable, they are also depicted as necessarily reliant upon prison rehabilitation programs in their efforts at self-redemption. Here, criminals are punished by alternatives but must rely on the alternatives in order to rehabilitate themselves.

Furthermore, with few exceptions, prisoners characterized as having undergone alternative forms of incarceration all show appreciation for their return to "normal" definitions of what is expected from them. For example, a nineteen-year-old who violated his probation and was consequently sentenced to serve time in Georgia's boot camp claimed in *People,* "When I came through the front door, I had to become a man in about 30 seconds. I wish I had come here the first time I got in trouble" (quoted in "Outside the Walls" 25). A twenty-five-year-old who was imprisoned for drug use and given the opportunity to leave prison under the auspices of an electronic home monitoring system declared in *USA Today,* "I now own my own deli. I do not do drugs and I will not go back to doing drugs. This program was a life-saver for me" (quoted in Scaglione 27).

The nature of the claims concerning the virtues of these systems remains fairly consistent throughout the period. Thus, after having undergone a program that, in addition to conditions of probation, forced him either to maintain steady employment or return to prison, an eighteen-year-old said that, after his first promotion, "I felt so proud. I went and told my mother, and she felt better, like, you know, maybe now I can get a new start" (quoted in "Outside" 27). The program provided him not only with a new start in the work force but with his family as well. Further, one in-house arrestee asserted simply that the alternative program "saved my life" (quoted in Lacayo, "Considering" 26). Free-lance writer Fred Scaglione, in another essay discussing alternatives to incarceration, provided the following scenario of an individual placed under the conditions of electronic home monitoring: "He gets to know his wife and kids, stops drinking or doing drugs, saves his money, and works around the house. Nine months later, they take off the monitor and he still comes home at night. He's got a job, a bank account, and a new relationship with his family" (27). Alternatives to incarceration are represented as a form of punishment that allows criminals to return voluntarily to the status quo definition of normality and to utter their gratitude for this opportunity. Moreover, such alternatives almost always work along the metaphor of the family. Hence, in a discussion of "therapeutic communities" (addiction-based programs in prisons) that are tied to furlough programs, *New York Times* reporter Peter Kerr notes that because the therapeutic community works to "change a person's values, thinking, moods, behavior, and spirituality," some have critiqued it as a form of brainwashing. However, for many prisoners, "the therapeutic community is the first family they have ever really had. In fact the prisoners call themselves a family" (24). Alternatives recreate the scene of the family; they keep people at home, where they are "supposed to be."

Concluding Observations

I would like to focus first on the notion of "just deserts" and the potential danger of such a philosophy given the historical backdrop shown in this work. In the period of discourse from 1969 to 1974, I observed the representation of moralities other than that of the status quo in the depiction of what I have labeled as the oppressed inmate. In this vein, the rhetoric and philosophy of "just deserts" claim to accept the existence of other moralities while reserving the right to punish the behavior that results from people acting on the basis of these other moralities. In effect, it is the claim of just deserts that, while as a culture we may accept the operation of multiple value and moral systems, we will judge individual behavior on the basis of a set of rules and contracts we have drawn up as a group. If these laws are violated, the offender will be punished only for the crime committed; he or she will not be forced to undergo rehabilitation programs, programs that suggest that everyone should be assimilated into a single shared value system. Hence, the philosophy of just deserts would appear to allow the celebration of "difference" up to the point that this celebration oversteps the boundaries of social law. Furthermore, while just deserts systems do not require rehabilitation of the criminal, they do provide the space and equipment for rehabilitation to take place. Rehabilitation is not required; it is allowed.

The dangers of such a configuration may be obvious. First, this discourse suggests that it is possible culturally to treat individuals equally according to their crimes and on that basis alone. Such an assumption ignores the influence of past stereotypes and rhetorical constructions on the present. It ignores, for example, that the way in which African-American males and other prisoners of color have been constructed in the past affects their current and future representations. It ignores as well the historic representation of prisoners by gender. As a result, the various prisoners constructed along the lines of race and gender are represented in public discourse as having different potentials for rehabilitation and as deserving different deserts.

The dangers of a just deserts system of rehabilitation reach far deeper than simply representing different prisoners as undergoing different forms of discipline, however. As I noted earlier, the early 1970s revealed a reliance on institutional programs as the only means by which prisoners could rehabilitate themselves. While moral autonomy and diversity are assumed under a philosophy of just deserts and while rehabilitation is theoretically a choice made by the prisoner, discursively, rehabilitation is still defined in terms of institutional rehabilitation programs in the present period. As a result, when prisoners choose to become normalized or rehabilitated, they must by necessity rely on prison programs to do so. What makes this especially dangerous is that the rhetoric of just deserts, unlike the rhetoric of rehabilitation of the 1950s, does not claim a universal moral system. However, due to the reliance on programs of rehabilitation and on the discourse that has constructed Caucasian male prisoners and female prisoners in general as redeemable, discipline in an era of just deserts assumes just such a universal morality. It normalizes the behavior of the prisoner according to the state's definition of normality while suggesting that the prisoner chooses on his or her own to "do the right thing," all the while indicating that there is room for a cultural diversity. In short, this configuration draws a picture in which, faced with a number of competing moralities, the criminal always "freely" chooses that of the state to improve his or her life, to become redeemed, and to rebuild his or her family.

In their study of the way in which mass media news reports represent order, Ericson, Baranek, and Chan note that "moral authority is always subject to consent, and legitimacy is always something that is granted. Law is crucial to making convincing claims to moral authority because, in modern administered society, questions of legitimacy revolve around procedural norms, procedural propriety, and the search for and sanctioning of procedural strays" (343). The moral authority of law found in the current configuration of public discussions of the prisoner is arguably more dangerous than it has been in the past precisely because it appears chosen rather than forced. Convicts appear to choose to rehabilitate themselves to culturally dominant norms rather than having those norms forced upon them. "Choice" is represented as a key term when in fact no other options are available. It is difficult to critique rehabilitation as an oppressive tool if we ignore the ways in which historical representations limit the options of choice in the present.

In 1948, Paul Lazarsfeld and Robert Merton suggested that mass media enforce social norms because "publicity closes the gap between 'private attitudes' and 'public morality' " (103). In the setting of this study, Lazarsfeld and Merton's claim is an extremely provocative one. They effectively suggest that when deviant behavior or thought is publicized, individuals within the culture must take a stand for or against it. In the end, they claim, publicity brings pressure to force a single rather than a dual morality. In the case of the discourse of prisoners, we have seen an interesting example of this "slimming" of moralities. As I have noted, the previous period saw the recognition of a separate morality or belief system of the African-American and minority prisoner in a segment of the public discourse. In this period, while we can assert that the philosophy of just deserts allows the continuance of different moralities, in effect only one morality exists. The redeemable prisoners swear by their improvement at the hands of the state, and the remaining prisoners, with their "different" moralities, are marginalized, their discourse unheard, and their voices deemed illegitimate.

Foucault notes that Western societies have persisted in using the "confessional" as one of the major modes of producing truth about individuals. He further suggests that the obligation to confess has become "so deeply ingrained in us that we no longer perceive it as the effect of a power that constrains us" (*History* 60). It may be true that we do not perceive the confession as a result of power when the focus is on those matters that have become socially acceptable forms of self-constitution. However, a number of examples of these public confessions of socially unacceptable behavior are easily pointed to in the array of morning and afternoon talk shows on television. The various abnormalities and problems that are confessed to by guests of *Donahue, Oprah,* or any other show of this genre all illustrate the power, glamour, and influence of the public confession. It is doubtful that anyone would suggest that these "free" confessions result from a constraining power.

However, in the case of alternative punishments, confession is utilized both to constrain overtly the individual who has committed crimes and to define for society at large what will and will not be accepted. The confessional, in its varied form as a means to punish, helps define what is accepted as normal behavior. In this vein, an Albany, Oregon, man who failed to appear in court on charges of theft was allowed to take out several ads admitting his crimes and apologizing to his community as a portion of his punishment. The district attorney who proposed the sentence asserted that he wanted to make the punishment "more direct, more public, and more embarrassing" (quoted in "Outside the Walls" 23). Furthermore, a child molester in Portland, Oregon, was ordered to post signs at his workplace and at his residence that read "Dangerous Sex Offender, No Children Allowed" ("Outside the Walls" 26). In Florida, those convicted of driving under the influence of alcohol are required to display a red and white glow-in-the-dark bumper sticker that reads: "Convicted DUI Restricted License." The judge who initiated the program noted that "if reputation is such a big thing, then maybe this can be a deterrent. Public humiliation is one of the big things that has been overlooked" (quoted in "Outside the Walls" 24). In each case, the criminal is forced to place his or her crimes in front of the public, to ask for forgiveness, and to present the crime as a truth of his or her essential being, allowing the rest of the community to know what will not be tolerated as normal behavior.

A long tradition of critical theorists has attempted to understand the relationship between mass-mediated forms of communication and human behavior, noting alternatively their potentially dominating, liberating, or altering influence on subjects. We may point to examples ranging from the extremes of Horkheimer and Adorno's warning of the impending ideological grasp of the cultural industries (239–47) and Althusser's dire concerns about the strength of ideological state apparatuses to more Gramscian-influenced work in cultural studies that provides for an active agent who can read liberating messages in virtually all mediated messages. Staking out an ambiguous middle ground, Foucault has observed that contemporary culture is becoming increasingly carceral; we have constructed a "panopticon-ish" society in which a normalizing gaze is persistently directed on each of us, and we learn to act as instruments of the gaze, disciplining each other's abnormal behaviors even while the option of rearranging this gaze, or loosely resisting it, is available. We are each normalized through standardized tests, rating systems, confessions, constant polling, television shows, and interpersonal cues (*Discipline* 293–308). We tightly constrain what behavior we will accept from each other and therefore, tightly constrain what we, as a "people," will be.[8]

Building from this notion, Poster has attempted to investigate the potential of new communication technologies to act as systems of surveillance. Combining his interest with Baudrillard's apocalyptic account of the effects of new communication instruments (computers, television, credit systems, and so forth), Poster warns that we may have entered the age of the "Super Panopticon," an age in which cases of surveillance are increased to a level at which resistance is impossible (123). With information about phone calls, library books, credit use, and everyday choices all recorded by computers, it is far easier for the subject to be monitored, for the spatial, temporal, and personality changes of an individual to be eyed immediately and simultaneously. If Poster's notion contains any degree of truth, an investigation of the rhetorical positioning of these new technologies as they pertain to actual forms of discipline and punishment is a high priority. In the case of electronic home monitoring devices and urine testing, for example, the publication of Maria Arnford's childlike adoration is a telling one. Maria Arnford, moreover, welcomes Poster's Super Panopticon, a system that persists in watching her every move, her bodily intake, as a desired parental influence. She testifies to the virtues not only of the whip but also of the gentle glove of culture.

Let me approach this subject through one more lexicon, that of Michel de Certeau. In his widely acclaimed *The Practice of Everyday Life*, de Certeau notes that "there is no law that is not inscribed on bodies. . . . From birth to mourning after death, law 'takes hold of' bodies in order to make them its text. Through all sorts of initiations (in rituals, at school, etc.), it transforms them into tables of the law, into living tableaus of rules and customs, into actors of the drama organized by a social order" (139). De Certeau is pointing to the dialectic of individual and culture, self and society. The law only has meaning after it becomes instantiated by human beings, and human beings only gain meaning or a legitimate sense of self as they emerge from the interstices of cultural norms, as they are defined by laws. As de Certeau goes on to note, "To make people believe is to make them act. . . . Because the law is already applied with and on bodies, 'incarnated' in physical practices, it can accredit itself and make people believe that it speaks in the name of the 'real.' It makes itself believable by saying: 'This text has been dictated for you by Reality itself' " (148). People act, he says, only when they believe. In the case under investigation here, even while working under a philosophy that says, "We will abdicate the stance of the Real," individuals are positioned as a result of multiple rhetorical, historical, cultural, political, and material forces to say, "The Law is real; I am given my proper sense of self in following the law as a parent. Only in following the law can I find the proper way to behave."

If we maintain a poststructural stance against essentialisms and argue that there are no truly base selves but discursively created subject positions that we experience, the implications of the public presentation of Arnford's adoration of the state-as-parent become clear. The conclusions of this investigation necessarily comment on the ways in which the rhetorical constructions of alternative systems of punishment encourage some members of our culture willingly to take on the subject positions and morals being offered while in effect asking, or even coercing, others (that is, males of color) to reject dominant morals. If we accept the assertion that a concept *is* as a concept *does,* this study becomes a theory of punishment in our society, a theory, moreover, with pervasive implications. Through the combinations, tensions, and influences of a large number of symbolic and material forces that surround the discourse of prisoners and punishment, a position emerges that binds a certain class of prisoners, mainly minority male ones, to be represented as paying their social debts in prison cells, while a certain number of "more responsible" primarily female and white male prisoners are able to avoid incarceration not only by representing their punishment as a just retribution for their mistakes but also by making a public declaration of suffering and a declaration that their activities now fit the confines of proper behavior, that they have "seen the light" and are thankful for their new position.

While I am not prepared to engage in a discussion that clearly delineates the virtues and faults of incarceration or its alternatives, it appears that those prisoners who are the product of a historical construction that posits them as irrational and violent are represented as being placed into the confines of prison cells, unable to gain a voice in the public forum. They are not invited to join the cultural body, to take on its norms. However, they are thereby able to critique their punishment and the institutions that discipline them because they have little, if any, need to show proof of their rehabilitation. The criminals provided with the alternatives, on the other hand, prefigured as rational and redeemable, must necessarily cease to critique the system as they rush to join it, reinforcing the notion that it is the right path after all, reaffirming their own representations within it, and giving "law-abiding citizens" the comfort of knowing that their own behavior is normal and beyond reproach.

7

Conclusions, Beginnings

Into the Future

If I were asked to provide a sound bite that would get at the heart of this study, that would aphoristically provide some sense of the meaning of "the cultural prison," I would in all likelihood simply repeat the Arnford narrative with which I began and to which I have referred throughout this examination of the "discipline of discipline." "The parent I never had," she said. Several years after first encountering her claim, I have tired neither of telling this story in the company of others nor of mulling it over in private. In some ways, it serves appropriately enough as both a beginning and an end.

However, in that I did not set out to close the book on "prisoners," prisons, or punishment but instead wanted this investigation to provoke, I want this final chapter to be an attempt to respond to some of the questions that served as the impetus for the study and a place to raise other issues; the chapter is meant to be reflective and active. I hope to begin and end, to reflect on the past and shape the parameters of the future.

Ending: The Story Cultural Discourses Have Told

One obvious and traditional way of ending such a study is to retell the story just told, to provide an integrated narrative of the discipline of discipline. Taking each era in turn, an integrated sketch of the historical transformations of the multiple representations of the prisoner, and the implications of these transformations on the present, comes to the fore. Such endings do serve a purpose.

Beginning again, then, the representation of the prisoner in the 1950s finds a culture that keeps faith with one dominant and homogeneous set of values. While the "real" culture was of course made up of many competing interests and values, its representation, as posited through dominant mass-mediated discourses that focused on prisoners and punishment, reflected the superiority and dominance of one set of values over all competing values. Within this set of discourses, "the prisoner" is represented as primarily Caucasian and male, imprisoned so that he may learn to behave in ways that will allow his reunion with the social whole. Although appearing far less often, the female prisoner is also represented, framed as "mother" and as the holder and defender of cultural values. Both male and female prisoners share the ability to use prison in order to find their way back to a "normal" state of being. Indeed, there is little if any critique of the seemingly homogeneous value system of the culture. Lifestyles and behaviors that lie outside of what is considered normal are either ignored (for example, that of African Americans) or are treated as something to be normalized (such as homosexuality). The discourse of discipline of this era, then, constructs a culture with one strongly held set of norms, one seemingly transcendent belief structure under which everyone is judged.

From 1960 to 1968, persistent riotous behaviors coupled with the apparent failure of rehabilitation programs serve as the planks upon which an alternative representation of the male prisoner is built. Hence, there appears not only a redeemable prisoner but also an irrational and violent one, seemingly immune to normalization. At the same time, the female prisoner's representation remains largely consistent with that of the earlier era; she is both mother and moral watchdog. When she is imprisoned, it is only so that she might rediscover her essence. The two representations of the male prisoner, however, operate in an irreconcilable tension with each other. That is, these two representations of the prisoner, one redeemable and treatable and the other irrational and violent, provide two competing definitions. As the period proceeds, these two representations are painted with racial tones so that Caucasian prisoners appear to be available for redemption and "minority" prisoners are depicted as "essentially" irrational and immoral.

The two competing depictions of the prisoner can only be simultaneously acceptable if an external means exists to differentiate them.

For a number of reasons, race becomes this agency. This means of differentiation has weighty consequences, as values and prisoners themselves are marginalized and judged on this basis. Thus, for example, when Caucasian prisoners riot, their behavior is represented as a response to an oppressive situation; they take the same action that any normal person would in the same situation. On the other hand, when African-American prisoners riot, they do so because their nature compels them to do so. While race provides a line by which to delineate value systems, then, it should be made clear that the judgments of these value systems, as represented in mass-mediated discourse, imply the existence of one transcendent morality, a homogeneous morality that judges one set of behaviors and one race as redeemable and others as immoral and irredeemable.

The complexity of the prisoner's dominant representation increases further during the next period of discourse. In addition to an increasing polarization of male prisoners on the basis of race and the stabilization of the redemptive and maternal character of the female prisoner, there is also the appearance on the public stage of yet another type of inmate, a male prisoner of color (generally African-American) represented as sentenced on unjust grounds. Imprisoned as the result of a system that is considered biased at base, this criminal has not been given a fair shake by the criminal justice process. Moreover, the actions for which he is imprisoned are often the same actions that are judged as legitimate within his own moral system, a moral system that happens to be, while neither better nor worse, inconsistent with the dominant cultural morality. Within this configuration, the prisoner implicitly represents a critique of the belief in a unified cultural morality.

While traditional stereotypes of prisoners on the basis of race persist, an apparent respect for cultural and moral diversity also emerges. One characterization that this move to a pluralism of values does change is the overall representation of the male prisoner of color as violent and nonredeemable. In effect, he is either marginalized because he is represented as violent, even if the violence is legitimate within the parameters of a different morality, or he is seen as irrational and violent when judged by traditional morality. Whether justified or not, then, his violent behavior is his defining characteristic.

It is also during this period that those rehabilitation programs designed by incarceration systems (that is, state and federal prisons) are characterized as the sole means by which prisoners can redeem themselves. While there is a growing belief that disciplinary systems should respect the moral autonomy of prisoners, rehabilitation begins to be situated as taking place only under the auspices of the state and its mechanisms, and prisoners are seen as redeemable only when they utilize the mechanisms provided by the state.

Finally, in contemporary discourses, the public discussion of prisoners, morality, and discipline is impacted by the popular and academic call for a practice of "just deserts." As an orientation, the policy of just deserts operates on the dual assumptions that discipline should be adjusted so that it is equivalent to the crime committed and that punishment should be the sole purpose of criminal justice. While rehabilitation may be offered to criminals, it cannot be a purpose or justification for disciplinary apparatuses. In essence, the idea of just deserts allows for the acceptance of cultural diversity while simultaneously maintaining the right of the state to constrict the behavior of individuals despite this acceptance.

It is in the discourse of this era, however, that one most clearly sees the weight of past representations of prisoners acting against the practical application of just deserts. For example, while just deserts might be claimed as policy, past depictions of African Americans as violent continue to exclude them from being represented in any mechanism of discipline other than prison. Past depictions of Caucasian males and of females in general, on the other hand, are more likely to situate both as inherently redeemable. Furthermore, and perhaps of more importance, when this redeemable nature is coupled with the rhetoric of just deserts, a rhetoric that makes rehabilitation voluntary, those particular white male prisoners and female prisoners in general who are represented as participating in alternative disciplinary programs testify that they have chosen their redemption and that they indeed appreciate the transformation that has taken place in their character and in their behavior. Because their rehabilitation is represented as freely chosen, the methods of redemption (primarily state rehabilitation programs) are represented as guideposts to a proper morality. On the other hand, depicted as violent, African-American male prisoners and other nonwhite male prisoners are not represented as eligible for or capable of rehabilitation programs or other alternatives to incarceration. Hence, they continue to hold the position of the Other, holder of an alternative morality. This configuration illustrates an uneasy acceptance of cultural diversity, an acceptance that is valid only when a morality does not interfere with dominant cultural norms. While pockets of resistance may exist, and while voices calling for diversity frequently may appear, the discourse of discipline reveals one way in which divergent voices are "disciplined."

While I do not want to deny that a system of home monitoring and urine testing could potentially remove some forms of human suffering by changing the patterns of an individual offender's life "for the better," this study illustrates that the rhetorical positioning of prisoners undergoing these forms of punishment results in the construction of punishment (and, more abstractly, of cultural norms and laws) as worthy of general appreciation and submission. The characterizations and representations discussed here tend to suggest that many criminals are preconstructed into a position that encourages them to praise that which reshapes them "for good or bad."

The testimonies of various criminals suggest a desire to be constituted according to a general cultural definition of normality and legality, an unwillingness to see cultural morality as contingent and open for critique. Those undergoing alternative forms of punishment are more likely to represent their previous orientations as warped and to see those of the "parental" program as closer to an objective morality. Equally important, their praise of the disciplinary procedures encourages every member of their culture to accept cultural norms, as codified by laws, as objective. The theory of just deserts posits the prisoner as having made the choice to undergo rehabilitation. Nevertheless, while it appears in mass-mediated discourse that such prisoners freely choose to be rehabilitated according to a particular system, in effect no other option is readily available. Thus, we are all encouraged to respect law, to look toward codified descriptions of behavior as guides for our own behavior.

This study is not meant to be a thesis in praise of anarchy; I am not suggesting that there is no need or utility for organization, laws, and norms. Rather, I am concerned that the testimony of Arnford and others concerning the pleasures of punishment, as articulated in popular journals and other media outlets, passes in and out of cultural consciousness with neither critique nor comment by the citizenry. The problem, as I see it, is more one of an inability or unwillingness to question or resist cultural definitions of normalcy and legal behavior than of an inability to rid ourselves of them completely. We exist in the interstices of such definitions. These definitions are comparatively more dangerous now than forty years ago because, unlike during the 1950s when rehabilitation was a matter of course for all represented prisoners, it now appears not only to be a choice, but one that is praised by the chosen and restricted by race and gender.

Ideally, definitions of proper moral behavior should be a matter of public debate, even by convicted criminals, rather than of unquestioned perpetuation. If we cannot see the judgment of morality inherent in legal definitions of right and wrong as culturally contingent, but rather as natural and something to be desired, there is little or no chance for the resistance to, or even the questioning of, existing cultural values. It is only when normalization is in the open that critique is possible. The most problematic move in this emerging construction of punishment, then, is that it presents itself as a process of desire.

In short, it is imperative that we reflect on the influences that the testimony of those criminals who undergo these alternative forms of punishment has on the mass cultural level. As I suggested at the opening of this book, cultural forms of mediated discipline reflect the beliefs of the larger culture. These reflections seem infinitely more interesting than what the statements say about individual criminals per se; if those who already abide by social laws witness outlaws testifying to the benefits of the prison system in incorporating them back into society, the law-abiding citizen is more likely to view his or her own behavior as unquestionably more agreeable, natural, and appealing. After all, these representations provide us with "criminals" who testify that the disciplinary system is useful, providing the discipline they *need,* encouraging a sense of responsibility.

No one is left unaffected by disciplinary procedures when they are constructed in this light. Even those who stand outside of formal systems of punishment are forced to confront the notion that disciplinary procedures as a whole exist for the benefit of everyone. By staying within the law, we behave as we should. Just as children learn to view their parents as omnipotent, so do we learn to view the repressive and ideological state apparatuses as both natural and loving. Indeed, even female prisoners, who are themselves positioned maternally and morally, turn to praise the state's disciplinary procedures as parental.[1]

Back to the Beginning: The Story to be Told

In the opening pages, I posed a number of questions that the story of Maria Arnford had initially prompted me to ask. I did not realize at the time how much the questions intermingled, nor did I realize that I was neglecting to put the stress on the last and most important question: What can be done once an attitude such as Arnford's becomes culturally predominant? That is, no longer am I solely interested in the conditions that allow the uncritical acceptance of such a claim, but I am now far more seriously interested in considering the ways in which one changes those conditions, and hence, the assumptions of the future.

"What are the rhetorical circumstances that create a reality in which a claim such as Arnford's could be published in *People,* a widely distributed popular journal, without exciting much attention?" "What is the cultural significance of the gender, the class, the race, the sexual orientation of Arnford, each at least implicitly suggested in the article (that is, Arnford is female, middle-class, Caucasian, heterosexual) in this representation of discipline?" These questions, the first and third with which I began, can no longer be tackled separately. Their answers are far more complex than I had originally imagined. In that they became the central questions, the driving force, of this project, the narrative summary I have recounted above in some part responds to both of them. The rhetorical circumstances—better, the cultural circumstances—are composed of the symbolic and material constraints that shape the way in which Arnford's comment is read. Remembering that this is the study of the "bricks and mortar" of culture, as well as the energy of its change, it has become evident that Arnford's claim rests at the end of a wide array of symbolic and material constraints. Indeed, this study itself surely only touches on a limited number of the conditions under which her claim is made. She speaks from within a dominant culture in which she is constructed as a moral guidepost and purveyor of "family values" (heterosexual married woman) and for which she speaks as a redeemable subject seeking to return to her natural state (the nexus of the female and Caucasian criminals).

The conditions of which Arnford speaks are shaped by a history of dominant discourses dealing with prisoners, with women, with Caucasians, and with each of these categories as they are linked with each other and with imprisonment. She speaks from a position that has been shaped by the civil rights movement, by the discourse and legal appeals of Black Muslims, by the shrinking budgets of the 1980s, by the discourse and policies of the War on Drugs, and by a multitude of other factors. She speaks, in other words, from a position far too complex to understand completely, even were she to choose to be self-reflective about it. More important, perhaps, she speaks, *and we listen,* from positions that shape our speaking and hearing strategies, our choice of style and our personal hermeneutics. While study and reflection allow some insight into speaking and receiving positions, the conditions are of epic proportions and difficult to change.

Addressing the remaining two questions forces me to take seriously the complexity implied by the first two: "What are the possible cultural effects of a shared reality that encourages such complete penetration of one of its participants, albeit a 'criminal' one?" "What type of social world is implied by our uncritical acceptance of her words, and what alternative visions might be offered?" Reflecting on the Arnford story, or indeed, the discussion about the third generation of surveillance that predicts that prisoners not only will have their bodies monitored but also will have chemical implants to allow law enforcement officers to monitor and change the chemical makeup of the criminal from a distance, our concern should not necessarily be with specific technologies or even with how these technologies are being used but instead with the fearful glee with which "criminals" invite the technology as the "only family they've ever known." That is, while we may not be surprised to find that cultural subjects are either passively or resistantly positioned as subjects of cultural disciplinary procedures, our surprise and (we hope) fear should be provoked by those representations of subjects who actively invite these disciplinary procedures. When one is resistant, at least passively, it is much easier to imagine utopian futures in which such opposition might play itself out. When one is the pursuer of dominant moralities and dominant discourses, it is far more difficult to envision a space for resistant discourses and moralities.

Envisioning an effective route of resistance or means of action to combat this representation of prisoners and punishment is difficult. While I am not quite sure that bell hooks would be comfortable with my invocation of her words in order to suggest one such means of imagination, they do appear fitting: "I was working," hooks notes " . . . to identify marginality as much more than a site of deprivation. In fact I was saying just the opposite: that it is also the site of radical possibility, a space of resistance" (341). Indeed, hooks wants us to envision the marginal as the site from which dominant discourses, moralities, and ideologies may be most readily critiqued and resisted, the site from which "creativity and power" have the greatest opportunity to emerge and provide resistant visions of future possibilities. Accordingly, while the African-American male prisoner is burdened by the bricks and mortar of a heavy dominant representation—violent, immoral, and irredeemable—he is also provided with the most radical possibilities for the use of the energy of rhetoric. Because the representation of this prisoner is the one placed most solidly on the margins, it is also the space where dominant ideology is not invited, the space where resistance to dominant ideology is most possible. While I do not mean to underestimate the human tragedy of life within prison bars, the strongest site of resistance may indeed lie somewhere deep within the walls restraining these inmates, at least as they are represented in dominant discourses. Locating such a site of resistance and allowing space for its representation are two different matters altogether, however, and matters not easily resolved.

A second route of change and possibility lies in the reimagination of the critical act itself. I began this work by noting that I hoped to add a practical edge to critical rhetoric, to make this work itself one that implies a radical and creative imagination, to serve as a warning that opens up spaces for future possibilities. In "The New Cultural Politics of Difference," Cornel West calls for a demystificatory criticism or "prophetic criticism." He notes that such a criticism begins with social structural analyses while also making its moral and political goals clear: "It is partisan, partial, engaged, and crisis-centered, yet always keeps open a skeptical eye to avoid dogmatic traps, premature closures, formulaic formulations or rigid conclusions. In addition to social structural analyses, moral and political judgments, and sheer critical consciousness, there indeed is evaluation" (31). If rhetorical criticism is to have a meaningful purpose, it must have analysis, evaluation, and action. Moreover, its purpose must be to act as a warning and as an introduction. Suggesting possibilities, *or opening up spaces for possibilities,* must become a common part of the goal and practice of criticism. Rhetorical criticism, and critical rhetoric, must in effect "do" poststructuralism rather than theorize it.

To that end, this work must be seen as a gathering of fragments, an interpretation, an attempt to add one sound bite among many others to the public debate over the meaning of the prisoner and the purpose of punishment. However, if I continue to heed the advice of Michael McGee and focus on my work as not only a critic but also a performing rhetorician, my work is not yet done (McGee, "Text"). The performative side of criticism, if it is going to have a significant influence culturally, must be highlighted in arenas that will heighten its strength. I cannot be satisfied with a list of the achievements and findings of this work in this concluding chapter; instead, it must be my task, and the task of critics in general, to increase the impact of criticism by finding outlets that increase its prominence as a cultural fragment, that aim toward opening up possibilities for a creative imaginary for the future. Only in this way can "critical rhetoric" take part in the universalizing function of discourse.[2]

In a preliminary sense, however, what openings, if any, does this work provide? When compared to other histories and theories of punishment, such as those discussed in chapter 2 and in appendix 1, the orientation taken here enables insights not provided elsewhere. Most obviously, while most histories trace out shifts in the perceived nature of prisoners and punishment from different perspectives (for instance, the viewpoint of the prisoner, criminal justice theories, orientations taken by prison administrators), this study provides a cultural understanding of the discourse surrounding prisoners and punishment from a more encompassing cultural point of view. While John Irwin attempts to provide an "insider's" perception of the ways prisoners understand their own positions, and while James Jacobs explains the workings of prison administrators, this orientation provides an awareness of how prisoners and punishment are represented in the dominant discourse of everyday life, a cultural mapping of the history of representations. This study is an attempt to illustrate for cultural self-reflection the ways in which the cultural representations of prisoners constrain current and future representations of prisoners. In this way, then, it provides space for the opening up of criticism.

More specifically, while most traditional histories of punishment and imprisonment are careful in their analysis of the reported makeup of prisoners by race, crime, age, gender, and so forth, they ignore the cultural racism that provides different images of the prison makeup than government statistics provide. While John Irwin and Larry Sullivan, for example, are careful to note the slow influx of African Americans into the prison system, they also say that, still, approximately 50 percent of inmates are Caucasian. In public discourse, this simply is not true. Because "prisoners," like most objects of discourse, become familiar to the public through fragmented representations, the cultural understanding of prisoners is developed from reading *People* magazine in the waiting room of the dentist's office, from viewing CNN before supper, or from conversing with friends. The mediated image has more rhetorical force than do federal statistics on how prisoners are understood culturally. Hence, this study allows an understanding of "prisoner" and "punishment" as historically fluctuating objects of discourse. Again, such an observation provides the space for critical reflection on the ways in which race, gender, and ethnicity are inscribed in cultural discourses and in some rather damaging ways.

On a different level, while Sullivan and other historians and theorists begin to probe alternatives to punishment, they conceptualize punishment generally in terms of its effects on those undergoing it. Although they may toss a cursory glance on its effects in stopping crime, they certainly do not begin to touch upon its possible rhetorical impact on the current and future configuration of mass culture. Ignoring for a moment questions concerning the rights of the individual being punished and the impact of that punishment on stopping or slowing the crime rate, I ask that we begin a process of reconceptualizing how we, as a culture, talk about punishment and prisoners in order to allow a wider range of ideas, about both laws and values. In brief, I want the readership of this book and the citizenry at large to question the voice with which our cultural body speaks about the relationship between law and morality.[3]

Historians of punishment as well as theorists have noted, prescribed, and resisted a move toward a neo-Kantian moral autonomy, a move that would have criminals accept blame for their crimes and take responsibility for bearing the punishment society has deemed equivalent to the crime. This autonomy encourages a representation of criminals as responsible for their own rehabilitation. This study would suggest instead that, while such a reconceptualization may ultimately take place on a cultural level, it will be a long time in coming simply because of the force of past discourses on the present. While we can claim culturally that individuals must take responsibility for their individual behavior, the force of past discourses in defining how we will conceptualize, say, the African-American prisoner or the female criminal will strongly mold how we will allow this person to act autonomously. We can claim autonomy for the criminal, but it is an autonomy constrained by cultural interpretations that influence how individual prisoners are represented and how they then constitute themselves. While this may seem an obvious lesson to those who study the power of discourse, it is one that often goes without mention in traditional treatises on punishment. As we have seen here, once placed into action, past discourses concerning the prisoner continue to influence present perceptions of the prisoner.

There is, and will continue to be, a need for increased understanding and awareness of institutional and cultural discipline. This work is one more step in a movement toward understanding the "bricks, mortar, and energy" of discipline in general; it is at the very least an attempt to take the question of institutional and cultural discipline seriously. If we as a culture can begin to question the ways in which the constitution of punishment and prisoners influences us culturally, we may begin to explain why the cultural configuration of disciplinary measures as "the parent we never had" may not be entirely positive. At the very least, we can be sure that such a claim will no longer go unchallenged when it is made.

Appendix 1. Theoretical Perspectives

This book is not an attempt to illuminate or critique the theoretical arguments concerning the purpose of punishment; however, this area is another that provides necessary background for the development of a "theory" of punishment as it exists in the public forum. While I pointed to DiIulio's delineation of theoretical perspectives into the old penology, the new penology, and the new old penology in chapter 2, here I hope to provide a brief reading of some contemporary theories of punishment in a different light. Furthermore, as Michael Shapiro illustrates in his critique of the work of James Q. Wilson, arguments over punishment emerging from the academy often attempt to claim to be value and ideologically free (370–78). While I would (perhaps predictably) contend that such a freedom is an impossibility, such academic works do differ in intent and function from those that appear in newspapers and magazines. To this degree, they allow an interesting comparison between arguments as they emerge within academic and policy realms and within public discussions.

The number of theoretical works dealing with approaches to crime and punishment is voluminous. My choices of works reflect an attempt to pursue those that have been influential both on academic and popular levels or have been influential in shaping public policy from the 1960s onward. In 1971, the American Friends Service Committee published its highly influential *Struggle for Justice,* a work that has become standard in discussions of the recent development of theories of punishment and public policy. The work is significant for a number of reasons, one of which is its authorship. Because it was published under the name and auspices of the Quakers or Society of Friends, the treatise reveals a major transition in opinion by one of the historically most visible groups that has persistently dealt with issues of imprisonment. Being forerunners in the "rehabilitation" and indeterminate sentencing movements, their shift to the formerly "conservative" policy of determinate sentencing and their preference for punishment over rehabilitation had a strong influence on changes in punishment policies in the present. The book's anonymous authors call for the creation of what will later be seen as a unity of the policies and positions of the left and right, a unity that leads to determinate sentences and a depiction of the criminal as a morally autonomous agent responsible for his or her choice of committing criminal acts and taking part in rehabilitation programs. A 1983 collection of essays edited by Tonry and Zimring clarified and sustained the mission of *Struggle for Justice.*

The "retribution" school of punishment also saw its fair share of representation in the 1970s. Classic statements of this thesis come from philosopher Ernest van den Haag (*Punishing Criminals: Concerning a Very Old and Painful Question*) and James Q. Wilson (*Thinking about Crime*). Both authors, while concurring with the contemporary liberal move against indeterminate sentencing, claim that punishment must be based on a principle of "paying back" the suffering imposed on the victims of crime. They prescribe punishment above all other methods. Van den Haag goes so far as to quote Scripture in support of his point: "He that spareth the rod hateth his son" (262).

In the 1980s, retribution was advocated by sources as diverse as James Boyd White (*Heracles' Bow*), James Q. Wilson and Richard J. Herrnstein (*Crime and Human Nature*), Igor Primoratz (*Justifying Legal Punishment*), and Andrew Von Hirsch (*Past or Future Crime*). Each of these authors frames the nature of the prisoner differently. While it would be unfair to characterize each as promoting a straight plan of retribution, each in some degree supports determinate sentencing. While the philosophical justification supporting each argument ranges from what is due the criminal to what is due the victim, the difference in policy is negligible. Taking a constructivist and rhetorical position, White sees the human subject as one essentially constituted in and through discourse. Wilson and Herrnstein, on the other hand, depict criminal behavior as determined both by the physical and genetic attributes of the criminal and by a socially determining context. Primoratz, in an attempt to attack utilitarianism's disregard for the individual, argues that punishment must always be for the purpose of hurting the individual who has brought harm to other individuals; it should never serve as a lesson for others or as a way to protect others. These functions may be helpful side effects of punishment, but by placing them at the top of the motive hierarchy, a culture disregards the individual for the benefit of the masses. In Primoratz's view, because criminals act by free choice, the most respect is shown for them when they are punished as freely acting agents and are not enslaved to social and physical conditions. While also positing a primarily free subject, Von Hirsch argues that agents are at least partially determined by their social surroundings. It is not possible and never will be possible to predict exactly when future crimes will occur and who will be responsible. Consequently, a responsible social body can only punish for retribution, never in order to prevent future crime by individuals who may never commit these crimes.

The use of community correction centers also has been posited from a number of perspectives. Two of the most noteworthy and influential arguments have come from Jessica Mitford (*The American Prison Business*) and Elliot Currie (*Confronting Crime*). A scathing attack on prisons as they existed in 1977, Mitford's book was influential in raising public awareness of the problems and corruption of American prisons. Mitford views the criminal as a thoroughly human subject, guilty or innocent, deserving respect as a human being. One of her solutions to the problems with existing prisons is the creation of community centers to which "nonviolent" criminals would be moved in the latter portions of their prison terms. More recently, liberal Elliot Currie has argued against the deterministic theses of James Q. Wilson. He suggests instead the thesis that criminal behavior is a product of the social conditions of individuals who find themselves with meaningless jobs, little direction, and few goals. Currie, like Mitford, suggests a need for community corrections and the provision of jobs that provide some sense of meaning to the lives of former prisoners.

Today, while explicit arguments for rehabilitation have fallen almost completely out of favor, a shade of the argument that prisoners not only need but deserve rehabilitation appears to be reemerging. Edgardo Rotman argues for viewing rehabilitation not as something granted to the criminal but as a human right. In his *Beyond Punishment: A New View on the Rehabilitation of Criminals* (1990), Rotman argues that it is the task of society to provide all outlets for the cultivation of human independence and self-determination. As this is a right for all human beings and not a privilege, outlets for rehabilitation should be available for all persons convicted of crime. Ideally, these outlets would be without moral directives and without ties to the release date of the prisoner; the prisoner must make a free choice to participate.

These works serve as a basis on which to reflect on the differences between public constructions of the "prisoner" and "expert" or academic constructions. The works allow a study of how arguments are transferred from the realm of the expert to public discussions. While this will not be my main focus, a cursory glance at the dialectics of the two fields of argument proves interesting.

Appendix 2. Differentiating Eras of Discourse

Given the nature of my assumptions and those of the sources I am drawing upon, it is somewhat difficult to provide clear distinctions between various "eras" of discourse as I have done throughout this work. Furthermore, my choice to describe or delineate four eras of discourse may seem to many to run counter to Foucault's attempts to break down continuities in history and to run against the grain of traditional histories. I wish to explain briefly, then, how I have derived these categories and why I have chosen to group them in an era-by-era system.

Foucault once noted that he would accept the historical groupings of discourse already suggested by historians only long enough to "subject them at once to interrogation; to break them up and then to see whether they can be legitimately reformed; or whether other groupings should be made" (*Archaeology* 26). While neither he nor others influenced by him generally create groupings as clearly delineated as those I have chosen here, there are good reasons for doing so.

First, I acknowledge that I am creating a narrative about the occurrence of cultural shifts. As one of my purposes is to posit my story as widely as possible and to make its implications understood by others, it appeared most "rhetorical" and appealing to posit the story in segments, in easily digested units of time. Furthermore, such units make an understanding of the way in which discourse works as a constraint all the easier to see.

Second, I have attempted to be as true to the discourse I have analyzed as is possible. In attempting to separate myself from the historical groupings I found in historical and theoretical works, I attempted to let the discourse arrange itself through my intervention. This is not to say that I do not recognize the power of my own biases, motives, base of knowledge, and critical orientation. I am of course aware that each of these factors affects my relationship with the discourse. Nevertheless, I feel confident that few members of our culture at large would read the same discourse and come up with a reading that radically contradicts this one. While readings could differ given the various orientations and motives of other readers, the patterns I have traced were ones that I could verify subjectively, and, in a very rough fashion, empirically. It is my assumption that the same themes would be observed by any typical reader, although some of my conclusions would not.

As for my procedure, on my first reading of the mass of articles, I made note of clear instances of some categories of characterizations and narratives concerning prisoners. These included violent actions, successful rehabilitation, the use of prisoners to save state finances, the savoring of privileges, homosexual behavior or rape, potential escapees, altruistic behavior, prisoners as failures, prisoners as "effects" of prison and social conditions, riotous behavior, prisoners categorized by race, prisoners categorized by gender, legal actions by prisoners, abnormal behavior, drug use, prisoner ignorance, prisoners as "effects" of abnormal childhoods, immoral and irrational behavior, prisoners as representations of middle-class values, prisoner affection for prison life, and religious behavior. As these categories were derived from a first reading of the discourse, I reread the material and coded it into the various categories. In addition, I took detailed notes and observations from each essay and filed them according to the above categories. I do not expect my categories and "numerical counts" necessarily to convince skeptical readers in search of statistical support. As Condit noted in providing evidence from a similar methodological orientation, "Private discourse and public discourse are both influenced by unique formal characteristics that make statistical tests misleading. Consequently, the author and reader are required to substitute judgment for statistical tests in assessing the significance of these numerical variations" (*Decoding* 223). The counts simply provide a form of categorization that I used in checking my reading. It is in this spirit that I offer this appendix.

Having worked with the material through numerous readings, not only was I able to draw out various themes, but I was also able to cluster the categories described above in order to verify my reading of the discourse. I recognize that another reader might choose to break the "history" of this discourse into different periods than I have chosen or, perhaps more likely, would choose to move the years of the period one or two years either way. Furthermore, I realize that other readers with different interests would develop different categories and read the discourse toward different ends. Nonetheless, the groupings do represent different shifts in the nature of the discourse. The closer one gets to the chronological edges of the eras I have chosen, however, the blurrier the distinctions between the periods become. The closer one gets to the center of a given period, the closer one finds oneself to the heart of the category I have described. No single event brings about a change in these eras; rather, they are the result of numerous forces, including my interpretation of their beginnings and endpoints.

Below, I will trace out the way in which my readings of the texts produced clustered characterizations. The clusters were not useful in every aspect of

Table 1. Characterizations of the Prisoner Organized into Clusters

Cluster A: Altruism

Cluster B: "Human" characteristics, redeemable

Cluster C: Criminal behavior as a result of prison or social surroundings

Cluster D: Homosexual behavior or rape

Cluster E: Immoral and irrational behavior and actions

Cluster F: Nonredeemable and violent prisoner

Cluster G: Racism

Cluster H: Drug use

Cluster I: Legal actions

Cluster J: Representations of female prisoners

my categorization. For instance, while there is a category that discusses specific instances of racism, there is not one breaking down each characterization by race. Instead, in the area of race, I took careful note of the introduction of African-American inmates and all instances of descriptions of the ethnic makeup of prisons. Furthermore, cluster C indicates that criminal behavior is the result of either social or prison conditions. This has different meanings for different prisoners. While it emphasizes that redeemable prisoners were socially coerced into their behavior, it also indicates the way in which African-American and other minority prisoners are coerced into behavior that causes their later imprisonment. I had to distinguish between the two in my interpretation of the discourse. Finally, there are cases in which I made the distinction based on other factors. For instance, I first ran across the use of the phrase "just deserts" in regard to a prisoner in 1975 (and, furthermore, many historians placed the advent of "just deserts" at or about 1975); hence, I began the movement toward this philosophy in 1975. Other matters of interpretation of this nature occurred several times throughout my reading and translation of the essays read for this study. In each case, I checked my initial impulse with the clusters, with my notes, and with the essays themselves.

In short, the four historical periods I have developed here are mandated by the representations of the prisoner found in the discourse itself. While someone else might break the periods up slightly differently, or while someone with different motives and a different orientation might create different categories, the distinctions I have drawn up work to provide the reader with a sense of change. Change is not as abrupt as chapter breaks may indicate. Indeed, the discourse suggests slower, less discernible changes. I leave it to the reader to bear this in mind throughout the text.

Table 2. Instances of Clustered Characterizations of the Prisoner

	A	*B*	*C*	*D*	*E*	*F*	*G*	*H*	*I*	*J*	*Totals*
1950	1	11	1	2	2	0	0	0	0	1	18
1951	5	7	3	3	1	2	0	0	0	1	22
1952	4	8	3	3	1	2	0	0	0	0	21
1953	4	12	8	4	2	1	1	1	1	3	37
1954	3	11	7	2	2	2	1	1	0	0	29
1955	3	5	5	0	2	2	1	0	0	0	18
1956	3	5	6	0	2	1	0	2	0	1	20
1957	2	9	1	2	3	0	0	0	0	2	19
1958	3	5	1	0	2	0	0	1	0	1	13
1959	1	8	2	0	2	1	1	0	0	0	15
1960	3	6	3	2	3	2	1	0	0	0	20
1961	3	5	1	0	2	3	2	1	1	0	18
1962	2	6	2	2	4	2	3	2	0	1	24
1963	5	5	1	1	2	3	2	0	2	1	22
1964	2	6	1	1	3	3	2	2	0	2	22
1965	1	4	1	2	2	3	2	0	1	0	16
1966	2	7	6	4	7	2	4	1	2	0	35
1967	1	8	2	1	3	3	3	1	1	0	23
1968	3	5	4	2	3	5	6	3	2	2	35
1969	1	10	7	1	5	4	5	1	1	0	35
1970	0	10	5	0	3	4	7	2	1	1	33
1971	1	14	14	2	8	7	13	1	8	2	70
1972	2	14	9	2	6	7	8	3	1	1	53
1973	1	10	11	1	7	7	6	1	2	4	50
1974	5	12	12	6	11	8	13	8	3	1	79
1975	0	12	7	2	7	6	3	2	1	1	41
1976	0	7	10	3	6	7	5	3	4	1	46
1977	0	15	3	3	6	8	5	4	2	1	47
1978	2	16	4	3	4	6	5	2	2	2	46
1979	0	9	10	3	5	8	4	4	1	2	46
1980	0	6	7	3	5	5	3	2	4	2	37
1981	0	5	5	1	5	6	2	0	2	0	26
1982	0	4	3	3	4	6	3	2	2	4	31
1983	1	7	2	1	2	5	4	1	2	2	27

(continued)

Table 2. Continued

	A	*B*	*C*	*D*	*E*	*F*	*G*	*H*	*I*	*J*	*Totals*
1984	0	1	7	1	3	4	2	2	3	0	23
1985	1	8	5	1	3	5	7	0	5	1	36
1986	0	5	5	1	3	4	6	0	2	2	28
1987	1	14	9	3	2	8	7	9	7	5	65
1988	0	9	4	2	3	4	5	5	5	3	40
1989	1	4	3	1	2	3	3	4	2	3	26
1990	0	3	3	1	3	3	5	5	5	2	30
1991	0	5	2	2	0	1	7	5	1	3	26
1992	0	9	5	5	0	4	4	9	0	3	39
1993	1	7	4	1	1	1	7	6	5	5	38
Total	68	349	214	83	152	168	168	96	81	66	1445

Appendix 3. Percentage of Prisoners in State and Federal Prisons by Race and Gender

Table 3. Percentage of Prisoners in Federal Prisons by Race and Gender

YEAR	*CAUCASIAN*	*OTHER*	*MALE*	*FEMALE*
1950	69	31	97	3
1955			96	4
1960	66	34	96	4
1965	65	35	96	4
1970	61	39	97	3
1975	64	36	96	4
1980	58	42	96	4
1985	56	44	96	4
1991	49	51	94	6

A few comments are in order about the sources of the above information. First, no information is available as far as I can discern about the racial composition of prisoners in 1955. Information about the racial makeup from 1950 through 1985 was taken from Patrick A. Langan (5). Information about race in 1991 was taken from United States (57). Information concerning the gender of prisoners was derived from Flanagan and Maguire (582) and that about gender in 1991 from United States (52–54).

Notes

1. The Historical Force of Rhetoric and the Disciplinary Force of Culture

1. It has perhaps become an impossibility to hold a discussion of either discourse or punishment, both central to this investigation, without invoking the name and work of Michel Foucault. While the inaccuracies of Foucault's history of punishment have outraged some, his thesis has become the norm for many studies of discipline, especially his discussion of the disciplinary procedures of everyday life in our own era. Foucault originally broaches this topic in his *Discipline and Punish.* For a brief discussion of the reactions to this work, see James Miller's account in his biography of Foucault (233–36) and that of Foss, Foss, and Trapp (208–11).

Here, however, I am far less interested in discussing Foucault's views on punishment than I am in borrowing from his views on discourse and how these views influence this study. Thus, while I do not rely on Foucault for answers to the questions that drive this study for numerous reasons (e.g., that we are dealing with different spatial and temporal cultures, different motivating interests), the assumptions he makes about discourse and its influence do provide some guidance to the "method" of this study. For explicit discussions of Foucault's value or use within rhetorical studies, see Gaonkar; Foss, Foss, and Trapp, 189–212; Blair and Cooper; Blair; Foss and Gill; Sholle; McKerrow, "Critical Rhetoric: Theory"; McKerrow, "Critical Rhetoric and"; and Biesecker.

2. The implications of the role of discourse in constraining and enabling can hardly be overstated. Gerald M. Erchak and Richard Rosenfeld's argu-

ment concerning dyslexia provides a practical example of both of these aspects of discourse. They argue that while the term *dyslexia* has little concrete meaning within the medical community, through reproduction and reshaping in popular media it has come to take on discursively concrete meanings in the reality of everyday life. Furthermore, the meaning of the term *dyslexia* has emerged as the result of a number of factors. First, there was an economic motive for specialists to arise from the medical community and claim expertise on the problem of dyslexia. Second, there were those parents who felt a need to label their offspring's learning problems as "diseases" so they could move away from the social stigma of either having a "slow" child or of being indicted for not spending enough time with their child at home. Finally, there were indeed children with "real" learning problems who needed and benefited from the expertise that emerged.

As a whole, however, the notion of dyslexia was created in the public forum without prior academic or medical support. In a way, academic legitimation was irrelevant. Even had the medical community had a stable meaning for the term, its "effective" meaning lies in how it is enacted in public fields of discourse. Having little reason to read medical journals on dyslexia, I am far more likely to take my meaning of the term from its public enactments on television, in magazines, in newspapers, and on the radio. Before a term exists culturally, no subject can be placed into its category; once it exists and an individual is labeled by it (e.g., as "dyslexic"), it becomes difficult for that individual to separate himself from the category. Dyslexia invites subjects to be defined under its auspices, and once this is done, both the dyslexic and dyslexia are material, more difficult to remove or change.

3. I am indebted to Thomas Lessl for his suggestion of this metaphor.

4. To trace out the history of this concept within rhetorical studies, one should see, in addition to Raymie McKerrow's original 1989 article on "critical rhetoric," McGee, "Text"; Hariman, "Critical"; Charland; Ono and Sloop; and McKerrow, "Critical Rhetoric and."

5. Robert Ivie has also been giving a great deal of comment to rhetorical performance in a series of editorials in the *Quarterly Journal of Speech.* See his "The Performance of Rhetorical Knowledge," "Scrutinizing Performances of Rhetorical Criticism," and "A Question of Significance."

6. The discussion of the fragmentation of contemporary culture can be found in McGee, "Text." One will find more than a passing resemblance between the idea of a "critical rhetoric" and the critical practice of Michel Foucault and his attempts to uncover and address the workings of power/knowledge within culture. This is certainly no coincidence, as McKerrow draws heavily upon Foucault in his attempt to describe this critical perspective.

7. For an excellent example of this type of research as applied to a historical rather than contemporary example, see McGee's "The Origins of 'Liberty': A Feminization of Power." Here, McGee argues that "conceptions of effective ideas should be 'socially material' instead of philosophical or 'socially ideal' " (25). He then proceeds to trace out the term *liberty* as it emerges in public discourses, rather than as defined by philosophers, during the revolutionary era in both England and the colonies.

8. Two other recent exemplary works in discursive analysis are Condit and John Lucaites's analysis of the historic development of the term "equality" (*Crafting*) and Cecelia Tichi's *Electronic Heart,* a discourse analysis of how "television" has been represented and struggled over in American popular culture.

9. As Ernesto Laclau and Chantal Mouffe have asserted, echoing Gramsci, it is mainly in the ideological struggles over the meanings of such terms that effective change takes place (135–37).

10. My methodological tactic closely resembles that followed by Condit in portions of her *Decoding Abortion Rhetoric: Communicating Social Change,* particularly chapters 2 and 4. She describes her methodological perspective on pages 220–25. Here, Condit executes a close analysis of the majority of articles in the *Reader's Guide to Periodical Literature* from 1960 to 1979 under the subject heading "abortion." For this study, I also included newspaper articles in available abstracts (including the computer database *Newsbank* for recent years) and films under the heading "Prison Films, United States" in *The Time Out Film Guide.* In viewing other media, my question is: Does this discourse parallel the popular periodicals or does it negate their arguments? How does it work differently? How does it add to or take away from theses that can be drawn from other popular media?

11. Before 1969, all discussions of male prisoners are listed under the title "Prisoners." After 1969, the *Reader's Guide* directs one to look under "Negro Prisoners" and then later "Black Prisoners" for articles dealing specifically with African Americans. Before 1975, female prisoners are listed under "Women Prisoners." In 1975, the *Reader's Guide* provides separate entries for articles dealing with female inmates. Similarly, in several years during the 1980s, there are separate listings for "Aged Prisoners." For consistency and thoroughness, articles listed under these headings were analyzed as well. Because one of my purposes in conducting this study is to understand the construction of "prisoners" in the United States, I have excluded all articles that have as their sole focus those prisoners, United States citizens or not, being held in foreign prisons.

12. Alexander Nehamas points out that Nietzsche always provided at least one moment in the text when he reminded the readers that his views were always, no matter how stridently stated, only his own (13–41). This could be read as such a moment in this text.

13. This activity is not just a public one. As Blair, Brown, and Baxter have recently argued, the review and editorial processes of our academic journals are one other way in which a particular style of writing is privileged at the expense of all others.

14. Turner (197–225) offers a historical review of how this transition has taken place.

15. Those interested in tracing out the ways in which the "weak" make use of dominant discourses in order to create space for resistance will find some of the more influential ideas in Michel de Certeau's *The Practice of Everyday Life,* Dick Hebdige's *Subculture: The Meaning of Style,* John Fiske's *Television Culture,* Stuart Hall's "The Rediscovery of 'Ideology,' " and Janice Radway's *Reading the Romance.*

16. Dana Cloud has taken a position one step further from "audience-oriented" studies in her recent critique of *Spenser: For Hire.* After analyzing the "ambivalent" nature of the character Hawk and audience receptions of that character, she argues that "we cannot simply assume that ambivalent or contradictory articulations of racial difference are in and of themselves subversive of such a structure" (322). By illustrating the ways in which the character Hawk's oppositional stance and persona, though subject to contradictory critical evaluations, continue to serve the needs of the dominant culture to construct specific racist stereotypes, Cloud illustrates that, regardless of audience readings, texts can still aid the dominant representation of race. Bonnie Dow, in her reading of the *Mary Tyler Moore Show,* also critiques audience studies in arguing that despite the show's popular reception as furthering feminist causes, the show provided a sexist portrayal of Mary through her behavior and relationships. As such, she argues that although audience research can only "enhance our conclusions and perhaps offer some sociological comprehension, it does not replace critical insight" (272).

In a different vein, but a very important one, Elspeth Probyn has made a very cogent argument for a "feminism with attitude." In short, while she makes the poststructural assumptions of a nonessential self, she continues to provide a space for the fashioning of various positions from which the subject may speak and articulate imaginary nonessential selves to be embodied in the future.

17. While I wish to emphasize that my depiction of the media is not meant to suggest that the media have the ability to constrain and discipline individuals and topics completely, I have gained many of my insights on the nature of the media as protectorates of the dominant ideology from recent critical theories with a post-Marxist orientation, theories that often employ language associated with such a view. If we can separate these terms from the theoretical baggage that arrives with the background of the theorists, we benefit in our understanding of the operations of culture. While a theorist like Goran Therborn may use a term like *state,* the term *culture* and the meanings that come with it may be more fitting for my purposes in this essay. In his *What Does the Ruling Class Do When It Rules?* Therborn provides the basis for an understanding of culture as essentially discursive and transformative rather than as a fixed product. Borrowing from Therborn, in my argument, the tasks of culture "may be defined as internal and external defense of a social formation, and supreme rule-making, rule-application and rule-adjudication" (63). Culture is "relatively autonomous" from the dominant or ruling class (147). It is not necessary that culture and public arguments be based on the economic in every instance; rather both may be seen at any given point as results of a historical, discursive articulation (105–14). Indeed, even classes and dominant discourses are discursive and argumentative rather than economically based.

This processual definition of the disciplinary function of ideology is also highlighted by Laclau and Mouffe's definition of hegemony and hegemonic articulations. Hegemony is delineated as a political "type of relation, a form . . . of politics," not a "determinable location within a topography of the social" (139). Hegemony signifies a set of articulatory practices, of floating signifiers that define and create subject positions, positions not necessarily constituted on the plane of the fundamental classes, but centered on one hegemonic articulation. Hegemony must be viewed as the set of dispersed articulatory practices that function to maintain a set of relations and subject positions that support a nondeterminate class in a position of power. What is most important and most intriguing to see in this definition is that the *rhetorical* or *ideological* is, while perhaps not determinate, most fully influential. Existing relations of power, then, are primarily maintained through ideological processes; these ideological processes, however, in turn give meaning to economic processes, political processes, and each individual's sense of self. I have also been influenced in thinking about the disciplinary or therapeutic function of individual behavior and mass media by Berger and Luckmann's discussion of therapy and nihilation (112–16).

18. Here, I am in no subtle way playing off of McGee's conception of "the people" as a rhetorical construct ("In Search").

19. For engaging discussions of the way in which "law" works to build community, see James Boyd White's *Heracles' Bow*, especially the foreword and chapter 2. In this work, White argues that law should be seen not as a set of rules or institutions or structures, but as a "rhetorical and literary activity" (x). White argues that through discussions of law, we create culture and community. Furthermore, for an example of two studies that have examined media representations about crime, law, and order with similar assumptions to those I have espoused here, see *Representing Order* by Richard Ericson, Patricia Baranek, and Janet Chan. Also see Hall et al., *Policing the Crisis,* a study of the moral panic seen in media representations of the "mugging crisis" that followed the Handsworth mugging in 1972. Arguments within the volume express the ways in which discussions of crime express an underlying racist perspective.

20. Celeste Condit has provided a rough "method" or orientation through which mass mediated articles might be organized and commented on in her *Decoding Abortion Rhetoric.* Condit investigates popular essays about abortion for three basic elements: ideographs, narratives, and characterizations (13–14). I focus on the latter two. Because my topic is one designating a group of people (prisoners) rather than an issue (abortion), the discourse is heavily coded in narrative and characterizations and less so in ideographs. While ideographs are of course present when questions of justifying punishment are raised, they are less prevalent in descriptions of the prisoner. I am partial to the extraction of narratives in this study because my understanding of narratives allows the following two assumptions. First, as Paul Ricoeur notes, narratives provide subjects with an understanding of the ultimate ending point for their lives and thus a way in which to characterize their existence now (175–79). For example, Christians may see their ultimate end as heaven and their essential character as children of God while physicists may see their ultimate end as a return to dust and their essential character as the product of proton collisions. In short, narratives give meaning to our lives. Narratives of prisoners allow us a means to constitute prisoners, their essential nature, and their eventual *telos.*

Second, and relatedly, narratives are the grounding for understanding characterizations. Narratives tend to build on one another and hence characterize the primary "actors." When several individual stories appear with similar theme and plot, stories often of the same event, a characteristic is created and elaborated (e.g., the narrative of the black rapist in prison, the narrative of the jailhouse lawyer). Moreover, even when narratives are not provided in articles about prisoners, the prisoners are often described in what turn out to be, once one is able to see patterns emerge, "characterized" forms. It is this characterization that acts as a rhetorical force, constraining the number of possible roles that particular types of inmates (e.g., African Americans, homosexuals, females) may take in future discourses concerning prisoners. Such characterizations play an active role in the text that follows.

21. Again, appendix 2 should be referred to for a "numerical" description of the organization of the following chapters. Be forewarned that the numerical description is not scientific but provides an idea of how I have derived my descriptions and representations.

2. Prelude to the Present: American Histories of Punishment

1. Historians of punishment and criminal justice are certainly indebted to Lawrence Friedman and his relatively recent *Crime and Punishment in American History.* While Friedman draws upon the work of numerous historians in order to provide a relatively comprehensive history of punishment in the United States from the colonial period to the present, he also provides something of a cultural history of punishment. That is, Friedman see his work as a "social history of crime and punishment"; it is not a history of criminal law, nor an intellectual history of penology or criminology, nor a philosophy of good and evil. Instead, it assumes that systems of punishment are made up of "social structure (the way society is organized) and social norms (people's ideas, customs, habits, and attitudes)" (6). In short, he sees crime as something that must be investigated rhetorically rather than philosophically.

Other works important to the historical narrative that I will weave are David J. Rothman's classic *The Discovery of the Asylum,* Adam Jay Hirsch's *The Rise of the Penitentiary,* and John DiIulio's "Understanding Prisons: The New Old Penology."

While I have noted my perspectival debt to the work of Michel Foucault in viewing discourse theoretically, I find his *Discipline and Punish* less useful in understanding the specific and local constructions of prisons and criminals in the United States. While he draws examples from discussions and artifacts outside of France, both the centering of his study in French discourse and its breadth make it less useful for understanding arguments specific to the United States' construction of its own prisoners. Even though both the French and the U.S. ideologies may in some ways be considered "liberal," cultural differences in media usage, the relationship between media and receivers, and indeed distinctions in the treatment of prisoners all work together to make the differences between the two cultures too great to allow the use of Foucault's ideas as if they were readily translatable to a study of the United States. One would doubtless note in my brief provision of the history of punishment striking similarities to Foucault's thesis. Such similarities exist for at least two reasons: (1) Foucault's historical research is simply compatible with those of others in terms of historical "fact," and (2) the way in which one reads "history" after Foucault orients the telling of history toward his perspective.

I have a related problem calling upon Thomas Dumm's history of punishment. Taking basically a Foucauldian viewpoint, Dumm argues that the penitentiary "arose at the transition from a social system in which juridical/sovereign relationships determined the limits of a common political reality to one in which power/knowledge does" (46). Once Dumm establishes this Foucauldian thesis, he is content to assume that Foucault is correct. While Dumm is in some ways illustrating that Foucault's thesis is valid for the United States as well as France, he does so in a "non-Foucauldian" way. That is, he comes to the discourse with Foucault's thesis in hand, never allowing the discourse to speak in any way except the way that his thesis says it should. If we wish to understand how the construction of prisoners (and prisons) has been transformed and where it is heading, we cannot do so by taking Foucault to the discourse. Instead, we must allow particular discourses to "speak" a thesis to us, to the degree that this is possible.

2. Other interesting historical works that one may wish to see include American Correctional Association, *The American Prison: From the Beginning . . . A Pictorial History;* this text provides an interesting and unique way to view prison life and proves useful as a check against the construction of prisoners in discourse. Norman Johnston's *The Human Cage: A Brief History of Prison Architecture* provides an engaging view of prisons by focusing on the ways in which the building and design of prisons have parallel relationships with the views of punishment dominant in the era of the building of each particular prison. Furthermore, Johnston focuses on the ways in which the structures of prisons affect the prisoners' psychological worldviews. There are also various regional prison histories, including David Lewis's *From Newgate to Dannemora: The Rise of the Penitentiary in New York, 1796–1848,* Martin and Ekland-Olson's *Texas Prisons: The Walls Came Tumbling Down,* and Rideau and Wikberg, *Life Sentences.* Each effort offers interesting background information, but none provides a well-rounded history of punishment and prisoners or a rhetorical perspective on punishment. I would also highly recommend that one visit Friedman's "Bibliographical Essay" as a sourcebook for works on crime and criminal justice (467–75).

3. For example, while Rothman centers his history of prisons on the Pennsylvania "Walnut Street Prison" and New York's "Auburn Prison" and argues that the motivation for imprisonment arises out of the mix of Cesare Beccaria's *On Crimes and Punishment* with post-Revolution, post-Calvinism, American liberal ideology (and blossoms with the Jacksonian emphasis on rehabilitation), Hirsch locates the birth of the prison with the Massachusetts "Castle Island Prison" (in addition to the Auburn and Walnut Street

Prisons) and in sixteenth-century English thought about rehabilitation and Puritanism. Moreover, he argues that the move toward rehabilitation existed in American thought much before the Jacksonian era.

4. Friedman points out that juries never sat in New Haven and only sat in other regions when the death penalty was at stake (24).

5. Again, I do not mean to ignore Hirsch's focus on the Massachusetts Castle Island Prison.

6. When I say an "equal justice shared by all," I of course realize that this means "all white male landowners." What is more important here, however, is the move law makes from being based on God's representative to a common link among citizens.

7. While I say "his or her," I do not want to overlook the race, class, or gender dimensions of punishment. As Lawrence Friedman notes, prisons and the court system only had to deal with white citizens during this period, as all others were subject to the "tyrannical rules" of whippings, execution, etc. Moreover, while women made up roughly 4 percent of the prison population at this time, often their male "guardians" (husbands, fathers) could be arrested for the crimes of the female, as the man was responsible for the women "in his charge" (211).

8. Some contemporary examples of the old penology can also be found. See, for example, Ernest van den Haag's *Punishing Criminals: Concerning a Very Old and Painful Question,* James Q. Wilson's *Thinking about Crime,* and Wilson and Herrnstein's *Crime and Human Nature.* In DiIulio's review essay, he cites as examples three new works: Useem and Kimball's *States of Siege: U.S. Prison Riots, 1971–86,* Kauffman's *Prison Officers and Their World;* and Toch and Adams's *Coping: Maladaptation in Prisons.*

9. One should not ignore the fact that such changes took place in fits and starts rather than simultaneously and in full. Moreover, such changes often took place differently in different geographical regions. For examples, in clandestine and open ways, blacks were still much more likely to be held to tyrannical punishment (e.g., whippings, lynchings) in the South than in other parts of the county.

10. For interesting case studies of such arguments, one should certainly see Michel Foucault's *I, Pierre Riviere, Having Slaughtered My Mother, My Sister, and My Brother, . . .* and Charles E. Rosenberg's *The Trial of the Assassin Guiteau.*

11. Other examples of contemporary works that can in some ways be termed the "new penology" include the American Friends Service Committee's highly influential *Struggle for Justice,* Larry Sullivan's *The Prison Reform Movement: Forlorn Hope,* Tonry and Zimring's edited volume *Reform and Punishment,* Edgardo Rotman's *Beyond Punishment: A New View on the Rehabilitation of Criminals,* Elliott Currie's *Confronting Crime,* and Jessica Mitford's bestselling and somewhat muckraking *The American Prison Business.*

12. One should be sure not to miss James B. Jacobs's influential study of the Stateville and Joliet penitentiaries in Illinois, as such stories in many ways act as a not altogether supportive case study in the transition from the "old penology" to the "new." While one of Jacobs's purposes is to explore one

of the few large penitentiaries that did not witness the unrest of other prisons in the 1950s and 1960s, he clearly creates a history of punishment similar to that of Irwin, explaining the cause and effects of such riots. When Joseph Ragen was the warden of the prison from 1936 to 1961, he held authoritarian control over every aspect of its operation and hence was able to prevent riots from erupting. However, after he left, Stateville encountered the same transitions and problems that other prisons had faced earlier. The riots and unrest that occurred after Ragen left as warden, especially as they were depicted in court cases involving the rights of Muslims in the prisons, led to a deterioration of control at the institutional level. No longer were prisons to be controlled by a single warden but were to be run from the level of the state. Because of political and popular pressure, Jacobs claims, the prison was transformed into a rational-legal bureaucracy, losing its local autonomy. Again, material and symbolic conditions came together jointly to reconfigure rhetorically the purpose of an individual prison and of punishment as a whole. Stateville's administration was "professionalized"; its tasks and roles at the administrative level proliferated. The prison administration was no longer either for or against rehabilitation; it simply wanted "a safe, clean, program-oriented institution which functions smoothly on a day to day basis and that is not in violation of code provisions, Administrative Regulations, or court orders" (103–4).

Jacobs blames at least a portion of this change on the impact of decisions by the courts concerning the rights of prisoners. Rather than having the time or resources to work on individual prisoners, the prison administration was forced to spend a large portion of its resources trying to create a rational system that could maintain the status quo while staying within legal limits. That is, prison administrators were being told that, to stay within legal boundaries, they needed to be sure that time and space were arranged for all religious groups, social groups, legal study groups, and so forth. As a result of attempting to cover these legal responsibilities, prison staff were simply unable to afford the time or fiscal resources to advance rehabilitation programs. Jacobs posits that these changes led to a more difficult position for the prison system as a whole; while prisoners escaped the horror of indeterminate sentencing, they came to be viewed as subjects to be maintained rather than humans to be provided with "help."

13. I deal more specifically with penological/criminal justice theory in appendix 1.

3. Rehabilitation and the Altruistic Inmate, 1950–1959

1. Green tells his daughter that "I got to have my freedom and get all that money that is put away and I have to get it for you and Ma and the kids" ("Siege" 17).

2. For other examples of this "human" element of prisoners, see Maisel 82; Elliott 81; Dolan 130.

3. For other examples of prisoners grateful for opportunities to rehabilitate, see Maisel 84; Yoder 81; Marine 477.

4. I am working here with Gronbeck's distinctions between factual, institutional, and symbolic realms of discourse in his study of political corruption.

5. See also McCorkle and Korn 88–98.

6. Other instances of female prisoners primarily represented as mothers are numerous. For the clearest examples, see the two I cite in the text or J. Martin, "The Case," and Bunzel (15–16).

7. I mention only African-American and Hispanic inmates because, with few exceptions, these are the only groups indicated other than whites. This will prove true throughout the periods covered in this study.

4. The Inmate Divide: Rehabilitation and Immorality, 1960–1968

1. Crump's case is also interesting in that it is the one relatively well known, and therefore anomalous, case of an African-American prisoner who is represented as rehabilitated and is supported for being so.

2. See, for example, "Prisoners Also Are People" 345; Conrad, "Prisons" 93; Moeller 81; Pearman 701–4; M. Alexander 98–99.

3. For other examples of this type of depiction, see "On the Outside"; Barton 33–37.

4. A reference back to chapter 2 would indicate that similar themes/characterizations of prisoners were present throughout the nineteenth century. See Friedman 61–260.

5. For more examples of this particular type of argument, see Davis 15; Conrad, "Violence" 113–14.

6. Furthermore, to the degree that people choose media sources that are consistent with their own viewpoints, they are probably more likely to be faced with one of these representations rather than the other.

7. For other examples of brief discussions of African-American inmates, see E. Smith, "I Don't"; Arc 58.

8. I am not maintaining that members of the Nation of Islam were practicing any brand of racism, only that the public representation of them did reflect this view.

9. Again, I am not making judgments about homosexuality here, but reporting on its representation. Homosexuality is rarely if ever represented in prison discourse as a neutral behavior; it is always negative, whether considered violent or perverted.

5. Rehabilitation, Revolution, and Irrationality, 1969–1974

1. For other calls for recreational services, see Flynn; Percy.

2. For other discussions of such programs, see A. Taylor; Kagan.

3. For other examples of such percentages, see Newton 32; England 36–37; Weiner 433; and B. Mason 192.

4. For other examples of this argument, see A. Taylor 172; Minton and Rice; E. Smith, "Pre-posthumous"; A. Anderson.

5. The list of examples of such discourse is not endless but could certainly go on much further. For a few other nice crystallizations of such ways of thinking, see Griswold et al. 23; Duncan 12–13; Barnwell 967; "Prison; Excerpts" 54.

6. The narratives of this occurrence can be found in Scheer; Ritter; "Support"; and "Warning."

6. The Meaning of Just Deserts: Valuing Our Discipline, 1975–1993

1. It is interesting to note that 1993 witnesses essays and articles that suggest that perhaps a medical model of punishment is on the return, although of course to a different rhetorical context. Hence, in a 1993 *New York Times Magazine* article, author Peter Kerr notes that "treatment programs" and "substance abuse programs" are regaining popularity in prisons nationally as a reaction to the 1980s "lock 'em up and throw away the key" attitude (24). Kerr notes that even the most stalwart proponents of "nothing works" (rehabilition does not work) are praising these new therapeutic communities. While there is not enough discourse to suggest a full-fledged transition, this development does offer space for some interesting speculation.

2. John DiIulio makes an interesting argument regarding the *Scared Straight* program in his attempt to argue against the "new penology." The program brings juvenile offenders into maximum security prisons in order to have a number of inmates, many of them life termers, lecture the juveniles about the harshness of prison life. DiIulio notes that the program does not work but that, even if it did, "it would still be a fitting monument to the new penology as the underlying intellectual justification for a situation in which, without any sense of personal shame, professional embarassment, or dereliction of public duty, government officials rely on prisoners to 'scare' potential clients with the officials' own failure to protect and guide—to govern—those in state custody" ("Understanding" 78).

3. While there is little point in repeating all of the examples that build this argument, some of those worth investigating are Astrachan, "Imprisoned"; Bonventre and Marbach; Bunker, "Fasting"; Coleman; Kravitz; Lieber; Magnuson; Press, "Inside"; Press et al., "When Prisons"; Press et al., "When Will."

4. For other examples of the prison's ability to dehumanize prisoners, see "Views From Behind Bars" and T. Mason.

5. For other examples, see W. Moore, "How to"; Keerdoja, Gayle, and Donosky; Baxter; "Tipping"; Sherrill; Suall.

6. For other discussions of rape or homosexuality in prisons during this period, see Astrachan, "Imprisoned" 12; Keerdoja, Gayle and Donosky 12; Stout; Press et al., "When Will" 70–75; Press, "Inside" 51; Press, "AIDS" 30.

7. Such an argument is made clearly in Celeste Condit's discussion of the use of visual images as arguments in public debates over abortion. She

notes that visual images cannot argue for themselves and are hence highly dependent on the words that accompany them (*Decoding* 85). That is, a fetus does not have hands, ears, etc., until someone labels sections of an ultrasound picture with these terms.

8. A nod should be read here in the direction of McGee, "In Search."

7. Conclusions, Beginnings: Into the Future

1. This study also speaks to a number of claims concerning the postmodern condition, specifically as discussed by Jean Baudrillard. In brief, Baudrillard's by now well-known theory of images argues that new technologies of reproduction influence our understandings of ourselves, consciousness, and culture in that they force individuals to acknowledge consciously that symbol systems work via an endless procession of simulacra (*Simulations*). While no connection may have ever existed between the signifier and the real, the contemporary modes of information produce a fragmented culture in which this lack of connection becomes evident, in which subjects find themselves lost without a solid ground on which to stand. Indeed, it provides a world that, according to Baudrillard, one might wish to grasp without being "tied to it by some kind of ideological enthusiasm, or traditional passions" (*Cool Memories*, cover). One recognizes that there is no longer a real with which to compare oneself.

Indeed, Baudrillard faults Foucault for desiring to keep at least a truth value associated with the terms Foucault utilizes in his discourse, terms, for instance, such as *power* (*Forget* 74). He claims that as subjects realize there is only an endless procession of simulacra, there is no longer any reason to believe that forms of surveillance work as discipline. He goes on to prescribe that individuals should feel "free," rather than oppressed, once they recognize the baselessness of all moral positions (*Forget* 74–78, 80–82). Once one takes on Baudrillard's perspective, there is no longer any real to be dealt with: one consequence of this lack of stability would be the inability to see a basis for laws or morality. Hence, punishment could and would be seen as arbitrary. To Baudrillard, this condition is inevitable and, hence, is one we should learn to work with rather than against.

While Baudrillard's impulse to discuss the proliferation of symbols is a useful one, this study suggests that it is not time for human subjects to turn to a conscious state of "giddiness." Rather, this brief exploration into the representation of human subjects who are being overtly disciplined indicates that the grasp of the rhetoric of discipline has only tightened, that discipline is indeed represented as desirable. Faced with the terror of the possibility of a contingent existence, perhaps we turn back to grasp all that our parents have taught us—we turn to whatever basis will allow us to claim a stable moral order, and we hold on tightly.

In essence, then, this conclusion is simply a restatement of what may seem obvious to those who have never encountered the nihilism of Baudrillard: the human subject emerges from a grounding, albeit a contingent and discursive one, and can only live a life without chaos and anomie when at least assuming grounding. The subject emerges in discourse but can only act in life if he or she is able to maintain a belief in stability and grounding. When individual human subjects express their appreciation and ultimate desire for discipline, they are simultaneously expressing a desire for grounding.

2. As Michel Foucault notes, "It is one of my targets to show people that a lot of things that are part of their landscape—that people think are universal—are the results of very precise historical changes . . . and show which space of freedom we can still enjoy and how many changes can still be made" (R. Martin 17).

3. I also feel comfortable rebutting a few particular claims made by historians and philosophers of punishment. For instance, while Irwin and Jacobs both suggest that the outbreak of multiple riots is one of the reasons that rehabilitation programs fell into disfavor at many prisons, this claim is not verified in public discourses. Instead of riots, which can be blamed on prison conditions, the violent nature of certain felons is considered the central cause for the failure of rehabilitation.

Similarly, these same historians argue that one of the major shortcomings of the move to determinate sentencing is that prisoners became framed as being in need of maintenance rather than care and rehabilitation. This, too, is not verified by public arguments. Instead, as we have seen, while this may be true for one depiction of the prisoner, for others, rehabilitation remains a requirement due to the force of past representations. Past constructions and knowledge about this prisoner strongly influence the choice of rehabilitation.

References

Abramson, Pamela. "Cops and Kids in Boise." *Newsweek* 21 June 1982: 42.

Against the Wall. Dir. John Frankenheimer. HBO Pictures, 1993.

Alexander, Myrl E. "What Life is Like in Today's Federal Prisons." *US News and World Report* 11 July 1966: 98–102.

Alexander, Shana. "Under the Rock." *Newsweek* 8 July 1974: 35.

Allen, Gina. "On the Women's Side of the Prison." *Humanist* Sept./Oct. 1978: 28–31.

Allen, Steve. "Let's Brainwash Our Criminals." *Science Digest* 63 (Apr. 1966): 34–40.

Alsop, Stewart. "Dangerous Poor." *Saturday Evening Post* 16 July 1966: 18.

"Alternatives to Prison." *Time* 24 July 1972: 55–57.

Althusser, Louis. "Ideology and Ideological State Apparatuses: Notes Toward an Investigation." In *Lenin and Philosophy and Other Essays.* Trans. Ben Brewster, 121–73. New York: Monthly Review P, 1971.

American Correctional Association. *The American Prison: From the Beginning . . . A Pictorial History.* College Park, MD: American Correctional Assn., 1983.

American Friends Service Committee. *Struggle for Justice.* New York: Hill and Wang, 1971.

Anderson, Alexandra C. "Art from the Inside." *Art in America* 61 (Mar. 1973): 14–15.

Anderson, George M. "Criminal Justice and Women." *America* 19 Apr. 1980: 339–42.

——. "D. C. Jail: The Crime of Punishment." *America* 12 May 1984: 353–57.

——. "Sick behind Bars: Health Care in Prison." *America* 10 Feb. 1990: 124–26.

Arc, M. "Prison Culture, from the Inside." *New York Times Magazine* 28 Feb. 1965: 52–63.
Astrachan, Anthony. "Imprisoned Americans." *New Republic* 20 Nov. 1976: 12–14.
——. "Standing Room Only." *New Republic* 27 Nov. 1976: 12–13.
Attica. Dir. Marvin J. Chomsky. American Broadcast Companies, Inc., 1980.
"Back From the Dead, A Jailhouse Lawyer Asks Why He's Doing Life." *People* 11 July 1988: 71.
Baldi, Frederick S. "What I've Learned About Convicts, Part I." *Saturday Evening Post* 5 Sept. 1953: 17–19, 52–54.
——. "What I've Learned About Convicts, Part II." *Saturday Evening Post* 12 Sept. 1953: 42–43, 92–101.
Banay, Ralph S. "Should Prisons Be Abolished?" *New York Times Magazine* 30 Jan. 1955: 13, 53, 56.
"Bar behind Bars." *Time* 22 May 1964: 88–90.
Barnwell, William H. "Concept: An Idea in Prison Reform." *Christian Century* 27 Sept. 1972: 966–67.
Bartollas, Clemens, Stuart J. Miller, and Simon Dinitz. "The Booty Bandit: A Social Role in a Juvenile Institution." *Journal of Homosexuality* 1 (1974): 203–14.
Barton, Edwin M. "The Day Sing Sing Licked Us." *Coronet* Dec. 1960: 33–37.
Baudrillard, Jean. *Cool Memories.* Trans. Chris Turner. New York: Verso, 1990.
——. *The Ecstasy of Communication.* Trans. Bernard Schutze and Coline Schutze. New York: Semiotext(e), 1988.
——. *Forget Baudrillard: An Interview with Sylvere Lotringer.* Trans. Phil Beitchman, Lee Hildreth, and Mark Polizzotti. New York: Semiotext(e), 1987.
——. *Simulations.* Trans. Paul Foss, Paul Patton, and Philip Beitchman. New York: Semiotext(e), 1983.
Baxter, Gordon. "Jail Birds." *Flying* Aug. 1980: 44–47.
"Be It Ever So Humble." *Time* 24 Dec. 1973: 18.
"Beating the Wall." *Time* 6 Jan. 1975: 75.
Beaumont, Gustave de, and Alexis de Tocqueville. *On the Penitentiary System of the United States and France.* Trans. Francis Lieber. Philadelphia: Carey, Lea, and Blanchard, 1833.
Beccaria, Cesare. *On Crimes and Punishments.* Trans. Henry Paolucci. Indianapolis: Bobbs-Merrill, 1963.
Bentham, Jeremy. *An Introduction to the Principles of Morals and Legislation.* London: Athlone P, 1970.
Berger, Peter, and Thomas Luckmann. *The Social Construction of Reality.* Garden City, NY: Anchor Books, 1967.
Berkeley, Norborne, Jr. "Forgotten Minority: Society and the Ex-Con." *Vital Speeches of the Day* 15 Oct. 1974: 28–31.
Best, Joel, ed. *Images of Issues: Typifying Contemporary Social Problems.* Hawthorne, NY: Aldine De Gruyter, 1989.
Biesecker, Barbara. "Michel Foucault and the Question of Rhetoric." *Philosophy and Rhetoric* 25 (1992): 351–64.

"Big-Hearted Guy." *Newsweek* 15 June 1953: 27.
Bishop, Gloria Wade. "Four and a Half Days in Atlanta's Jails." *Atlantic* July 1964: 68–70.
Bistro, Bob. "#1770, Conrad Maas Artist." *Coronet* Nov. 1957: 54–58.
"Black Men Six Times More Likely to Get Prison Term." *Jet* 19 Aug. 1985: 39.
Blair, Carole. "The Statement: Foundation of Foucault's Historical Criticism." *Western Journal of Speech Communication* 51 (1987): 364–83.
Blair, Carole, Julie Brown, and Leslie A. Baxter. "Disciplining the Feminine." *Quarterly Journal of Speech* 80 (1994): 383–409.
Blair, Carole, and Martha Cooper. "The Humanist Turn in Foucault's Rhetoric of Inquiry." *Quarterly Journal of Speech* 73 (1987): 151–71.
Bonventre, Peter, and William D. Marbach. " 'Hell' in Texas." *Newsweek* 15 Jan. 1979: 74.
Boyd, Frederick V., and Wilson F. Minor. "Prison Watchdog." *Newsweek* 7 May 1979: 105–6.
Boyle, Wanda. "Helping (Children) to Grow Physically, Mentally, and Spiritually Isn't an Amateur's Job." *Ladies Home Journal* Sept. 1972: 68–69.
"Boys and Girls Together." *Newsweek* 23 July 1973: 23–24.
"Braille in Jail." *Ebony* Nov. 1972: 82–85.
"The Break That Failed." *Commonweal* 4 Feb. 1955: 467–68.
Brecher, Ruth, and Edward Brecher. "They Volunteered for Cancer." *Reader's Digest* Apr. 1958: 62–66.
Bricker, Rebecca. "A Demure English Professor Who Fights for the Freedom of Her Husband, a Convicted Cop Killer." *People* 9 Feb. 1981: 76–80.
Brown, Charles J. "Technology and Crime Reduction." *Futurist* Dec. 1984: 27–30.
Brown, Chip. "The Transformation of Johnny Spain." *Esquire* Jan. 1988: 72–81.
Bunker, Edward. "Fasting in Prison: The Mess-Hall 'Insurrection.' " *The Nation* 11 Dec. 1976: 627–28.
——. "The Lynching of Vinson Harris." *The Nation* 17 May 1986: 681, 697–99.
——. "Open Letter From Prison: Eddie Bunker Wants to Go Straight." *The Nation* 18 Dec. 1976: 657–58.
——. "Writer in Prison: The Catch in Rehabilitation." *The Nation* 16 Feb. 1974: 205–7.
Bunzel, Peter. "The Outcry of a Woman Condemned." *Life* 8 Dec. 1958: 115–18.
Burdman, Milton. "Realism in Community-Based Correctional Services." *Annals of the American Academy* 38 (1969): 71–80.
Burger, Warren E. "For Whom the Bell Tolls." *Vital Speeches of the Day* 15 Mar. 1970: 322–25.
Burke, Kenneth. *A Grammar of Motives.* Berkeley: U of California P, 1962.
Burkhart, Kitsi. "Women in Prison." *Ramparts* June 1971: 20–29.
Byrn, Robert M. "The Morality of Punishment." *America* 15 Jan. 1972: 39–41.
Byron, Dora. "Georgia Rockpile." *The Nation* 29 June 1957: 568–69.
Cahill, Tom. "Rape behind Bars." *Progressive* Nov. 1985: 32–34.
"The California Plan: How One State Is Salvaging Its Convicts." *US News and World Report* 24 Aug. 1970: 44–47.

Cameron, Gledhill. " 'I Take the Girls to Prison.' " *Collier's* 30 May 1953: 9–11.
Cape, Bruce. "One Man's Break from Prison's Vicious Cycle." *US News and World Report* 23 Apr. 1984: 46.
"Captive Class." *Newsweek* 8 Nov. 1965: 78.
"Captive Congregation in a Calaboose." *Life* 23 Nov. 1955: 105, 108.
Carlson, Cathy M. "Friends Not Authority Figures." *Aging* 1987: 23.
Carlson, Peter. "Killing Time on Death Row." *The Nation* 25 June 1977: 774–75.
Carroll, Ginny. "An Ugly Silence in a Prison Death." *Newsweek* 4 Aug. 1986: 19.
Carty, William H. "You've Got to Be Tougher than the Toughs." *Collier's* 5 Mar. 1954: 70–75.
"The Case of Paul Crump." *Christian Century* 1 Aug. 1962: 929.
Castelli, Jim. "Inside the Prison-Industrial Complex." *Commonweal* 5 Nov. 1971: 124–25.
"Catalogue of Savagery." *Time* 20 Sept. 1968: 54.
Chaneles, Sol. "Growing Old behind Bars." *Psychology Today* Oct. 1987: 46–51.
Charland, Maurice. "Finding a Horizon and *Telos:* The Challenge to Critical Rhetoric." *Quarterly Journal of Speech* 77 (1991): 75–78.
Chaze, William L. "Death Row: 'This Ain't Just a Bad Dream.' " *US News and World Report* 1 Apr. 1985: 68–69.
Christianson, Scott. "In 1976: The Lesson Not Learned." *The Nation* 4 Dec. 1976: 586–88.
Christopher, Maura. "When Mothers Serve Time." *Scholastic Update* 9 Feb. 1987: 8.
Cleaver, Eldridge. "Address." *Ramparts* 14 Dec. 1968: 6–10.
Clemmer, Donald. *The Prison Community.* 1940. Rpt. New York: Rinehart, 1958.
Cloud, Dana. "The Limits of Interpretation: Ambivalence and the Stereotype in *Spenser: For Hire.*" *Critical Studies in Mass Communication* 9 (1992): 311–24.
Coan, Peter M. " 'They Used to Call Me McEnroe.' " *World Tennis* May 1987: 20–21.
"Coed Incarceration." *Time* 16 Sept. 1974: 84.
Cohen, Duffie. "The Struggle to Cap Sky-High Prison Costs." *Scholastic Update* 9 Feb. 1987: 10–11.
Coleman, John R. "What I Learned Last Summer." *Psychology Today* Nov. 1980: 14–21.
"Comments on Bobby Seale's *Seize the Time.*" *Ramparts* June 1970: 17–29.
Condit, Celeste. *Decoding Abortion Rhetoric: Communicating Social Change.* Urbana: U of Illinois P, 1990.
——. "Democracy and Civil Rights: The Universalizing Influence of Public Argumentation." *Communication Monographs* 54 (1987): 1–18.
——. "The Rhetorical Limits of Polysemy." *Critical Studies in Mass Communication* 6 (1989): 103–22.
Condit, Celeste Michelle, and John Louis Lucaites. *Crafting Equality: America's Anglo-African Word.* Chicago: U of Chicago P, 1993.

Congdon, Thomas B. "The Convict Volunteers." *Saturday Evening Post* 2 Mar. 1963: 62–64.
Conrad, John P. "Prisons and Prison Reform." *Current History* 53 (Aug. 1967): 88–93, 117.
———. "Violence in Prison." *Annals of the American Academy* 364 (1964): 113–19.
"Convicts Bone Up on Stocks." *Business Week* 18 Jan. 1969: 22.
"Convicts Bully a Sovereign State." *Life* 5 May 1952: 27–33.
Coons, William R. "Attica Graduate Tells His Story." *New York Times Magazine* 10 Oct. 1971: 20–21, 92–98.
Corn, David. "Justice's War on Drug Treatment." *The Nation* 14 May 1990: 659–62.
"Corporal Punishment vs. Solitary Confinement." *Intellect* Dec. 1974: 146.
"Court Upholds $100,000 for 'Jailhouse Lawyer.' " *Jet* 20 May 1985: 12.
Cowley, S. W. "Gospel Behind Bars." *Newsweek* 29 Mar. 1976: 84.
Cozart, Reed. "Our Prisons Need Not Fail." *Saturday Evening Post* 8 Oct. 1955: 17–18, 121–22.
Creighton, Linda. "Nursery Rhymes and Hard Time." *US News and World Report* 8 Aug. 1988: 22–24.
"Crime Cures." *The Nation* 23 Feb. 1974: 230.
"The Crimes of Punishment." *Progressive* Feb. 1985: 12–13.
"Crisis Builds in America's Crowded Prisons." *US News and World Report* 7 Aug. 1978: 32.
Crittenden, Ann. "Prison Can Be a Dumb Solution." *New York Times* 29 Dec. 1989.
"Crusading Cons." *Time* 4 Oct. 1968: 60.
Cuddy, Edward. "College for Convicts." *Progressive* Feb. 1977: 53–55.
Currie, Elliott. *Confronting Crime: An American Challenge.* New York: Pantheon, 1985.
Davis, Alan J. "Sexual Assaults in the Philadelphia Prison System and Sheriff's Vans." *Transaction* Dec. 1968: 2, 8–16.
de Certeau, Michel. *The Practice of Everyday Life.* Berkeley: U of California P, 1984.
"Death Row: A New Kind of Suspense." *Newsweek* 11 Jan. 1971: 23–27.
"Death-Row Murderers Could Be Lifesavers." *Newsweek* 9 Jan. 1989: 49.
The Defiant Ones. Dir. Stanley Kramer. Lomitas Productions and Curtleigh Productions, 1958.
Dellinger, Robert. "The Grape Seed and Fried Ice Cream Game." *Psychology Today* Jan. 1974: 89–90.
Deming, Barbara. "In the Birmingham Jail. . . . " *The Nation* 25 May 1963: 436–37.
Dent, Lewis. "The Social Structure of the Underworld: Who's Who in Prison Life." *Harper's* May 1953: 21–27.
Dickey, Christopher. "A New Home for Noriega?" *Newsweek* 15 Jan. 1990: 66–69.
Dickson, Phil. "The Inmate Press." *The Nation* 27 Apr. 1974: 527–30.
DiIulio, John. "Punishing Smarter." *The Brookings Review* Summer 1989: 3–12.

———. "Understanding Prisons: The New Old Penology." *Law and Social Inquiry* 16 (1991): 65–100.
DiLeo, Michael. "Writer with Convictions." *Mother Jones* Jan./Feb. 1991: 36–38, 83–85.
DiSpoldo, Nick. "Halfway Houses: A Prison Alternative." *America* 20 Apr. 1985: 319–21.
———. "Prisoners and the Law." *America* 5 Nov. 1983: 269–71.
Dolan, George. "Convicts Take the Cure." *American Mercury* Oct. 1953: 130–31.
Douglas, Carlyle C. "How Justice Shortchanges Blacks." *Ebony* Oct. 1974: 76–84.
Dow, Bonnie. "Hegemony, Feminist Criticism, and *The Mary Tyler Moore Show.*" *Critical Studies in Mass Communication* 7 (1990): 261–74.
"Down on the Farm." *Newsweek* 20 Feb. 1967: 101–4.
Doyle, Barrie. "Jesus in Jail." *Christianity Today* 5 July 1974: 44–46.
"Drug Tests behind Bars." *Business Week* 27 June 1964: 58–62.
Drury, Michael. "A Prison Was My Classroom." *McCall's* July 1962: 45, 127–28.
Duffy, Clinton T. "San Quentin Is My Home, Part One." *Saturday Evening Post* 25 Mar. 1950: 19–21, 147–52.
———. "San Quentin Is My Home, Part Two." *Saturday Evening Post* 1 Apr. 1950: 34–35, 95–99.
———. "San Quentin Is My Home, Part Three." *Saturday Evening Post* 8 Apr. 1950: 42–43, 95–100.
———. "San Quentin Is My Home, Part Four." *Saturday Evening Post* 15 Apr. 1950: 42–43, 92–104.
———. "San Quentin Is My Home, Part Five." *Saturday Evening Post* 22 Apr. 1950: 34, 134–36.
———. "San Quentin Is My Home, Part Six." *Saturday Evening Post* 29 Apr. 1950: 34, 118–22.
———. "San Quentin Is My Home, Part Seven." *Saturday Evening Post* 6 May 1950: 34, 162–66.
———. "San Quentin Is My Home, Part Eight." *Saturday Evening Post* 13 May 1950: 34, 178–82.
Duffy, Gladys. "Warden's Wife." *Good Housekeeping* Sept. 1959: 60–61, 174–223.
Dumm, Thomas L. *Democracy and Punishment.* Madison: U of Wisconsin P, 1987.
Duncan, Don. "America's Devil Island." *Ramparts* 25 Jan. 1969: 8–14.
Earley, Pete. *The Hot House: Life inside Leavenworth Prison.* New York: Bantam, 1992.
Eddy, L., and Tom Runyon. "Iowa's Convict Fishermen." *Saturday Evening Post* 9 Sept. 1950: 17.
Einstein, Charles. "Fish of Death Row." *Coronet* Aug. 1960: 146–48.
Elliott, Lawrence. "World within Walls." *Coronet* Feb. 1952: 69–84.
"The Employees Who Got a Second Chance." *Nation's Business* Apr. 1967: 90–95.

England, Ralph W. "Is the Prison Becoming Obsolete?" *Current History* 61 (1971): 35–39, 50.

Erchak, Gerald M., and Richard Rosenfeld. "Learning Disabilities, Dyslexia, and the Medicalization of the Classroom." In *Images of Issues: Typifying Contemporary Social Problems.* Ed. Joel Best, 79–98. Hawthorne, NY: Aldine De Gruyter, 1989.

Ericson, Richard V., Patricia M. Baranek, and Janet B. L. Chan. *Representing Order: Crime, Law, and Justice in the News Media.* Toronto: U of Toronto P, 1991.

The Executioner's Song. Dir. Lawrence Schiller. Virgin Films, 1982.

Faber, Nancy. "An Unusual Experiment at Stanford Dramatizes the Brutality of Prison Life." *Life* 15 Oct. 1971: 82–83.

Fagin, Alane, and Arlene Reid. "Moms in Jail." *Children Today* Jan./Feb. 1991: 12–13.

Farbar, Bernard. "My Life Inside." *Esquire* Sept. 1988: 146–54.

Farrell, Barry. "A New Way to Run the Big House." *Life* 8 Sept. 1972: 32–36, 41.

Felder, Carol L. "NOW Goes to Jail: Reaching through the Bars." *Ms.* Jan. 1975: 21.

Fiske, John. *Television Culture.* New York: Methuen, 1987.

Flanagan, Timothy J., and Kathleen Maguire, eds. *Sourcebook of Criminal Justice Statistics 1989.* Washington, DC: Hindeland Criminal Justice Research Center, 1990.

Fleming, Robert. "Drugging Inmates: God in Pill Form." *Encore American and Worldwide News* 1 Oct. 1979: 44.

Flynn, Edith E. "Recreation—A Privilege or a Necessity?" *Parks and Recreation* Sept. 1974: 34–36, 57–59.

Footlick, Jerrold K., Frederick Boyd, and Holly Camp. "Death Watch." *Newsweek* 12 June 1978: 105.

Foss, Sonja K., Karen A. Foss, and Robert Trapp. *Contemporary Perspectives on Rhetoric.* Prospect Heights, IL: Waveland Press, 1985.

Foss, Sonja K., and Ann Gill. "Michel Foucault's Theory of Rhetoric as Epistemic." *Western Journal of Speech Communication* 51 (1987): 384–401.

Foucault, Michel. *The Archaeology of Knowledge.* Trans. A. M. Sheridan Smith. New York: Pantheon, 1972.

———. "Clarifications on the Question of Power." In *Foucault Live.* Trans. James Cascaito. Ed. Sylvere Lotringer, 179–92. New York: Columbia UP, 1989.

———. *Discipline and Punish: The Birth of the Prison.* Trans. Alan Sheridan. New York: Pantheon, 1977.

———. *The History of Sexuality.* Vol. I: *An Introduction.* Trans. Robert Hurley. New York: Vintage, 1980.

———. "Nietzsche, Genealogy, History." In *The Foucault Reader.* Trans. C. Porter. Ed. Paul Rabinow, 76–100. New York: Pantheon, 1984.

———. "The Order of Things." In *Foucault Live.* Trans. John Johnston. Ed. Sylvere Lotringer, 1–10. New York: Columbia U, 1989.

———. "Truth and Power." In *Power/Knowledge: Selected Interviews and Other Writings 1972–1977.* Trans. Colin Gordon, Leo Marshall, John

Mepham, and Kate Soper. Ed. Colin Gordon, 109–33. New York: Pantheon, 1980.
——, ed. *I, Pierre Riviere, Having Slaughtered My Mother, My Sister, and My Brother . . . A Case of Parricide in the 19th Century.* Trans. Frank Jellinek. New York: Pantheon, 1975.
Fox, Vernon, and Bill Fay. "How I Broke the Michigan Prison Riot." *Collier's* 12 July 1952: 11–13, 48–49.
Freeman, Jean Todd. "My Baby Was Born in Prison." *Ladies Home Journal* July 1979: 31–34, 130.
Friedman, Lawrence M. *Crime and Punishment in American History.* New York: BasicBooks, 1993.
Friedman, Robert. "Death Row." *Esquire* Apr. 1980: 84–92.
"GE Opens a Prison Door with Computer Training." *Business Week* 20 Nov. 1966: 96–103.
Gaddis, Thomas E. "Home at Last: The Prison Habit." *The Nation* 5 June 1972: 719–21.
Gallagher, Dorothy. "The Teacher Who Chose to Go to Jail." *Redbook* Jan. 1971: 58–59, 160–64.
"The Gang's All Here." *Time* 23 Apr. 1973: 39.
Gaonkar, Dilip Parameshawar. "Foucault on Discourse: Methods and Temptations." *Journal of the American Forensic Association* 18 (1982): 246–57.
Gerber, Toni. "Letters to Gary Gilmore." *Psychology Today* May 1980: 33.
Gest, Ted. "Personalized Penalties." *US News and World Report* 20 Nov. 1989: 75–76.
——. "Teaching Convicts Real Street Smarts." *US News and World Report* 18 May 1987: 72.
Ginzburg, Ralph. "Castrated: My Eight Months in Prison." *New York Times Magazine* 3 Dec. 1972: 38–39, 143–50.
Goldfarb, Ronald L. "No Room in the Jail." *New Republic* 5 Mar. 1966: 12–14.
——. "Rapping with Convicts." *New Republic* 19 July 1969: 21–23.
Goldinger, Milton, ed. *Punishment and Human Rights.* Cambridge, MA: Schenkman P, 1974.
"The Good Life in Stir." *Newsweek* 25 Feb. 1974: 55.
"Good Samaritan." *Time* 15 June 1953: 24.
Gottfredson, Michael R., Michael J. Hindeland, and Nicolette Parisi, eds. *Sourcebook of Criminal Statistics 1977.* Albany, NY: Criminal Justice Research Center, 1978.
Greenfeld, Lawrence A. *Women in Prison.* Washington, DC: U.S. Department of Justice, 1991.
Gribben, Bruce. "Prison Education in Michigan City, Indiana." *Phi Delta Kappan* May 1983: 656–58.
Griswold, H., et al. "Eye for an Eye." *New Republic* 4 July 1970: 23–24.
Gronbeck, Bruce. "The Rhetoric of Political Corruption: Sociolinguistic, Dialectical, and Ceremonial Processes." *Quarterly Journal of Speech* 64 (1978): 155–72.
"Halfway Help." *Christianity Today* 6 Nov. 1970: 35.
Hall, Sarah Moore. "A Teenager's Traffic Tickets End in a Jailhouse Tragedy—and Boise, Idaho Wonders Why." *People* 21 June 1982: 36–37.

Hall, Stuart. "The Rediscovery of 'Ideology': The Return of the Repressed in Media Studies." In *Culture, Society, and the Media.* Ed. Michael Gurevitch, Tony Bennett, James Curran, and Janet Woollacott, 56–90. London: Methuen, 1982.

Hall, Stuart, Chas Critcher, Tony Jefferson, John Clarke, and Brian Roberts, eds. *Policing the Crisis: Mugging, the State, and Law and Order.* New York: Holmes and Meier, 1978.

Hammer, Richard. "Role Playing: A Judge is a Con, A Con is a Judge." *New York Times Magazine* 14 Sept. 1969: 56–70.

Hariman, Robert. "Afterward: Relocating the Art of Public Address." *Rhetoric and Popular Culture in 19th Century America.* Ed. Thomas W. Benson. East Lansing: Michigan State UP, in press.

——. "Critical Rhetoric and Postmodern Theory." *Quarterly Journal of Speech* 77 (1991): 67–70.

Harmer, Ruth Mulvey. "They Turn Criminals into Craftsmen." *Reader's Digest* Jan. 1959: 128–32.

Harris, Jean. "The Babies of Bedford." *New York Times Magazine* 28 Mar. 1993: 26–27.

——. "Inside Story." *New York* 13 June 1983: 24–29.

——. "Life in Prison." *McCall's* Sept. 1982: 73–75, 121–22.

Hebdige, Dick. *Subculture: The Meaning of Style.* New York: Methuen, 1979.

Hinson, Sandra. "Terry Jean Moore Fights to Keep Her Baby in a Florida Prison." *People* 21 May 1979: 63–64.

Hirsch, Adam Jay. *The Rise of the Penitentiary: Prisons and Punishment in Early America.* New Haven, CT: Yale UP, 1992.

Holden, Constance. "Patuxent: Controversial Prison Clings to Belief in Rehabilitation." *Science* 10 Feb. 1978: 665–68.

——. "Prisons: Faith in 'Rehabilitation' is Suffering a Collapse." *Science* 23 May 1975: 815.

Hollister, Hal W. "An Ex-Convict's Scheme for More Practical Prisons." *Harper's* Aug. 1962: 14–20.

——. "How to Succeed in Jail." *Saturday Evening Post* 6 Oct. 1962: 74–77.

——. "What Convicts Are Made Of." *Reader's Digest* Nov. 1961: 103–8.

——. "Why Prisoners Riot." *Atlantic* Oct. 1955: 65–67.

hooks, bell. "Marginality as Site of Resistance." *Out There: Marginalization and Contemporary Cultures.* Ed. Russell Ferguson, Martha Gever, Trinh T. Minh-ha, and Cornel West, 341–44. New York: New Museum of Contemporary Art, 1990.

"Hope for Criminals Who Are Mentally Abnormal." *Science Newsletter* 17 June 1961: 371.

Hopkins, J. V., and L. L. Hopkins. "Seven in Death Row. *The Nation* 1 Dec. 1956: 476–78.

Horkheimer, Max, and Theodor Adorno. *Dialectic of Enlightenment.* Trans. John Cumming. New York: Continuum, 1988.

Horn, Patrice. "On Fitting Inmates for Release." *Psychology Today* Apr. 1973: 88.

——. "Personal Graffiti—The Rogue's Tattoo." *Psychology Today* Jan. 1974: 26–27.

———. "A Rule That Keeps Competent Defendants from Trial." *Psychology Today* Feb. 1978: 29–33.
Horowitz, Irving L. "Alias 'Mad Bomber Sam.' " *Commonweal* 16 June 1972: 327–31.
"How a Prisoner Became a Writer." *Ebony* Nov. 1962: 88–94.
Howard, Lucy, Gerald C. Lubenow, and Stephan Lesher. "What Prisons Should Do." *Newsweek* 10 Feb. 1975: 36.
Huie, Virginia A. "Mom's in Prison." *Progressive* Apr. 1992: 22–23.
"Hypnopaedia." *The Nation* 25 Jan. 1958: 62.
"In Prison, An Ex-Actor Stages the Watergate Tapes." *People* 14 Apr. 1975: 22–23.
"Into the Fire." *The Nation* 7 Mar. 1981: 260–61.
"Iron Bars a Cage." *Time* 10 Dec. 1956: 23–24.
Irving, Clifford. "Jailing." *Playboy* Nov. 1977: 168–72, 187–92.
Irwin, John. *Prisons in Turmoil.* Boston: Little, Brown, 1980.
Ivie, Robert. "The Performance of Rhetorical Knowledge." *Quarterly Journal of Speech* 80 (1994): 128.
———. "A Question of Significance." *Quarterly Journal of Speech* 80 (1994): 382.
———. "Scrutinizing Performances of Rhetorical Criticism." *Quarterly Journal of Speech* 80 (1994): 248.
Jackson, Bruce. "Our Prisons Are Criminal." *New York Times Magazine* 22 Sept. 1968: 44–47.
———. "Prison: The New Academy." *The Nation* 6 Dec. 1971: 584–89.
Jackson, Bruce, and Diane Christian. "Death Row." *Society* Nov. 1979: 53–61.
Jackson, George. "The Last Words of a Soledad Brother." *Esquire* Mar. 1972: 111, 157.
Jackson, Paul. "Prison Heroes Conquer Malaria." *Coronet* Nov. 1950: 40–42.
Jacobs, James B. *Stateville: The Penitentiary in Mass Society.* Chicago: U of Chicago P, 1977.
Jacoby, Tamara. "The Lady on Cell Block 112A." *Newsweek* 5 Sept. 1988: 60.
"The Jailhouse Lawyers." *Newsweek* 2 Sept. 1974: 74–75.
"Jaycees in Prison." *Time* 20 Sept. 1971: 60–61.
Jennes, Gail. "Saved from the Electric Chair, Hank Arsenault Warns Kids That Crime Pays Only in Heartbreak." *People* 23 Oct. 1978: 55–57.
"Jobs behind Bars: Boon to Prisoners and Taxpayers." *US News and World Report* 20 June 1977: 60.
Johnson, Lawrence. "The Executioner's Bias." *National Review* 15 Nov. 1985: 44.
Johnston, Norman. *The Human Cage: A Brief History of Prison Architecture.* New York: Walker, 1973.
Jones, Ann. "One Woman Who Chose to Say No." *The Nation* 17 Apr. 1982: 456–59.
"Judges vs. Jailers." *Time* 16 Sept. 1966: 69.
Junger, Victor. "Psychiatrist Emilee Wilson Treats Rape, but Her Patients Are the Victims." *People* 16 Oct. 1978: 60–62.
"Jungle Rats." *Time* 27 June 1969: 78.
"Justice Department Explores Black Prisoner's Death." *Jet* 25 Aug. 1986: 33.

"Justice within Prison Walls." *Newsweek* 9 Sept. 1974: 54.
Kagan, Julia. "Working to Stay Out of Jail." *McCall's* July 1974: 35.
Kaszycki, Andrea Charlene. "Don't Expect More of Your Children than You Do of Yourself." *Ladies Home Journal* Sept. 1972: 60–62.
Kauffman, Kelsey. *Prison Officers and Their World.* Cambridge: Harvard UP, 1989.
Keerdoja, Eileen, Stephen H. Gayle, and Lea Donosky. "Soledad Nephew." *Newsweek* 27 Feb. 1978: 12.
Kellett, Mike. "Convicts Also Have Hearts." *Coronet* Mar. 1961: 173–76.
Kellogg, M. A. "Enterprise: The Delancey Street Gang." *Newsweek* 23 Sept. 1974: 81–82.
Kelly, Kathy. "A Note from Prison." *America* 14 Oct. 1989: 230.
Kenney, Anne. "Capital Punishment: Just or Cruel?" *Scholastic Update* 9 Feb. 1987: 13.
Kerr, Peter. "The Detoxing of Prisoner 88A0802." *New York Times Magazine* 27 June 1993: 22–27, 58–59.
"Kids of Women Prisoners Must Bear Emotional Scars." *Jet* 27 May 1985: 32.
Knight, Cook. "Family Prison." *Cosmopolitan* Mar. 1960: 62–67.
Kort, Michelle. "A Tough Assignment—Working Out Inside." *Ms.* Oct. 1987: 32.
Krajick, Kevin. "Electronic House Arrest." *Psychology Today* Oct. 1985: 72–73.
Kravitz, Lee. "Our Crowded Prisons: Do They Cause Crime or Cure It?" *Scholastic Update* 9 Feb. 1987: 4–5.
LaBarre, Harriet. "The California Institute for Women." *Cosmopolitan* Oct. 1957: 52–57.
Labat, Edgar. "My Fourteen Years on Death Row." *Look* 19 Mar. 1968: 80–88.
Lacayo, Richard. "Considering the Alternatives." *Time* 2 Feb. 1987: 60–61.
———. "Our Bulging Prisons." *Time* 29 May 1989: 28–31.
Laclau, Ernesto, and Chantal Mouffe. *Hegemony and Socialist Strategy: Towards a Radical Democratic Politics.* New York: Verso, 1985.
Lamott, Kenneth. "Cells as Second Homes." *Holiday* Feb. 1966: 12–21.
———. "Lung-gom Runner." *New Yorker* 23 Apr. 1960: 151–63.
———. "Socrates at San Quentin." *New Yorker* 2 May 1959: 130–47.
———. "We Have to Live Here, Too." *New Yorker* 12 Mar. 1960: 142–45.
Langan, Patrick A. *Race of Prisoners Admitted to State and Federal Institutions, 1926–86.* Washington, DC: U.S. Department of Justice, 1991.
"The Last Mile?" *Time* 20 July 1962: 22.
Lazersfeld, Paul F., and Robert K. Merton. "Mass Communication, Popular Taste, and Organized Social Action." In *The Communication of Ideas.* Ed. Lyman Bryson, 95–118. Binghamton, NY: Institute for Religious and Social Studies, 1948.
"Lester's Open House." *Newsweek* 1 May 1967: 24.
Lewis, W. David. *From Newgate to Dannemora: The Rise of the Penitentiary in New York, 1796–1848.* Ithaca, NY: Cornell UP, 1965.
"Library Service for Prisons Aim of New Organizations." *Library Journal* 1 Jan. 1972: 20.
Liddy, G. Gordon. "Serving Time in America." *Esquire* Dec. 1977: 138–40, 222–26.

Lieber, James. "The American Prison: A Tinderbox." *New York Times Magazine* 8 Mar. 1981: 26–35, 56–61.
"Life in Prison." *Commonweal* 6 Mar. 1953: 543–44.
Little, Tim. "I Care, You Care, He Cares." *Harper's* Apr. 1964: 170.
"Lock Them Up!" *Senior Scholastic* 12 Mar. 1973: 11.
Lyotard, Jean-François. *The Postmodern Condition: A Report of Knowledge.* Trans. Geoff Bennington and Brian Massumi. Minneapolis: U of Minnesota P, 1984.
MacCormick, Austin. "Behind Those Prison Riots." *Reader's Digest* Dec. 1953: 97–101.
Magnuson, Ed. "Prison Nightmare." *Time* 8 June 1981: 16–18.
Maisel, Albert Q. "No Locks in This Prison." *Reader's Digest* Feb. 1953: 81–84.
Marine, Gene. "Part-Time Jail." *The Nation* 21 Dec. 1957: 477.
Marousek, Theresa. "Work Release: A Step toward Eliminating the Atticas." *Christian Century* 12 Apr. 1972: 428–31.
Martin, John Bartlow. "America's Toughest Prison, Part I." *Saturday Evening Post* 20 Oct. 1951: 19–21, 52–53.
——. "America's Toughest Prison, Part II." *Saturday Evening Post* 27 Oct. 1951: 38–39, 64–68.
——. "America's Toughest Prison, Part III." *Saturday Evening Post* 3 Nov. 1951: 34, 160–62.
——. "The Case of Anne Milton, Ex-Convict." *Saturday Evening Post* 7 July 1957: 30–31, 70–72.
——. "Why Did It Happen: The Riot at Jackson Prison, Part I." *Saturday Evening Post* 6 June 1953: 17–19, 46–51.
——. "Why Did It Happen: The Riot at Jackson Prison, Part II." *Saturday Evening Post* 13 June 1953: 42–43, 130–36.
——. "Why Did It Happen: The Riot at Jackson Prison, Part III." *Saturday Evening Post* 20 June 1953: 36–37, 62–67.
——. "Why Did It Happen: The Riot at Jackson Prison, Part IV." *Saturday Evening Post* 1 Aug. 1953: 30, 146–50.
Martin, Rux. " 'Truth, Power, Self: An Interview with Michel Foucault." In *Technologies of the Self.* Eds. L. H. Martin, H. Gutman, P. H. Hutton. Amherst: U of Massachusetts P, 1988.
Martin, Steve J., and Sheldon Ekland-Olson. *Texas Prisons: The Walls Came Tumbling Down.* Austin: Tulist Strategy, 1972.
Mason, B. J. "Coed Cons." *Ebony* Nov. 1973: 192–99.
Mason, Tommy Ray. "Prison Life: One Convict's Story." *Scholastic Update* 9 Feb. 1987: 6–7.
"Matching Ex-Convicts to Jobs They Like." *Business Week* 8 Nov. 1976: 106.
McCall, Cheryl. "A Jailhouse Lawyer Brags about the Cons He Springs—But So Far Not Himself." *People* 23 Oct. 1978: 55–57.
McCarthy, Belinda, ed. *Intermediate Punishments: Intensive Supervision, Home Confinement and Electronic Surveillance.* Monsey, NY: Criminal Justice P, 1987.
McConnell, Michael. "Locked Down in Lockup." *Progressive* Jan. 1986: 16–17.

McCorkle, Lloyd W., and Richard R. Korn. "Resocialization within Walls." *Annals of the American Academy* May 1954: 88–98.
McGee, Michael Calvin. "The 'Ideograph': A Link between Rhetoric and Ideology." *Quarterly Journal of Speech* 66 (Feb. 1980): 1–16.
———. "In Search of the 'People': A Rhetorical Alternative." *Quarterly Journal of Speech* 61 (June 1975): 235–49.
———. "A Materialist's Conception of Rhetoric." In *Explorations in Rhetoric: Studies in Honor of Douglas Ehninger.* Ed. Ray E. McKerrow, 23–48. Glenview, IL: Scott, Foresman, 1982.
———. "The Origins of 'Liberty': A Feminization of Power." *Communication Monographs* 47 (1980): 23–45.
———. "Text, Context, and the Fragmentation of Contemporary Culture." *Western Journal of Speech Communication* 54 (1990): 274–89.
McKerrow, Raymie E. "Critical Rhetoric: Theory and Praxis." *Communication Monographs* 56 (June 1989): 91–111.
———. "Critical Rhetoric and the Possibility of the Subject." In *The Critical Turn: Rhetoric and Philosophy in Postmodern Discourse.* Ed. Ian Angus and Lenore Langsdorf, 51–67. Carbondale: Southern Illinois UP, 1993.
Melossi, Dario, and Massimo Pavarini. *The Prison and the Origins of the Penitentiary System.* London: Macmillan, 1981.
Miller, James. *The Passion of Michel Foucault.* New York: Simon and Schuster, 1993.
Mills, Michael, and Norval Morris. "Prisoners as Laboratory Animals." *Society* July 1974: 60–66.
Milne, Tom. *The Time Out Film Guide.* London: Penguin, 1989.
Minton, Robert, and Stephen Rice. "Using Racism at San Quentin." *Ramparts* Aug. 1970: 18–24.
Mitford, Jessica. *The American Prison Business.* Middlesex, England: Penguin, 1977.
———. "Experiments behind Bars." *Atlantic* Jan. 1973: 64–73.
———. "Torture Cure." *Harper's* Aug. 1973: 16–29.
Moeller, H. G. "Continuum of Corrections." *Annals of the American Academy* Jan. 1969: 81–88.
Moore, Jo Anne A. "A Mother Who Cries Out, 'I Don't Understand My Daughter,' Actually Means, 'I Have Never Tried.' " *Ladies Home Journal* Sept. 1972: 58–59..
Moore, Winston E. "How to Solve Prison Sex Problems." *Ebony* Nov. 1976: 83.
———. "My Cure for Prison Riots: End Prison Racism." *Ebony* Dec. 1971: 84–95.
Morris, Joe Alex. "Don't Label Them Incorrigible." *Saturday Evening Post* 18 Nov. 1961: 98–101.
———. "A Municipal Hot Potato." *American City and County* Feb. 1990: 29.
Morris, Norval. "From an Expert—Some Ideas on What's Needed to Fight Crime." *US News and World Report* 20 June 1977: 61–66.
Muth, Edmund H. "Prison Recreation in 1990." *Parks and Recreation* Sept. 1974: 34.

"Nathan Leopold After Thirty-two Years." *Life* 4 Mar. 1957: 61–69.
Neese, Robert. "Photos by a Con of a Con's Grim Life." *Life* 20 Apr. 1959: 109–15.
Nehamas, Alexander. *Nietzsche: Life as Literature.* Cambridge: Harvard UP, 1985.
"New Congregation." *Newsweek* 9 Oct. 1972: 98.
"New Jails: Boom for Builders, Bust for Budgets." *Business Week* 9 Feb. 1981: 74–75.
"A New Life for Women Inmates." *Ebony* Apr. 1970: 105–9.
"New York Gov. Nixes Death Bill; NBA, NAACP Laud Decision." *Jet* 7 Apr. 1986: 33.
Newton, Huey P. "Revolutionary Suicide: My Days in Solitary." *Ramparts* May 1973: 29.
Nordyke, Lewis. "These Convicts Make Fun of Themselves." *Saturday Evening Post* 3 Jan. 1953: 24–25, 36–37.
Nowlen, Chuck. "A Prison on Trial." *Progressive* Apr. 1980: 25–28.
Nussbaum, Albert F. "The Rehabilitation Myth." *American Scholar* Aug. 1971: 674–76.
O'Brien, Patrick J. "Convicts Can Be Heroes." *Today's Health* May 1952: 29, 55.
O'Gorman, Samuel F. "Our Overcrowded Prisons." *Senior Scholastic* 13 Nov. 1981: 14–17.
"The Ominous Hours." *Newsweek* 31 Jan. 1955: 24.
"On the Outside." *Newsweek* 30 Dec. 1963: 18–20.
"One in Four." *New Republic* 26 Mar. 1990: 5–6.
Ono, Kent A., and John M. Sloop. "Commitment to *Telos:* A Sustained Critical Rhetoric." *Communication Monographs* 59 (1992): 48–60.
"Organizing behind Bars." *Time* 13 May 1974: 93–94.
Orloski, Richard J. "Prison: No Fun Place to Visit." *America* 9 Sept. 1972: 152–53.
"Outside on the Job." *Time* 14 Sept. 1962: 33.
"Outside the Walls." *People* 1 Feb. 1988: 20–25.
Panik, Martha A., and Tony A. Mobley. "Bottle and the Tube: Leisure for the Convicted." *Parks and Recreation* Mar. 1977: 28–30, 54–55.
Paumier, Kay. "Serving Time, Family Style." *Ms.* May 1976: 47.
Pawelek, Dick. "Decide on the Death Penalty." *Scholastic Update* 9 Feb. 1987: 12.
Pearce, Donn. "Life-Styles: Building Time." *Esquire* Apr. 1969: 130–34.
Pearman, Robert. "Arkansas Prison Farm: The Whip Pays Off." *The Nation* 26 Dec. 1966: 701–4.
Peck, Keenen. "High-Tech House Arrest." *Progressive* July 1988: 26–28.
Pell, Eve. "The Soledad Brothers: How a Prison Picks Its Victims." *Ramparts* Aug. 1970: 31, 48–52.
"Pennsylvania Death Row Inmates Take System to Court." *Jet* 25 Aug. 1986: 32.
Percy, Charles H. "Rehabilitating a Captive Audience." *Parks and Recreation* Sept. 1974: 24–25, 73–74.
Pinsky, Mark. "Alarms on the Prison Grapevine." *The Nation* 5 Oct. 1974: 294.
"Players from Prison." *Time* 8 Apr. 1974: 61.

Playfair, Giles. "Without Bars: Some Bold (and Some Timorous) Experiments." *Harper's* Apr. 1964: 171–75.

Poster, Mark. *Critical Theory and Poststructuralism: In Search of a Context.* Ithaca, NY: Cornell UP, 1989.

Press, Aric. "AIDS: A Bad Way to Die." *Newsweek* 23 Mar. 1987: 30.

——. "Inside America's Toughest Prison." *Newsweek* 6 Oct. 1986: 46–61.

Press, Aric, Ron LaBrecque, Peggy Clausen, and Donna Foote. "When Prisons Go Coed." *Newsweek* 11 Jan. 1982: 66.

Press, Aric, Michael Reese, Vern Smith, Vincent Coppola, Diane Camper, and Emily F. Newhall. "When Will It Happen Again?" *Newsweek* 18 Feb. 1980: 68–76.

Press, Aric, and David Friendly. "Where to Kill with Impunity." *Newsweek* 3 May 1982: 88–90.

"The Price of Repression." *The Nation* 31 Aug. 1970: 130–31.

Primoratz, Igor. *Justifying Legal Punishment.* Atlantic Highlands, NJ: Humanities P, 1989.

Pringle, Henry F., and Katharine Pringle. "Convicts in Skirts." *Saturday Evening Post* 25 Nov. 1950: 34–35, 68–78.

"Prison; Excerpts." *Publisher's Weekly* 13 Mar. 1972: 53–54.

"Prisoner Power: A Radical Turn." *Newsweek* 27 Sept. 1971: 38.

"Prisoners Also Are People." *America* 12 Mar. 1966: 344–45.

"Prisoners 'On Strike'—The Meaning." *US News and World Report* 2 May 1952: 20–21.

"Prisoners' Plaint." *America* 22 Oct. 1955: 89.

"Prisons: Bridge to the Outside." *Newsweek* 28 May 1973: 92–94.

Probyn, Elspeth. *Sexing the Self: Gendered Positions in Cultural Studies.* New York: Routledge, 1993.

"Psychiatry in Prison." *Time* 25 Apr. 1960: 78.

Quinn, Barbara. "Jail Overcrowding: A Systems Problem." *American City and County* June 1988: 78.

Radway, Janice. *Reading the Romance: Women, Patriarchy, and Popular Literature.* Chapel Hill: U of North Carolina P, 1984.

Railsback, Celeste. "The Contemporary American Abortion Controversy: Stages in the Argument." *Quarterly Journal of Speech* 79 (1984): 410–24.

Reed, R. R. "A Criminal Saved My Life." *American Mercury* Nov. 1958: 88–92.

Reekie, Isabel M. " 'J. D.', about a Canadian Who Has Devoted His Life to Fighting Crime and Its Causes with Kindness." *Rotarian* June 1958: 32–33.

Reid, Dee. "High-Tech House Arrest." *Technological Review* July 1986: 12–14.

Ricoeur, Paul. "Narrative Time." In *On Narrative.* Ed. W. J. T. Mitchell, 165–86. Chicago: U of Chicago P, 1981.

Rideau, Wilbert, and Ron Wikberg. *Life Sentences: Rage and Survival behind Bars.* New York: Times Books, 1992.

"Rights for Prisoners." *Time* 5 Jan. 1968: 46–47.

Riot. Paramount Pictures and William Castle Productions, 1968.

Ritter, Jesse P. "Nightmare for the Innocent in a California Jail." *Life* 15 Aug. 1969: 51–54.

Roberts, Steven V., and Ted Gest. "A Growing Cry: 'Give Them Death.' " *US News and World Report* 26 Mar. 1990: 24–25.

Rogers, Cornish. "Biomedics, Psychosurgery and Laissez-Faire." *Christian Century* 31 Oct. 1973: 1076–78.
Rosen, Charley. "Basketball behind Bars." *Sport* May 1986: 30–31.
Rosenberg, Charles E. *The Trial of the Assassin Guiteau: Psychiatry and Law in the Gilded Age.* Chicago: U of Chicago P, 1968.
Ross, Jack. "The Convict Who Broke into Prison." *Coronet* Mar. 1953: 102–6.
Rothman, David J. *Conscience and Convenience: The Asylum and Its Alternatives in Progressive America.* Boston: Little, Brown, 1980.
———. *The Discovery of the Asylum: Social Order and Disorder in the New Republic.* Boston: Little, Brown, 1971.
Rotman, Edgardo. *Beyond Punishment: A New View on the Rehabilitation of Criminals.* Westport, CT: Greenwood P, 1990.
Rubinstein, Jonathon. "To Russia with Love." *New Yorker* 9 Nov. 1992: 80–83.
Russell, Dick, and David Nevard. "The Good/Hood Samaritan." *Family Health* May 1976: 36–38, 66–67.
Sachs, Georgine. "Anastassia's 1,000 Fathers." *Coronet* Apr. 1961: 114–15.
Salholz, Eloise, Lynda Wright, Clara Bingham, Tony Clifton, Ginny Carroll, Spencer Reiss, and Farai Chidey. "Women in Jail: Unequal Justice." *Newsweek* 4 June 1990: 37–38, 51.
Samuels, Gertrude. "Forgotten Youth: The 'Detained.' " *New York Times Magazine* 1 July 1956: 12–13, 21.
———. "Open Doors for Young Prisoners." *New York Times Magazine* 12 Feb. 1961: 41–48.
Sanz, Cynthia. "Bedford Hills, 10507." *People* 16 Mar. 1992: 75–78.
Satchell, Michael. "The Toughest Prison in America." *US News and World Report* 27 July 1987: 23–24.
Savold, David. "Electronic Jailer." *Science 84* Sept. 1984: 80–82.
Scaglione, Fred. "You're Under Arrest—at Home." *USA Today* Nov. 1988: 26–28.
"Scandal in Virginia." *Newsweek* 15 Nov. 1971: 39.
Scared Straight. Arnold Shapiro Productions, 1978.
Scheer, Robert. "A Night at Santa Rita." *Ramparts* Aug. 1969: 50–51.
Seidman, David. "The Prisoner and the Union." *The Nation* 5 July 1971: 6–7.
"The Shame of the Prisons." *Time* 18 Jan. 1971: 48–59.
Shapiro, Michael. "The Rhetoric of Social Science: The Political Responsibilities of the Scholar." In *The Rhetoric of the Human Sciences.* Ed. John S. Nelson, Allan Megill, and Donald N. McCloskey, 363–78. Madison: U of Wisconsin P, 1987.
Shelly, Gordon, and David Mazroff. "Draughts of Old Bourbon." *American Mercury* June 1952: 118–25.
Sherrill, Robert. "Death Row on Trial." *New York Times Magazine* 13 Nov. 1983: 80–83, 98–116.
Shockley, Donald G. "Reforming Prison Reform." *Commonweal* 24 Sept. 1971: 497–98.
Shockley, Donald G., and Richard L. Freeman. "Johnny Cash on Prison Reform." *Christian Century* 31 Aug. 1970: 1157.
Sholle, David J. "Critical Studies: From the Theory of Ideology to Power/Knowledge." *Critical Studies in Mass Communication* 5 (1988): 16–41.

"Should Experimentation on Prisoners Be Stopped?" *Senior Scholastic* 3 Nov. 1969: 11–12.

"The Siege of Cherry Hill." *Time* 31 Jan. 1955: 17.

Skoler, Daniel L. "There's More to Crime Control than the 'Get Tough' Approach." *Annals of the American Academy* Sept. 1971: 28–39.

Slack, Ruth M. "Breaking Down Barriers." *Independent Woman* June 1956: 14, 27.

Slade, Margot. "Jailhouse Mothering." *Psychology Today* Dec. 1978: 35–36.

Sloop, John M. " 'Apology Made to Whoever Pleases': Cultural Discipline and the Grounds of Interpretation." *Communication Quarterly* (1994): 345–62.

Small, Collie. "My Convict." *Coronet* Sept. 1958: 64–68.

Smith, Edgar H. "I Don't Want to Die." *Saturday Evening Post* 7 Sept. 1968: 10–11.

——. "A Pre-posthumous Conversation with Myself." *Esquire* June 1971: 112–15, 14, 20–24.

Smith, R. H. "Inmate Manuscripts." *Publisher's Weekly* 7 Dec. 1970: 29.

Smith, Ralph Lee. "Research behind Bars." *New York Times Magazine* 4 Dec. 1960: 39–42.

Smolowe, Jill. "Bringing Decency into Hell." *Time* 14 Dec. 1992: 60–62.

——. "Race and the Death Penalty." *Time* 29 Apr. 1991: 68–69.

Snarr, L. Glenn. "A Prisoner Invents His Way to Freedom." *Coronet* Oct. 1952: 126–29.

Social Science Research Council. *Theoretical Studies in the Social Organization of the Prison.* New York: SSRC, 1960.

Sommer, Robert, and Barbara A. Sommer. "Showcase Prisons: The Best Are a Waste." *The Nation* 19 Oct. 1974: 369–72.

"Spiderman's Net." *Time* 14 Oct. 1985: 93.

Stanford, Phil. "A Model, Clockwork-Orange Prison." *New York Times Magazine* 17 Sept. 1972: 9, 71–84.

Starr, Mark. "The Ballot Box Goes to Prison." *Newsweek* 25 Jan. 1988: 63.

Stein, Loren, and Veronique Mistiaen. "Pregnant in Prison." *Progressive* Feb. 1988: 18–21.

Steinman, Clay. "The Case of the Frightened Convict." *The Nation* 3 Dec. 1973: 590–93.

Stewart, Gordon C. "Worship and Resistance: The Exercise of Freedom." *Christian Century* 13 Mar. 1974: 290–92.

Stout, Robert Joe. "Going Straight." *Commonweal* 16 Jan. 1981: 16–18.

Suall, Irwin. "Extremist Groups Seek Recruits in Prisons." *USA Today* Sept. 1987: 22–28.

Sullivan, Larry E. *The Prison Reform Movement: Forlorn Hope.* Boston: Twayne, 1990.

Sullivan, Robert E., Jr. "Reach Out and Guard Someone: Using Phones and Bracelets to Reduce Prison Overcrowding." *Rolling Stone* 29 Nov. 1990: 51.

"Support Your Local Police." *New Republic* 21 June 1969: 9.

"Sweet Dreams." *Newsweek* 30 Dec. 1957: 21.

Sykes, Gresham M. *The Society of Captives.* Princeton, NJ: Princeton UP, 1958.

Szulc, Tad. "George Jackson Radicalizes the Brothers in Soledad and San Quentin." *New York Times Magazine* 1 Aug. 1971: 10–11, 16–23.
Taggart, Robert. "Manpower Programs for Criminal Offenders." *Monthly Labor Review* Aug. 1972: 17–24.
"Talking Pillows." *Commonweal* 27 Dec. 1957: 326.
Taylor, Andress. "Beyond Rehabilitation: The Federal City College Lorton Project—A Model Prison Higher Education Program." *Journal of Negro Education* 43 (1974): 172–78.
Taylor, Victor E. "Heroin and the Black Community." *American Scholar* 40 (1971): 691–94.
"Teaching Law behind Bars." *Time* 13 Sept. 1976: 57.
Telander, Rick. "Sports behind the Walls." *Sports Illustrated* 17 Oct. 1988: 82–92.
Therborn, Goran. *What Does the Ruling Class Do When It Rules?* London: Verso, 1980.
Thomas, J. Parnell. "Red Hunter's Red Jailmates." *Life* 4 Oct. 1954: 138–53.
Tichi, Cecelia. *Electronic Hearth: Creating an American Television Culture.* New York: Oxford UP, 1992.
"Tipping Justice's Scale." *Newsweek* 13 Sept. 1982: 76.
Titus, Harold. "Michigan's Happy Convicts—They Improve the State's Great Parks." *Collier's* 19 Aug. 1950: 18–19, 58, 60.
Toch, Hans, and Kenneth Adams, with J. Douglas Grant. *Coping: Maladaptation in Prisons.* Rutgers, NJ: Transaction P, 1989.
Tomkins, Calvin. "Crime-Breeding Prisons." *Newsweek* 25 Apr. 1960: 108.
Tonry, Michael, and Franklin E. Zimring, eds. *Reform and Punishment.* Chicago: U of Chicago P, 1983.
Torok, Lou. "A Convict Looks at Crime and Criminals." *America* 13 Jan. 1973: 10–14.
"Treatment behind Bars." *Time* 9 July 1973: 35–36.
Turner, Graeme. *British Cultural Studies: An Introduction.* New York: Routledge, 1992.
U.S. Department of Justice. *Correctional Populations in the United States, 1991.* Washington, DC, 1993.
Useem, Bert, and Peter Kimball. *States of Siege: U.S. Prison Riots, 1971–1986.* New York: Oxford UP, 1989.
van den Haag, Ernest. *Punishing Criminals: Concerning a Very Old and Painful Question.* New York: Basic, 1975.
"Views from behind Bars." *Time* 30 June 1975: 23.
"Voice of the Convict." *Harper's* Apr. 1964: 164–70.
"Volunteers behind Bars." *Time* 12 July 1963: 72.
Von Gottfried, Johanna. "Diary from the Fresno County Farm." *America* 13 Oct. 1973: 262–66.
Von Hirsch, Andrew. *Past or Future Crimes.* New Brunswick, NJ: Rutgers UP, 1985.
Walker, Dan. "In the Interest of Public Safety." *Parks and Recreation* Sept. 1974: 19–20.
Walker, Lynn. "Employment Problems of Ex-Offenders." *Essence* Sept. 1973: 20.

Walsh, Denny. "The Gorilla Cowed His Keepers." *Life* 25 June 1971: 42–52.
"Warning from Berkeley." *The Nation* 16 June 1969: 747–48.
Waskow, Arthur I. " . . . I am not Free." *Saturday Review* 8 Jan. 1972: 20–21.
Wasserstrom, Richard A., ed. *Morality and the Law.* Belmont, CA: Wadsworth, 1971.
Weiner, Bernard. "The Clockwork Cure." *The Nation* 3 Apr. 1972: 433–36.
Weintraub, Adam. "To Build or Not to Build?" *Arkansas Gazette* 25 Apr. 1989.
Wertham, Fredric. "The Delinquents." Rev. of *Life Plus 99 Years,* by Nathan Leopold. *Saturday Review* 15 Mar. 1958: 18.
West, Cornel. "The New Cultural Politics of Difference." In *Out There: Marginalization and Contemporary Cultures.* Ed. Russell Ferguson, Martha Gever, Trinh T. Minh-ha, and Cornel West, 19–36. New York: New Museum of Contemporary Art, 1990.
West, Dorothy. " 'I Was Afraid to Shut My Eyes.' " *Saturday Evening Post* 13 July 1968: 23.
Wharton, Don. "Jim Waite's Prison Camp: Here First Offenders Get a Second Chance." *Reader's Digest* Sept. 1953: 61–64.
———. "Prisoners Who Volunteer Blood, Flesh, and Their Lives." *American Mercury* Dec. 1954: 51–55.
"What Life is Like for Women in Prison." *US News and World Report* 28 Nov. 1977: 79.
"What Are Prisons For?" *Time* 13 Sept. 1982: 38–55.
White, James Boyd. *Heracles' Bow.* Madison: U of Wisconsin P, 1985.
Whitehill, Joseph. "The Convict and the Burgher: A Case Study of Communication and Crime." *American Scholar* 38 (1969): 441–51.
"Why Convicts Riot." *US News and World Report* 19 Dec. 1952: 18–21.
Williams, Raymond. *The Long Revolution.* New York: Columbia UP, 1961.
Willis, Paul. "Shop Floor Culture, Masculinity and the Wage Form." In *Working Class Culture: Studies in History and Theory.* Ed. John Clarke, Chas Critcher, and Richard Johnson, 185–98. London: Hutchinson, 1979.
Wilson, Donald Powell. "My Six Convicts." *Life* 22 Jan. 1951: 90–106.
Wilson, Donald Powell, and Harry Elmore Barnes. "Riot Is an Unnecessary Evil." *Life* 24 Nov. 1952: 138–50.
Wilson, James Q. *Thinking about Crime.* Rev. ed. New York: Vintage, 1975.
Wilson, James Q., and Richard J. Herrnstein. *Crime and Human Nature.* New York: Simon and Schuster, 1985.
Wilson, Paul E. "A Square's Night behind Bars." *The Nation* 15 Feb. 1971: 200–206.
Winkler, Max. "Walking Prisons: The Developing Technology of Electronic Controls." *The Futurist* July–Aug. 1993: 34–36.
"Women in Prison Plead: 'Help Your Daughters.' " *Ladies Home Journal* Sept. 1972: 58–69.
Worthy, William. "The Anguish of Martin Sostre." *Ebony* Oct. 1970: 122–32.
"Writing to Rehabilitate." *Time* 18 Mar. 1974: 71–72.
Yancey, Philip. "Love Made the Difference." *Reader's Digest* Nov. 1978: 27–32.

Yoder, Robert M. "Wisconsin Throws Them Out of Jail." *Saturday Evening Post* 4 Feb. 1956: 25, 80–83.
Zimbardo, Philip G. "Pathology of Imprisonment." *Society* Apr. 1972: 4–8.
Zinn, Howard. "Incident in Hattiesburg." *The Nation* 18 May 1964: 501–4.
Zuckerman, Laurence. "They Put Him in Writer's Block." *Time* 29 Aug. 1988: 66.

Index

About the Series

STUDIES IN RHETORIC AND COMMUNICATION
General Editors:
E. Culpepper Clark, Raymie E. McKerrow, and David Zarefsky

The University of Alabama Press has established this series to publish major new works in the general area of rhetoric and communication, including books treating the symbolic manifestations of political discourse, argument as social knowledge, the impact of machine technology on patterns of communication behavior, and other topics related to the nature of impact of symbolic communication. We actively solicit studies involving historical, critical, or theoretical analyses of human discourse.

About the Author

John M. Sloop is Assistant Professor, Department of Communication Studies and Theatre, Vanderbilt University. He received his bachelor's degree from Appalachian State University, his master's from the University of Georgia, and his doctorate from the University of Iowa.